KU-134-347

LIFELONG LEARNING IN EUROPE

Equity and efficiency in the balance

Edited by Sheila Riddell, Jörg Markowitsch and
Elisabet Weedon

First published in Great Britain in 2012 by

The Policy Press
University of Bristol
Fourth Floor
Beacon House
Queen's Road
Bristol BS8 1QU
UK
Tel +44 (0)117 331 4054
Fax +44 (0)117 331 4093
e-mail tpp-info@bristol.ac.uk
www.policypress.co.uk

North American office:

The Policy Press
c/o The University of Chicago Press
1427 East 60th Street
Chicago, IL 60637, USA
t: +1 773 702 7700
f: +1 773-702-9756
e:sales@press.uchicago.edu
www.press.uchicago.edu

© The Policy Press 2012

British Library Cataloguing in Publication Data
A catalogue record for this book is available from the British Library.

Library of Congress Cataloging-in-Publication Data
A catalog record for this book has been requested.

ISBN 978 1 44730 013 7 hardcover

The right of Sheila Riddell, Jörg Markowitsch and Elisabet Weedon to be identified as editors
of this work has been asserted by them in accordance with the 1988 Copyright, Designs and
Patents Act.

All rights reserved: no part of this publication may be reproduced, stored in a retrieval system,
or transmitted in any form or by any means, electronic, mechanical, photocopying, recording, or
otherwise without the prior permission of The Policy Press.

The statements and opinions contained within this publication are solely those of the editors
and contributors and not of The University of Bristol or The Policy Press. The University
of Bristol and The Policy Press disclaim responsibility for any injury to persons or property
resulting from any material published in this publication.

The Policy Press works to counter discrimination on grounds of gender, race, disability, age and
sexuality.

Cover design by The Policy Press
Front cover: image kindly supplied by istock
Printed and bound in Great Britain by MPG Book Group
The Policy Press uses environmentally responsible print partners

FSC
www.fsc.org
MIX
From responsible
sources
FSC° C018575

Contents

List of figures, tables and case studies   iv

Notes on contributors   vii

List of contributors, by country, to the EU Sixth Framework Project   x
'Towards a Lifelong Learning Society in Europe: The Contribution of the
Education System' (LLL2010)

one   Lifelong learning and the generation of human and social capital   1
two   Lifelong learning and the wider European socioeconomic context   17
three   Neoliberal and inclusive themes in European lifelong learning policy   39
four   Formal adult education in the spotlight: profiles, motivations and   63
         experiences of participants in 12 European countries
five   The sociodemographic obstacles to participating in lifelong learning   87
         across Europe
six   The qualification-providing enterprise? Support for formal adult   103
         education in small and medium-sized enterprises
seven   Reducing or reinforcing inequality: assessing the impact of European   125
         policy on widening access to higher education
eight   Conclusion: the role of lifelong learning in reducing social inequality 151
         at a time of economic crisis

Technical annex to Chapter Four   168
Glossary of terms and abbreviations   171
Index   177

List of figures, tables and case studies

Figures

2.1	Inequality in OECD countries as measured by the Gini co-efficient	19
2.2	Percentage of households at risk of poverty after social transfers	20
2.3	Employment rates by educational attainment, 2010 (25-64 years of age)	21
2.4	Highest educational attainment of participants in formal adult education (25-64 years of age) for LLL2010 partner countries	22
4.1	Bounded agency model (Rubenson and Desjardins, 2009)	63
4.2	Intrinsic versus extrinsic reasons for participation by ISCED level of current course	69
4.3	Intrinsic versus extrinsic reasons for participation by country/region	70
4.4	Age distribution of adult learners by country/region	71
4.5	Initial educational attainment of adult learners by country/region	71
4.6	Admission requirements by ISCED level of current course	73
4.7	Modular system by ISCED level of current course	74
4.8	Class sizes of 21 and over by ISCED level of current course	75
4.9	Perception of the classroom environment by country/region	77
4.10	Experience of satisfaction by country/region	78
4.11	Variation in satisfaction by country clusters	80
5.1	Participation in formal adult learning by level of initial education	89
5.2	Participation in formal adult learning by labour force status	91
5.3	Participation in formal adult learning by labour market integration	91
5.4	Participation in formal adult learning by interruption of studies	92
5.5	Rates of participation in formal adult education by gender	93
5.6	The impact of interruption of studies on participation in formal education, based on a gap of less than five years	97
6.1	Participation in formal adult education of employed persons and proportion of employees with (some) support from the enterprise	107
7.1	Proportion of 30–34 year olds with tertiary education, 2005 and 2010	133
7.2	Proportion of the population with tertiary education (ISCED 5-6) by age, 2007	133
7.3	Percentage who have completed tertiary education (ISCED 5-6) by age and gender, 2007	134
7.4	Percentage of those aged 25+ who have completed tertiary education (ISCED 5-6) by level of educational background of parents and by gender, 2005	136
7.5	Net entry rate (%) by age, ISCED 5A, 2006	137
7.6	Percentage of students entering higher education via non-traditional route, 2006	137
7.7	Percentage of students studying part time by age	138

7.8   Employment rates by educational attainment, 2010 (25–64 years of age) 139
7.9   Employment rates by educational attainment and gender, 2010   139
        (25–64 years of age
7.10   Percentage of people with tertiary level education, aged 25–34, by level 140
        of occupation and gender, 2007
8.1   Risk of poverty by educational level in different European countries   158

Tables

2.1   Key characteristics in relation to the economy, labour market and   28
        educational achievement of the EU LLL2010 countries
4.1   The motivational dimensions based on the Education Participation Scale   68
5.1   The occurrence or non-occurrence of demographic obstacles in   95
        19 AES countries
5.2   The occurrence or non-occurrence of socioeconomic obstacles in   95
        19 AES countries
5.3   Demographic and socioeconomic obstacles to participation in formal   96
        education
5.4   Obstacles to participation in formal adult education: observed   98
        indicators and casual effects
6.1   Types of support for participation in formal adult education of   109
        employees in small to medium-sized enterprises
6.2   Typology of patterns in supporting formal adult education in   111
        enterprises
6.3   Reactive versus expansive training cultures – defining characteristics 115
6.4   Cross-tabulation of training cultures and support patterns in case   118
        study enterprises
7.1   Students in Austrian state tertiary educational institutions by   126
        socioeconomic status
7.2   Participation in different types of tertiary-level education in Flanders 127
        by socioeconomic status, percentages, cohort born 1976
7.3   Main categories monitored on social dimension in LLL2010 countries   131
        as recorded in EACEA (2010)
7.4   Proportion of women graduates in mathematics, science and   135
        technology, 2000 and 2005
A1   Micro and meso level variables influencing learner satisfaction: detailed 168
        results of the regression analysis summarised in Figure 4.11

Case studies

6.1   Metal production enterprise, Norway   112
6.2   Copper production enterprise, England   112
6.3   Chemical production enterprise, Slovenia   113
6.4   Chemical production enterprise, Austria   113

6.5	Packaging enterprise, Ireland	115
6.6	Chemical research and distribution enterprise, Russia	116
7.1	An elite Scottish university	141
7.2	A Slovenian university	142
7.3	An Estonian research-intensive public university	143
7.4	An Austrian university of applied sciences	144
7.5	A Flemish college of higher education	145

Notes on contributors

Dr Ellen Boeren is research associate at the Research Institute for Work and Society at the KU (Katholieke Universiteit) Leuven (Belgium). She successfully defended her PhD thesis 'Participation in adult education: a bounded agency approach' in May 2011. Her research interests focus on participation issues in adult education, motivational psychology, education policy and classroom perceptions. During Winter 2009/10, she was a visiting scholar at the University of Nottingham School of Education. She published the theoretical framework of her PhD in the *International Journal of Lifelong Education*. In May 2012 Ellen Boeren took up a Chancellor's Fellowship at the University of Edinburgh.

Günter Hefler is senior project manager at 3s Unternehmensberatung GmbH in Vienna and researcher at the Danube University Krems, Department for Continuing Education Research and Educational Management. He studied Philosophy, Sociology, and Political Science at the University of Vienna. His areas of research include comparative studies on lifelong learning and continuing vocational training, workplace learning, and adult learning and development.

John Holford is Robert Peers Professor of Adult Education and Director of the Centre for Research in Higher, Adult and Vocational Education at the University of Nottingham, England. His main current research interests are in lifelong learning policy, especially in Europe, in adult learning of citizenship, and in the history of adult education. He is an Editor of the *International Journal of Lifelong Education*, and a convenor of the Policy Studies Network for the European Society for Research in the Education of Adults.

Jörg Markowitsch is founder and senior partner of 3s Unternehmensberatung GmbH, and research manager at the Danube University Krems, Department for Continuing Education Research and Educational Management. He studied Mathematics at the Technical University of Vienna and Philosophy at the University of Vienna. His areas of research include comparative studies in vocational education and training, lifelong learning, European education policy, theories of skills acquisition, skills taxonomies, and skills forecasting.

Vida Andreja Mohorčič Špolar was Director of the Slovenian Institute for Adult Education, and is currently an assistant lecturer at the University of Ljubljana, Faculty of Arts, Department of Educational Sciences. For many years she has been involved in policy development and research on adult learning in Slovenia and in the EU. Currently she is a member of the Slovenian National Commission for UNESCO and ESREA Policy network.

Professor Ides Nicaise has a background in economics and is head of the unit of education and lifelong learning at HIVA (Research Centre for Work and Society), a multidisciplinary research institute of KU Leuven (Flemish Louvain). His early background was in economics but he further specialised in social policy and is particularly interested in the relationships between education, labour market policy and social inclusion in rich as well as developing countries. He has been involved in a large number of projects at national, European and international levels dealing with education, ranging from educational funding to lifelong learning and initial education for socially excluded groups. Besides his professional activities, he chairs the Belgian Resource Centre for the Fight against Poverty, a centre created by law as an interface between the government, the civil society and grassroots organisations defending the interests of the poor. This centre is linked with the Centre for Equal Opportunities and for the Fight against Racism.

Sheila Riddell is Director of the Centre for Research in Education Inclusion and Diversity at the Moray House School of Education, University of Edinburgh. Her research interests are in the broad field of equality and social inclusion, with particular reference to gender, social class and disability in education, training, employment and social care. She has published extensively in these areas and sits on policy advisory committees on disability and equal rights in the UK and Scotland.

Péter Róbert is a Full Professor at the Faculty of Economics, Széchenyi István University, Györ, Hungary. He is also a Senior Research Fellow at the Institute for Political Science (HAS) and a project-based Program Manager at the TARKI Social Research Institute, Budapest. His research interests include social stratification and mobility with a special focus on educational inequalities and life-course analysis. He also does research on attitudes toward social inequalities and political preferences. Recent publications examine the educational transition from secondary to tertiary school, a comparison of students' performance in state-owned and church-run schools, early careers of young graduates and participation in adult education.

Eve-Liis Roosmaa (MA) is a researcher in the Department of Social Stratification at the Institute of International and Social Studies, Tallinn University, and doctoral student in sociology at Tallinn University, Estonia. Her main fields of study are education, labour market and lifelong learning. She has published in books and journals on social justice issues and participation in non-formal learning.

Ellu Saar is a Professor at the Institute for International and Social Studies, Tallinn University, Estonia. She coordinated the EU Sixth Framework Project 'Towards a Lifelong Learning Society in Europe: The Contribution of the Education System' (LLL2010). Her research areas are social stratification and mobility, educational inequalities and life course studies. She is a member of the Editorial Board of

European Sociological Review and a member of the Steering Committee of the European Consortium of Sociological Research.

Elisabet Weedon is Deputy Director of the Centre for Research in Education Inclusion and Diversity at the Moray House School of Education, University of Edinburgh. Her main research interests are in the area of adult learning and equality in education. She is currently involved in projects on workplace learning and educational experiences and outcomes for Muslim pupils in England and Scotland.

List of contributors, by country, to the EU Sixth Framework Project 'Towards a Lifelong Learning Society in Europe: The Contribution of the Education System' (LLL2010)

Country	Contributors
Estonia – coordinating team	Ellu Saar (Tallinn University, Institute for International and Social Studies – TLU IISS), team leader
	Eve-Liis Roosmaa (TLU IISS)
	Triin Roosalu (TLU IISS)
	Rein Vöörmann (TLU IISS)
	Jelena Helemäe (TLU IISS)
	Auni Tamm (TLU IISS)
	Margarita Kazjulja (TLU IISS)
	Kristina Lindemann (TLU IISS)
	Marii Paškov (TLU IISS)
	Larissa Jõgi (TLU Institute of Educational Sciences)
	Katrin Karu (TLU Institute of Educational Sciences)
	Marin Gross (TLU Institute of Educational Sciences)
	Liis Roodla (TLU Institute of Educational Sciences)
	Merily Murd (TLU IISS)
	Uno Saar (TLU IISS)
Austria	Jörg Markowitsch (3srl, Danube University Krems), team leader
	Günter Hefler (3srl/Danube University Krems)
	Stephanie Rämmel (Danube University Krems)
	Paul Ringler (3srl/Danube University Krems)
	Sylvia Benda-Kahri (3srl)
	Regina Gottwald
Flanders, Belgium	Ides Nicaise (HIVA, KU Leuven)
	Ellen Boeren (HIVA, KU Leuven)
	Ella Desmedt (HIVA, KU Leuven)
	Katleen De Rick (HIVA, KU Leuven)
	Loes Vandenbroucke (HIVA, KU Leuven)
	Lode Vermeersch (HIVA, KU Leuven)
	Walter Van Trier (HIVA, KU Leuven)
	Heidi Knipprath (HIVA, KU Leuven)
	Zhipeng Chen (HIVA, KU Leuven)

Country	Contributors
Bulgaria	Pepka Boyadijeva (Bulgarian Academy of Science)
	Galin Gornev (Bulgarian Academy of Science)
	Valentina Milenkova (Bulgarian Academy of Science)
	Kristina Petkova (Bulgarian Academy of Science)
	Diana Nenkova (Bulgarian Academy of Science)
	Valery Todorov (Bulgarian Academy of Science)
England (UK)	John Holford (University of Surrey/University of Nottingham), team leader
	Linda Merricks (University of Surrey), team leader
	Peter Jarvis (University of Surrey)
	Stephen McNair (University of Surrey/NIACE)
	Guy Hannan (University of Surrey)
	Fiona Aldridge (NIACE)
	Swati Nettleship (NIACE)
	Laura Engel (University of Nottingham)
	Agata Mleczko (University of Nottingham)
	Alison Kington (University of Nottingham)
	Thushari Welikala (University of Nottingham)
Hungary	Péter Róbert (team leader) (TARKI)
	Anikó Balogh (TARKI)
	Éva Tót (TARKI)
	Saida Ayupova (TARKI)
	Janka Salát (TARKI)
	Matild Sági (TARKI)
	Ágnes Szölősi
	Anna Józan
Ireland	Paul Downes (St Patrick College, Dublin City University), team leader
	Catherine Maunsell (St Patrick College, Dublin City University)
	Catherine Dooley (St Patrick College, Dublin City University)
	Valerie McLoughlin (St Patrick College, Dublin City University)
	Jane Carrigan St Patrick College, Dublin City University)
Lithuania	Leta Dromantiene (Mykolas Romeris University), team leader at MRU
	Meilute Taljunaite (Social Research Institute), team leader at SRI
	Sarmite Mikulioniene (Mykolas Romeris University)
	Irena Zemaitaityte (Mykolas Romeris University)
	Vida Kanopiene (Mykolas Romeris University)
	Natalija Kasatkina (Social Research Institute)
	Renata Sutinyte (Social Research Institute)
	Liutauras Labanauskas (Social Research Institute)
	Jurate Terepaite-Butviliene (Social Research Institute)
	Loreta Blazeviciene (Social Research Institute)
	N Norvile (Mykolas Romeris University)

Country	Contributors
Norway	Odd Bjørn Ure (FAFO), team leader
	Marianne Dæhlen (FAFO)
	Skule Sveinung (FAFO), team leader
	Bjørg Eva Aaslid (FAFO)
	Ole Anders Stensen (FAFO)
Russia	Vladimir Kozlovsky (St Petersburg State University), team leader
	Anisya Khokhlova (St Petersburg State University)
	Andrey Nevsky (St Petersburg State University)
	Maria Veits (St Petersburg State University)
	Ekaterina Saburova (St Petersburg State University)
	Oksana Golenskaja (St Petersburg State University)
Slovenia	Vida A. Mohorčič Špolar (Slovenian Institute for Adult Education), team leader
	Angela Ivančič (Slovenian Institute for Adult Education)
	Marko Radovan (Slovenian Institute for Adult Education)
	Peter Beltram (Slovenian Institute for Adult Education)
	Jasmina Mirceva (Slovenian Institute for Adult Education)
Scotland (UK)	Sheila Riddell (University of Edinburgh), team leader
	Elisabet Weedon (University of Edinburgh)
	Linda Ahlgren (University of Edinburgh)
	Jim Crowther (University of Edinburgh)
	Judith Litjens (University of Edinburgh)
	Richard Purves (University of Edinburgh)
The Czech Republic	Martin Dobeš (National Training Fund), team leader
	Petra Jedličková (National Training Fund)
	Miroslava Mandíková (National Training Fund), team leader
	Zdeněk Palán (National Training Fund)
	Ivana Sládková (National Training Fund)

LLL2010 Advisory Board	Kjell Rubenson (UBC, Vancouver)
	Palle Rasmussen (Aalborg University)
	Philip O'Connell (Economic and Social Research Institute (ESRI), Ireland)
	Sadiq-Kwesi Boateng (Eurostat)
	Sue Waddington (EAEA/NIACE)

ONE

Lifelong learning and the generation of human and social capital

Sheila Riddell and Elisabet Weedon, Centre for Research in Education Inclusion and Diversity, University of Edinburgh

Introduction

This book takes a retrospective and prospective look at the contribution of lifelong learning to economic growth and social cohesion across Europe. It draws on comparative data from the EU Sixth Framework Project 'Towards a Lifelong Learning Society in Europe: The Contribution of the Education System' (LLL2010), which ran from 2005 to 2011 and involved 12 European countries and Russia. The countries participating in the project allowed for contrasts to be drawn between the experiences of old member states located in Northern and Western Europe and new member states in Central and Eastern Europe. Throughout the book there is a focus on the part played by lifelong learning in challenging social exclusion, which takes very different forms in old and new member states. The Eastern European post-communist countries experienced considerable change in the early 1990s with the collapse of the Soviet Union and the transition from planned, state-regulated economies to less regulated economies and labour markets. This led to increases in unemployment and also a dismantling of existing social institutions such as child-care and adult education networks. By 2007, all the LLL2010 post-communist countries had joined the European Union (EU). This provided access to funding in a range of areas, including lifelong learning, and obligations to increase participation rates. The economy of the EU was buoyant until mid-2007, but was subsequently hit by successive waves of financial crisis that threaten the progress made in widening access to lifelong learning opportunities across Europe. At the time of writing (December 2011), the ongoing economic crisis raises fundamental questions about the political and social goals of the EU, particularly the feasibility of harmonising social and education policy across member states. While some countries, such as Germany, are arguing for greater fiscal and social integration, other countries, such as the UK, are seeking to repatriate powers from Europe, particularly in areas such as employment and training. The forward momentum of the European project is clearly faltering, raising the possibility that the high-water mark of European integration has been achieved, with implications for many aspects of education and social policy, including lifelong learning.

In this introductory chapter, we set out the broad problematic of the book, which explores how lifelong learning is understood and enacted across Europe and how this is changing over time. We investigate tensions between the use of lifelong learning as a means of promoting economic growth through the development of human capital, and as a means of promoting social inclusion through the development of social capital. Different conceptions of lifelong learning, the learning society and social inclusion are examined, and we question the extent to which the EU is on track to achieve its goal of 'smart, sustainable and inclusive growth', as reflected in the Lisbon strategy of 2000 and reiterated in the subsequent Europe 2020 education and training strategy. It should be noted that the book does not use a precise definition of lifelong learning, but rather explores the way in which the term is understood in post-16 education and training systems across Europe. We have a particular interest in the formal education system reflected in the qualifications frameworks adopted in different countries. At the same time, we note that the boundaries between formal (award-bearing) and non-formal education systems vary greatly between countries, with strict boundaries in countries such as Austria and many Eastern European countries, compared with a much more permeable interface in Ireland and the UK.

Globalisation, neoliberalism and the knowledge economy

It is important to consider the particular set of social, economic and political conditions that have led to the emergence of lifelong learning as a travelling policy. As we noted in an earlier publication (Riddell et al, 2001), the rise of interest in lifelong learning must be understood in the context of the rise of global capitalism. In the words of Castells (2000):

> For the first time in history, the whole planet is either capitalist or highly dependent on capitalist economic processes. (Castells, 2000, p 52)

The new global economy is dependent on, and has emerged as a result of, new information and communication technologies, allowing capital to be moved around the globe almost instantaneously, with consequent implications for national, regional and local labour markets. Summarising the interconnection of capital, people and ideas, Green et al (2007) define globalisation as 'the rapid acceleration of cross-border movements of capital, labour, goods, knowledge and ideas'. While the present wave of globalisation, dating from the 1970s, has been driven by technological and scientific advances, it has also been driven by a political movement towards trade liberalisation and market deregulation, sometimes referred to as neoliberalism. Economists of the Chicago School such as Milton Friedman maintained that unregulated market forces should be allowed to determine the course of national and global financial affairs, leading to an ongoing process of creative destruction whereby outdated forms of production would be replaced by new and vibrant industries.

Stiglitz (2010), in his account of the collapse of the global economy, describes the inter-linkage between the global economy, neoliberalism and the knowledge society in the following way. As a result of the philosophy of neoliberalism, the burgeoning financial services industry of the 1990s was allowed to develop in a largely unregulated fashion. In both the US and the UK in the late 1990s and early 2000s, loans were made to individuals who had very little chance of repaying them. The loans were disguised within complex financial instruments such as Credit Default Swaps (CDSs), which were regarded as very secure by market ratings agencies such as Moodys. Using the new technology, these complex packages of debt were traded at amazing speed within financial markets in an uncontrolled manner. While these synthetic instruments were intended to limit risk by spreading it throughout the global financial system, they actually had the opposite effect, as was realised with hindsight, spreading risk and contagion globally. Massive defaults led to the near collapse of the global economy in 2008. National governments across Europe committed public money to bailing out the stricken banks, and subsequently, by 2011, a banking crisis had morphed into a sovereign debt crisis. Within the eurozone, the combination of high government borrowing to fund public services combined with the banking crisis had a particularly toxic effect, threatening the break-up of the eurozone and/or the ceding of fiscal control from member states to the EU. The epic boom and bust of the first decade of the 21st century forms the backdrop to this book. As discussed above, the crisis emerged as a result of the coupling of the political ideology of neoliberalism with the emergence of the globalised financial services industry, itself a product of the new technology and the knowledge society. While lifelong learning flourished across the developed world during the boom years, it is likely that the years of austerity to follow will see a reduction in all forms of publicly funded education and training, particularly since governments across the developed world have turned their backs on Keynesian economics, which would have suggested the need for counter-cyclic investment.

As noted by Sennett (2006), globalisation has not simply affected macroeconomics but has also had a profound effect on workers' identities. Deregulated labour markets, which are most strongly evident in the Anglo-Saxon world, require workers to engage in an ongoing process of upskilling in order to secure ongoing employment, creating a permanent sense of insecurity and alienation. Those who cannot adapt to the demands of rapidly changing labour markets are likely to find themselves excluded both socially and economically. Just as the new global economy generates great prosperity for some, it also intensifies the social and economic exclusion of continents, countries, regions, localities and social groups. As illustrated by the financial and political crisis that is engulfing Europe at the time of writing, the new global economy generates huge problems for politicians. Global markets appear to be uncontrollable by national governments, leading to fears that nation states may be unable to control their own financial affairs. Unelected transnational bodies, such as the International Monetary Fund, clearly enjoy increasing power in the new global order, with consequent challenges for democracy. Green et al (2007) have noted that national governments still have considerable power over tax regimes and redistributive spending, and that the power of the global markets may sometimes be used as an excuse to conceal political inaction or to justify major public spending cuts, as are taking place in many countries at the time of writing. Nonetheless, since the 1990s, as the power of the global markets has grown, politicians have placed increasing emphasis on lifelong learning as one of the few policy levers available to governments to secure their country's economic survival.

Social commentators have described the radical changes in individual and group identity arising as a result of globalisation. Beck (1992, 2000), for instance, suggests that, whereas in the past an individual's life course was strongly determined by social structures relating to social class and gender, the new global economy provides opportunities to exercise a much greater degree of individual agency, weakening traditional identities rooted in local communities or areas of work. At the same time, the uncertainty accompanying rapid labour market change may engender a deep sense of insecurity, particularly in those at the social margins who experience an abundance of risk. Education and lifelong learning play a key part in allowing individuals to forge new identities for themselves through social mobility, although some theories of individuation fail to recognise sufficiently the extent to which such opportunities are socially structured. For many, engaging in lifelong learning does not offer opportunities for social advancement, but merely of basic economic survival. As we illustrate in subsequent chapters, lifelong learning reflects the wider paradox of education, having the potential to transmit and intensify inequality across generations, but also to disrupt this process, opening up possibilities of social transformation. Individuals and policy makers are currently grappling with the problem of how to control, rather than be controlled by, the new global economy, and in this book we focus on the potential of lifelong learning to act as a socially transformative force, rather than simply reflecting or amplifying existing inequality. However, at a time of growing social inequality and reduced social transfers (OECD, 2008), the promise that the new global economy would unleash new opportunities for the majority of EU citizens seems somewhat far-fetched.

Throughout the book, we attempt to place the development of European policy on lifelong learning within a wider historical, economic and political context. As discussed more fully by Holford and Mohorčič Špolar in Chapter Three, the economic focus of the European Community meant that education and lifelong learning did not feature prominently in its early activities, but assumed a higher profile over time. The Treaty of Maastricht, signed in 1992, gave the European Union a modest role in education, particularly in the sphere of vocational education and training, which was seen as closely interconnected with the labour market. At the same time, it was reaffirmed that competence in education lay with member states. Since then education and lifelong learning has assumed an increasingly central position within European policy, contributing to attempts to achieve greater social and economic integration (CEC, 2006, 2007). As noted by a range of writers (for example Boshier, 1998; Field, 2006, Robertson, 2009) throughout the 1990s European policy on education and lifelong learning tended to focus on their contribution to utilitarian economic objectives rather than to wider social goals, often referring to the challenges of globalisation and the danger of Europe being overtaken by the emerging economies of China, India and Brazil. Robertson (2009) suggests that the focus on lifelong learning as a generator of human capital, which characterised EU political discourse from the 1990s onwards, reflects an ideological shift away from Keynesianism, with its emphasis on managed markets, towards neoliberalism, with its emphasis on free markets and transnational production.

Despite the primacy of the link between lifelong learning and human capital formation, Europe's commitment to the social dimension of lifelong learning resurfaces in the EU 2020 education and training strategy, where member states are invited to ensure 'equitable education and training systems that are aimed at providing opportunities, access, treatment and outcomes that are independent of socio-economic background and other factors which may lead to educational disadvantage' (Council of the European Union, 2010). The aim of removing the association between social background and educational outcomes across the EU is clearly highly ambitious, particularly at a time when public sector funding is being slashed following the collapse of the European banking system. A major focus of this book is to examine the extent to which lifelong learning systems are playing a part in equalising educational outcomes.

The new focus on the social dimension of lifelong learning seems to have been achieved by challenging the tensions between equity and efficiency, which were often assumed by neoliberal economic models. Writers such as Wilkinson (1996; and Wilkinson and Pickett, 2009) argue that more economically equal societies perform better on many measures including health, wellbeing and levels of violence. In other words, achieving reasonable levels of social cohesion should be seen as an essential precondition for economic prosperity. Reflecting these arguments, the 2006 Communication from the Commission to the Council and the European Parliament (CEC, 2006) maintained that social inequality carried serious economic costs and risks. Rather than being regarded as dichotomous, efficiency and equity in education and training systems should be seen as complementary, with greater equity leading to greater efficiency and vice versa.

Clearly, if efforts to achieve economic prosperity and social equality and cohesion can be aligned, then lifelong learning and education may be used to achieve not only more prosperous, but also more equal societies. However, not all commentators are equally sanguine that conflicting interests may so easily be resolved. For example, Rizvi and Lingard have argued that over the past three decades there has been 'an almost universal shift from social democratic to neoliberal orientations in thinking about educational purposes and governance, resulting in policies of corporatization, privatization and commercialization on the one hand, and on a greater demand for accountability on the other' (Rizvi and Lingard, 2010, p 3). They argue that economic efficiency now appears to be regarded as a metavalue, 'subsuming within its scope aspirations such as social equality, mobility and even social cohesion' (Rizvi and Lingard, 2010, p 85). As indicated above, the central question of this book is the extent to which lifelong learning is, on balance, serving the interests of global capitalism in the extraction of profit, or whether it is able to foster a more humane and benign version of capitalism that values individuals' aspirations for personal growth through education and regards social cohesion as an end in itself, not simply as a means of maximising economic outputs. In addressing this question, we are aware that, although lifelong learning may be seen as a manifestation of travelling policy, which is evident across the developed world, it also exists as embedded policy, adopting various forms in specific national and local contexts (Ozga and Lingard, 2007).

Our investigation of lifelong learning and social inequality focuses on a range of variables including social class, using a range of proxy measures such as individuals' and parents' levels of prior educational attainment. We also investigate experiences and outcomes of lifelong learning in relation to other individual characteristics such as gender, age and disability. Race/ethnicity and religion are also clearly very important aspects of inequality in access to lifelong learning, particularly in the context of growing anxieties about immigration. However, there is a lack of agreement on common definitions, and surveys such as the Adult Education Survey do not ask questions relating to these variables. As a result, the qualitative data presented in the book address equality issues as broadly as possible, whereas the quantitative data are unavoidably more limited in scope.

Lifelong learning and the building of human and social capital

As mentioned above and discussed further in Chapter Three, lifelong learning is regarded at European and national level as fulfilling a number of key social functions. These are, of course, by no means mutually exclusive. First, lifelong learning is seen as a generator of human capital, enabling states and individuals to maintain their economic competitiveness by constantly updating skills and competences. Second, lifelong learning is seen as a generator of social capital, bringing people together to engage in a shared endeavour that nurtures collective identity in an increasingly fragmented and individualised world. The generation of human and social capital are of course intertwined, since the acquisition of knowledge and skills for employment promotes social capital development through the formation of relationships in the workplace and the support of family and community life. Third, lifelong learning is seen as playing a key role in the European liberal education tradition, in which learning is valued for its own sake and is seen as a means of attaining personal growth and development, as well as contributing to the greater social good. This tradition is reflected in the existence of ancient universities in many countries, dedicated to the advancement of knowledge and sometimes opposed by the Church and the state. It has also formed a part of adult education systems in many European countries, and can often be seen as overlapping with a social capital approach. Finally, lifelong learning may be seen as an instrument of social control (Coffield, 1999), mediating particular value systems and compelling benefits claimants to engage in education and training as a condition of (minimal) state support.

The particular slant on lifelong learning in different countries depends on their history and current social, political and economic context. Enhancing economic growth is the major concern of states that have recently joined the EU (for example Bulgaria, Estonia, Slovenia, the Czech Republic, Lithuania). In the older parts of the EU (England, Scotland, Flanders, Austria and Ireland), the principal concern seems to be retaining position in the economic 'pecking order', as manufacturing continues to decline and greater emphasis is placed on high-tech, high-value added production. At the same time, particularly during the boom years of the 1990s and early 2000s, lifelong learning was seen as the means of opening up educational opportunities to non-traditional learners. Norway, although not officially a member of the EU, has much in common with the old member states of Northern and Western Europe in terms of welfare systems and economic development. With its small population and wealth derived from North Sea oil and gas, Norway has many economic assets, but is still clearly concerned about safeguarding its national prosperity into the future when the oil runs out. However, as in other Nordic countries, lifelong learning is also seen as a means of extending educational opportunity across a wide social spectrum, with the overarching goal of promoting social cohesion. The Russian Federation has a number of economic commonalities with some of the new member and candidate EU states, sharing with them common Soviet traditions. However, the scale and cultural diversity of the country means that it faces particular challenges in managing economic liberalisation. While the Russian Federation couches its policies in terms of adult education rather than the learning society, it is evident that the building of human capital is increasingly emphasised. In addition, the push to promote lifelong learning throughout Europe (including the Russian Federation) is due to the problems posed by a declining and ageing population, and the related need to enlarge the age groups available for active participation in the labour market. Furthermore, a high proportion of younger people in Europe are from migrant groups, some of whom lack the necessary paperwork to be legally employed in the EU. Migrant workers and their children pose particular challenges for social inclusion, which lifelong learning policies are only just beginning to address.

The nurturing of social capital has become increasingly important in old member states, for example the Republic of Ireland and the UK, as rising prosperity is coupled with growing social exclusion, which is seen as a threat to social stability. In countries like Ireland, with strong voluntary traditions, there is an emphasis on the need to nurture social cohesion through the incorporation of lifelong learning into neighbourhood regeneration strategies (see, for example, the Irish Green Paper on Adult Education, 1998). Sometimes, lifelong learning in this context is seen as a good in itself, and at other times it is portrayed as the vehicle for the development of human capital. The social control functions of lifelong learning are evident in the growth of links to welfare benefit systems and in the uses of lifelong learning to promote particular ideologies. Older EU member states tend to have relatively generous levels of social welfare, and there are major concerns that these may produce incentives towards economic inactivity, rather than efforts to upskill and rejoin the labour market. As a result, in countries such as the UK, Belgium and Austria, receipt of social security benefits is tied to requirements to participate in upskilling and 'active labour market' activities. In Austria conscious efforts were made in the post-war period to use lifelong learning and other types of education to re-educate people away from adherence to national socialism. In new and accession member states the emphasis on the value-free nature of the learning society, in contrast with the obvious ideological character of former Soviet-style education, may occlude the presence of less obvious ideological aspects, including the hegemony of market values.

Lifelong learning, social inclusion and equality

As we argue below, while neoliberal economic policies tend to lead to growing levels of economic inequality across Europe, there are anxieties about their propensity to erode the social fabric, ultimately compromising rather than promoting economic efficiency. For example, Green and Janmaat (2011) note the 'subtle and insidious' effects of extreme inequality on social cohesion, increasing the social distance between groups, undermining inter-group trust and reducing the sense of common citizenship. In the US, and increasingly in less equal European societies such as the UK, Green and Janmaat comment on the tendency of the rich to insulate themselves from the rest of society, avoiding taxes, living in privately policed, gated communities, and avoiding public services such as state-funded education and healthcare, which the rest of the population depend upon. This might be seen as a voluntary form of social exclusion, but it has a weakening effect on public services, which may come to be regarded as a safety net for the poor rather than part of the social wage used by all citizens. At the other end of the social spectrum, a growing body of people excluded from the labour market are at risk of involuntary social exclusion. Levitas (2005) noted that social exclusion may be attributed to poverty, worklessness or a failure to subscribe to dominant social values. While politicians often attempt to attribute social exclusion to the moral failure of individuals or social groups, the urban riots and anti-capitalist occupations of 2011 point to growing social unrest, particularly amongst young people whose job prospects appear to be particularly bleak.

In considering the uses of lifelong learning to tackle social exclusion in different countries, there is a need to identify which groups of individuals experience systematic social and economic inequality, so that positive measures may be appropriately targeted. The protected equality grounds recognised within

European policy and legislation (gender, race, disability, sexual orientation, religion/belief and age) relate to individuals' characteristics, circumstances or culture. Social class is of a slightly different order, in that it is both an outcome of the labour market and part of the transmission mechanism that affects how people's lives develop. Occupational social class is strongly associated with educational outcomes, so that even at pre-school age, children from middle-class backgrounds have better scores on tests of vocabulary and problem solving (Bradshaw, 2011). These children are more likely to obtain higher level educational qualifications and subsequently find work in better paying jobs, thus ensuring that social class advantage is reproduced across generations.

Many theorists have acknowledged the need to pay attention to economic injustices, associated with the politics of social class, and to cultural injustices, associated with the politics of identity, in order to understand and remedy the situation of socially marginalised groups (for example, Sen, 1985; Young, 1990; Fraser, 1997). The exploration of barriers to learning based on analysis of the International Adult Education Survey (see Chapter Five) investigates the relationship between demographic and social factors. Of course, there are often intersections between different types of inequality, so that, for example, recent immigrants and some minority ethnic groups, such as Gypsy Travellers or Romany people, may be particularly vulnerable to both economic inequality and cultural disrespect. Education and lifelong learning have the potential to amplify or ameliorate inequality in economic, social and cultural domains, and social justice initiatives need to take account of the specific barriers encountered by particular social groups. One of the challenges of monitoring inequality in access to lifelong learning and targeting initiatives effectively is to develop common definitions of particular social categories. As discussed in Chapter Seven on access to higher education, there is currently a lack of shared understandings of variables such as race/ethnicity across Europe, and this has hindered the establishment of shared benchmarks and indicators.

The LLL2010 research project

As noted earlier, this book draws on data gathered as part of a European project on policy and practice on lifelong learning (LLL2010), which formed part of the European Commission's Sixth Framework Research Programme. The project sought to understand how lifelong learning policies are understood and implemented across Europe and how these policies impact on equality and social inclusion. Various elements of the research are used, including a review of policy and statistics; a survey-based analysis of the experiences and motivations of returners to formal education; case studies of the cultures of workplace learning in small to medium-sized enterprises (SMEs) and institutional approaches to widening access in different countries.

The LLL2010 research project had a number of specific objectives including the following:

- understanding the role of lifelong learning in knowledge-based societies, particularly with regard to managing the tensions between social inclusion and economic efficiency;
- investigating the implementation of lifelong learning policy in particular national and local contexts within the overarching framework of EU enlargement and globalisation;
- analysing the role particular parts of education systems (for example higher education, workplace learning, community education) play in the enhancement of lifelong learning;
- investigating the motivations of adult returners to formal education and the factors which influence their satisfaction with the courses on which they enrol;
- exploring the adequacy of lifelong learning policies for different social groups, in particular those at risk of social exclusion;
- considering the extent to which lifelong learning has the potential for social transformation, as opposed to the intensification of inequality.

These objectives were achieved through the following sub-projects:

- sub-project 1 consisted of a review of statistics and policies on lifelong learning across Europe;
- sub-project 2 entailed a secondary analysis of Labour Force Survey and Adult Education Survey data;
- sub-project 3 involved the conduct of a large-scale survey in 12 of the partner countries;
- sub-project 4 centred on the analysis of approaches to workplace learning in SMEs in the partner countries, along with case studies conducted in each country;
- sub-project 5 focused on approaches to widening access to different types of lifelong learning, including higher education.

A total of 13 countries – Russia, Estonia, Lithuania, the Czech Republic, Hungary, Bulgaria, Slovenia, Flanders, Austria, Norway, Ireland, England and Scotland – participated in the project. Six of these countries are new EU member states located in Central and Eastern Europe, and, as we discuss in greater depth in Chapter Two, little is known about their emergent welfare states. Norway, as one point of comparison, is part of the Scandinavian group of very prosperous countries with high taxes and relatively generous welfare states. England, Scotland and Ireland form an Anglo-Celtic group where neoliberalism has been increasingly influential over the past three decades. Austria and Flanders form part of a continental group of countries with high trade union membership and worker support, but with relatively high levels of social exclusion. Two countries that participated in the project – Norway and Russia – are not members of the EU. While much of the analysis focuses on these 13 countries, some chapters draw on data from across Europe and from other OECD countries. Chapter Five, for example, using data from the Adult Education Survey to identify barriers to participation in formal education, is important because it enables an additional layer of comparison to be introduced, allowing the countries selected for in-depth study to be placed within a wider international context.

The research took place between 2005 and 2011, the second half of the decade dedicated to the implementation of the Lisbon Strategy, which aimed to make the EU 'the most competitive and dynamic knowledge-based economy in the world capable of sustainable economic growth with more and better jobs and greater social cohesion' (CEC, 2000). The timeframe of the research spanned a phase of economic growth across Europe, followed by a major economic recession of which the aftershocks are still being felt within the eurozone and beyond. At the same time as these major economic upheavals were taking place, many Central and Eastern European countries were still adjusting to the shift from a planned to a market-based economy. Across Europe, but particularly in countries where financial services formed a significant part of the economy, a large amount of public money was diverted into preventing the meltdown of banks and other financial institutions (at least a trillion pounds in the UK). Subsequently, governments across Europe have embarked on a programme of public sector cuts, which are likely to have a disproportionately adverse effect on institutions delivering non-statutory services, particularly in the post-compulsory phase. Much of the data gathered for the LLL2010 project took place prior to the recession, but our analysis and discussion attempts to take account of the opportunities and challenges for lifelong learning as economic and political problems intensify across Europe.

Our focus in the book is mainly, but not exclusively, on formal education and training, which refers to education and training delivered in the regular system of schools, universities and colleges in each country. Formal learning may include a number of very different activities, such as adult basic education for those who lack numeracy and literacy skills; language classes for recent immigrants; courses for employees delivered in the workplace or on day release to colleges; university degrees delivered on a full-time or part-time basis. Courses of study range from basic education (ISCED levels 1 and 2) through to degree and postgraduate study (ISCED levels 5 and 6). Informal learning, by way of contrast, can be intentional, for example attending short lectures or participating in a book club. It can also be unintentional, occurring by chance or as a by-product of everyday activities. Inevitably, informal learning is very difficult to define, since it might refer at its broadest to all aspects of human existence and interaction, which involve growth and development throughout life. Our focus on formal learning was partly related to the difficulty in defining informal learning, but also because formal learning has become increasingly important in modern societies, acting as a positional good that plays a major role in legitimating the distribution of economic wealth.

The structure of the book

The structure of the book is as follows. Chapter Two (Riddell and Weedon) examines the broad social and economic context in which lifelong learning in Europe is located, in particular the global trend towards growing economic inequality. Since success in initial education is both a cause and an effect of wider social inequality, we identify the trends that are evident in different countries. We consider the broad purposes that have been ascribed to lifelong learning, including its role in generating human and social capital, as a means of individual intellectual development, and as the vehicle for social control. We also consider understandings of social inclusion and equality across Europe, and the contribution which lifelong learning may make to the achievement of a more equal society. Throughout this book we draw on the concept of bounded agency developed by Rubenson and Desjardins (2009). These writers argue that the chances of participation in adult learning are linked not only to individual motivation, but also to the social context in which the individual learner is located. The approach to social welfare and lifelong learning within specific countries forms a crucial part of the backdrop against which individual decisions on participation are made. We therefore briefly review existing ways of categorising different countries with regard to their approaches to social welfare and lifelong learning, before presenting the typology that has informed our work.

Chapter Three (Holford and Mohorčič Špolar) explores the developing European understanding of lifelong learning over time. While social cohesion is generally acknowledged to be one of the aims of the EU's lifelong learning policy, it is typically seen as subordinate to the 'growth' and 'knowledge economy' dimension. The chapter explores the relative role and framing of the 'economic' and 'social' dimensions in EU policy on lifelong learning, focusing on the period since 1995. It suggests that while vocational and labour market concerns have always predominated, the EU has ensured that social concerns remain on the agenda. However, the nature of these 'social' concerns requires interrogation. Sometimes, such notions as 'active citizenship' and 'social inclusion' have been reduced almost entirely to characterising an individual's level of engagement with the labour market. The open question is to what extent EU policy has maintained, expanded, or creatively reframed the social dimension of education and lifelong learning.

In Chapter Four, Boeren, Nicaise, Roosmaa and Saar analyse differences between individuals and groups in relation to their motivations for participating in adult education, drawing on bounded agency theory (Rubenson and Desjardins, 2009). According to EU policy documents, lifelong learning mainly serves the following four purposes: enhancing or maintaining employability, promoting personal development, fostering social cohesion and developing active citizenship. It is generally believed that fulfilling labour market requirements (employability) account for more than 80% of all learning activities. Whereas this may apply to learning as a whole, this analysis finds that national systems differ widely with regard to the scope of courses on offer and the reasons for participation in formal adult learning are far more diverse, so that individuals are not simply calculating the financial return for further study.

On the basis of survey data collected from 12,000 adult learners in 12 European countries, the profile of participants in formal adult education is compared. Two key issues are addressed. Firstly, the factors determining adults' motivation to learn are identified. Determinants at individual, school and system level are included in the analysis, and we conclude that the quality of the courses (characteristics of the learning environment as well as the learning process) exert a decisive influence on learner satisfaction and motivation. Lessons can be drawn from this analysis as regards the key determinants of quality in (formal) adult education. Secondly, the authors examine differences in motivation by sociodemographic and socioeconomic background. The findings appear to contradict some old stereotypes, for example about the more extrinsic motivation of those with low levels of initial education and the more intrinsic motivation of highly-educated learners. Needless to say, insights into the patterns of motivation are essential to inform policies aiming to boost participation in lifelong learning, especially among disadvantaged groups.

As noted earlier, an individual's decision to participate in adult learning is not simply a reflection of their individual motivation, but also of the social and economic structures which frame their lives. These structures may either promote or inhibit access to lifelong learning, and in Chapter Five Róbert uses Adult Education Survey data from 2007 to examine patterns of participation in lifelong learning and the socioeconomic and demographic variables that influence these outcomes. The chapter examines the way in which social and demographic barriers intersect in specific national contexts and in groups of countries. The extent to which particular countries can be fitted into broad groupings related to their approach to social welfare and lifelong learning is considered. It is argued that there is a need to examine the way in which general policies such as lifelong learning are embedded differently in different contexts.

Workplace learning in SMEs is the topic of Chapter Six, contributed by Hefler and Markowitsch. Within the existing literature, there is wide acceptance of the crucial role of the workplace as a site of learning and of employers in providing non-formal training. However, far less attention has been paid to the role of employers and workplaces in providing access to formal education. This chapter uses case studies of SMEs to analyse the relationship between approaches to lifelong learning and organisational learning cultures. It is argued that participation in formal adult education in enterprises is influenced simultaneously by: (a) the education system and its articulation with the labour market, (b) a set of institutional factors driving the application of training activities, and (c) the agency of individual firms and learning cultures. It is suggested that the astonishing array of formal adult education opportunities available in all European countries cannot be understood as the result of converging economic needs, but arises as a result of competing legitimacy claims of different education systems and their impact on social stratification.

Higher education has been identified by the EU as an area of great importance both in terms of producing workers with high level skills and in promoting social cohesion and fairness by promoting cross-generational social mobility. One of the goals of the most recent EU education and training strategy is that by 2020 at least 40% of EU citizens should have tertiary level qualifications, on the grounds that labour market forecasts suggest a decline in low-skilled jobs and a growth in jobs requiring medium and high level skills. Chapter Seven (Weedon and Riddell) begins with an overview of European policy on higher education, with its encouragement of student mobility through the Socrates programme and the standardisation of qualifications through the Bologna process. Despite the hope that the expansion of higher education would contribute to much greater opportunities for social mobility, the analysis of EU statistics suggests that across all countries there are strong associations between parental educational background and the chances of achieving a higher level qualification. Similarly, those who obtain a tertiary level qualification are much more likely to be in employment than others and to achieve higher level of earnings across the life-course. Although women are generally more likely to participate in higher education than men, this is not always the case. For example, in the UK and Slovenia women are more likely to have higher level education qualifications than men, and in other countries such as Austria the reverse is the case. Across Europe, disabled people appear to be very disadvantaged in accessing higher education and are also less likely to obtain employment than non-disabled people with similar qualifications. The chapter concludes by presenting case studies of widening access initiatives in different European countries. Overall, it is argued that while higher education often legitimates and perpetuates existing social inequalities, it also has the potential to open up new opportunities for previously excluded individuals and groups. At the same time it cannot compensate for the general trend towards widening inequality across Europe, which has coincided with the expansion of access to higher education.

In the concluding chapter we return to the central theme of the book with regard to the understanding and enactment of lifelong learning in different national contexts and within the wider context of the new global economy. This theme is considered in relation to the issues addressed in different chapters, including the reasons adults return to education, the way in which the institutional architecture of national education systems promotes or inhibits lifelong learning, and the extent to which lifelong learning is currently promoting or inhibiting progress towards social justice across Europe. Evidence from different chapters is used to explore the expression and resolution of central tensions between neoliberalism and inclusive liberalism in lifelong learning policy and practice. Future EU policy options in the sphere of lifelong learning are examined in the light of the recession and the retrenchment of the welfare state.

References

Beck, U. (1992) *The risk society,* London: Sage.

Beck, U. (2000) *What is globalization?,* Cambridge: Polity Press.

Boshier, R. (1998) 'Edgar Faure after 25 years: down but not out', in J. Holford, P. Jarvis and C. Griffin (eds) *International perspectives on lifelong learning,* London: Kogan Page, pp 3-20.

Bradshaw, P. (2011) *Growing up in Scotland: changes in child cognitive ability in the pre-school years, Research Findings No 2/2011,* Edinburgh: Scottish Government.

Castells, M. (2000) *The rise of the network society,* 2nd edn, Oxford: Blackwell.

Coffield, F. (1999) 'Breaking the consensus: lifelong learning as social capital'. *British Educational Research Journal,* vol 25, no 4, pp 479-99.

CEC (Commission of the European Communities) (2000) *Lisbon European Council 23 and 24 March 2000, Presidency Conclusions,* Brussels: CEC.

CEC (Commission of the European Communities) (2006) *It is never too late to learn,* Communication from the Commission to the Council, the European Parliament, the European Economic and Social Committee of the Regions, Brussels: CEC.

CEC (Commission of the European Communities) (2007) *Action plan on adult learning: it's always a good time to learn,* Communication from the Commission to the Council, the European Parliament, the European Economic and Social Committee of the Regions, Brussels: CEC.

Council of the European Union (2010) 'Council conclusions on the social dimension of education and training', *Official Journal of the European Union* (2010/C 135/02), Brussels: CEC.

Field, J. (2006) *Lifelong learning and the new educational order,* 2nd edn, Stoke on Trent: Trentham Books.

Fraser, N. (1997) *Justice interruptus: critical reflections on the post-socialist condition,* London: Routledge.

Green, A. and Janmaat, J.G. (2011) *Regimes of social cohesion: societies and the crisis of globalisation,* Basingstoke: Palgrave Macmillan.

Green, A., Little, A., Kamat, S., Oketch, M. and Vickers, E. (eds) (2007) *Education and development in a global era: strategies for 'successful globalisation'* London: Department for International Development.

Irish Green Paper on Adult Education (1998) *Education in era of lifelong learning,* Pn 6394, Dublin: Department of Education and Science.

Levitas, R. (2005) *The inclusive society? Social exclusion and New Labour,* 2nd edn, Basingstoke: Palgrave Macmillan.

OECD (2008) *Growing unequal? Income distribution and poverty in OECD countries,* Paris: OECD.

Ozga, J. and Lingard, B. (2007) 'Globalisation, education policy and politics', in B. Lingard and J. Ozga (eds) *The RoutledgeFalmer reader in education policy and politics,* London: RoutledgeFalmer, pp 65-82.

Riddell, S., Baron, S. and Wilson, A. (2001) *The learning society and people with learning difficulties,* Bristol: Policy Press.

Rizvi, F. and Lingard, B. (2010) *Globalizing education policy,* London: Routledge.

Robertson, S. (2009) 'Europe, competitiveness and higher education', in R. Dale and S. Robertson (eds) *Globalisation and Europeanisation in education*, Oxford: Symposium Books, pp 65-83.

Rubenson, K. and Desjardins, R. (2009) 'The impact of welfare state regimes on barriers to participation in adult education: a bounded agency model', *Adult Education Quarterly*, vol 59, no 3, pp187-207.

Sen, A. (1985) *Commodities and capabilities*, Oxford: North-Holland.

Sennett, R. (2006) *The culture of the new capitalism,* New Haven: Yale University Press.

Stiglitz, J. (2010) *Freefall: free markets and the sinking of the global economy.* Allen Lane: London.

Wilkinson, R. (1996) *Unhealthy societies: the affliction of inequality,* London: Routledge.

Wilkinson, R. and Pickett, K. (2009) *The spirit level: why more equal societies almost always do better,* London: Allen Lane.

Young, I. (1990) *Justice and the politics of difference,* Princeton: Princeton University Press.

TWO

Lifelong learning and the wider European socioeconomic context

Sheila Riddell and Elisabet Weedon, Centre for Research in Education Inclusion and Diversity, University of Edinburgh

Introduction

The aim of this chapter is to examine the relationship between lifelong learning systems and the wider socioeconomic context in which they are located at national and European levels. We describe the growth of economic inequality across much of Europe, which has coincided with the emergence of the knowledge economy. As demonstrated by Wilkinson (1996), Wilkinson and Pickett (2009) and Green and Janmaat (2011), countries with higher levels of inequality are much more prone to a range of problems associated with loss of trust and weak social cohesion. Education and lifelong learning are often charged with ameliorating these problems, but there are questions about the extent to which education can compensate for social and economic inequality. At the same time as common economic trends can be identified across all European countries, with knock-on effects for welfare regimes and systems of lifelong learning, there is also great variation between individual countries and groups of countries. As noted by Green et al (2007), one of the central debates within the literature on globalisation concerns the extent to which there is a growing trend towards the homogenisation of national cultures, reflected, amongst other things, within national systems of education and lifelong learning. An alternative view is that nation states, as a reaction to globalisation, may seek to intensify their cultural differences that are reflected strongly within education systems. Over recent years, through the Open Method of Coordination, the EU has sought to encourage member states to harmonise their education and lifelong systems with a view to facilitating the free movement of labour across national boundaries (see Chapter Three for further discussion). Understanding the similarities and differences between national systems as they react to global economic forces is therefore important in assessing progress towards a single harmonised system of European lifelong learning, particularly within the context of the ongoing economic crisis that may engender a less, rather than a more united Europe.

This chapter is underpinned by an understanding that different varieties of capitalism (Hall and Soskice, 2004), reflected in different approaches to social welfare and lifelong learning, are critical in facilitating or discouraging participation in lifelong learning. Adults who are motivated to learn will only be able to do so if systems and support are in place to facilitate their return to education after a break (Green et al, 2007; Rubenson and Desjardins, 2009). The typology of countries that is presented here and referred to in subsequent chapters highlights different approaches to social welfare and lifelong learning regimes, which are closely intertwined. The lifelong learning systems of some countries (specifically the Scandinavian countries and the Anglo-Celtic liberal market regimes) encourage lifelong learning as the means of boosting economic competitiveness and social inclusion. By way of contrast, adult education systems within corporate continental countries are more rigid and social transfers rather than lifelong learning systems are seen as the main way of achieving social cohesion. Finally, countries in Central and Eastern Europe, which are still making the transition from socialist to market economies, are at a much earlier phase in the development of lifelong learning. They are generally much poorer than the old member states and often spend less on lifelong learning and social transfers. While many typologies of lifelong learning and social welfare tend to group these countries together on the grounds that it is too early to discern clear differences between them, an attempt is made here to draw out some of the distinguishing features which are emerging.

The trend towards growing inequality

There are a variety of ways of measuring inequality, one of which is the Gini coefficient, which is an international summary indicator of economic inequalities. It can take values from zero to 100 (in percentage terms) or from zero to one. Zero indicates perfect equality, with every household or individual having the same amount. A value of 100 or of one would imply that one household or individual had all of the country's income or wealth. This measure does not take account of the very richest or very poorest in a country and therefore does not provide a complete picture of the extent of inequality. Nonetheless, it is commonly used by bodies such as the Organisation for Economic Cooperation and Development (OECD) and is useful as one means of drawing cross-country comparisons. As illustrated by **Figure 2.1**, relatively poor countries, such as Mexico and Turkey, have very high levels of inequality, as do English-speaking countries with deregulated labour markets, such as the US, the UK and New Zealand. Since the mid-1970s, according to the OECD (2008), there has been an increase in household income inequality across Europe, particularly in countries with liberal market economies, such as the UK and Ireland, which tend to have less progressive taxation systems and less generous social transfers.

The percentage of households at risk of poverty is another way of shining a light on the extent of social inequality within a country. Within Europe, a relative measure is used, so that households are described as being at risk of poverty if their equivalised income is less than 60% of the median. As illustrated

Figure 2.1: Inequality in OECD countries as measured by the Gini co-efficient

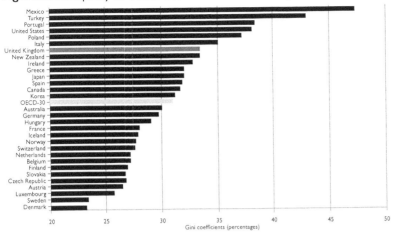

Source: Hills et al (2010); aggregated data from mid-2000s

in **Figure 2.2**, there is considerable variation among the LLL2010 countries in relation to the proportion of households that are at risk of poverty. In countries with liberal market economies, such as the UK and Ireland, the risk of poverty is relatively high. This is also the case in Estonia and Lithuania, which rapidly adopted features of the market economy, such as flat tax regimes and deregulated labour markets, in the post-socialist era. Bulgaria has seen a rapid increase in households at risk of poverty since joining the EU. **Figure 2.2** shows that in countries such as the UK and Ireland, where the economy has shrunk rapidly since 2008, there has, counter-intuitively, been a decrease in households at risk of poverty. This reflects the fact that there are fewer higher income earners and so the gap between those at the top and bottom has decreased, although those at the bottom are likely to be worse off in real terms than they were before the economic crisis. However, from 2012 onwards, higher rates of unemployment and reductions in benefits are likely to lead to an increase in household and child poverty.

Wilkinson and Pickett (2009) have argued that, in developed countries, levels of public health and other indicators of social cohesion such as violence and trust are strongly influenced by income distribution rather than the absolute level of GDP. They suggest that this may be due to the adverse psychological effects of high levels of inequality on individuals across the social spectrum, but with particularly negative effects for those at the social margins. Income distribution reflects the spread of educational qualifications and skills across the population, since more highly qualified individuals are generally paid more than those with lower qualifications. The distribution of educational opportunities and outcomes therefore plays a role in fostering or inhibiting economic inequality. It is worth noting that countries such as the US and the UK, with a high proportion of well-qualified people, may also have high levels of inequality because of the skewed distribution of educational qualifications (see Chapter Seven for further discussion of the significance of the expansion of higher education). It may also be

Figure 2.2: Percentage of households at risk of poverty after social transfers

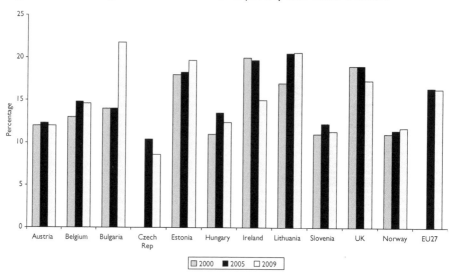

Source: Eurostat, EU-SILC (http://appsso.eurostat.ec.europa.eu/nui/show.do?dataset=ilc_li02&lang=en), accessed 2 August 2011

the case that people with higher educational qualifications may not be employed in graduate-level jobs, particularly where a hierarchy of institutions has emerged and the supply of graduates outstrips the available opportunities. For example, in Greece and Ireland many highly qualified young people are either unemployed or working in entry-level jobs, creating high levels of frustration. As argued by Brown and Lauder (1996), in order to avoid the emergence of a damaging culture of competitive individualism, there is a need for the state to intervene to ensure that educational qualifications are fairly distributed and adequate support is available for less qualified people.

The OECD (2008) comments that while the trend towards greater inequality is significant, particularly in the English-speaking world, it would have been much greater in the absence of large-scale social transfers through taxation and welfare payments that occurred in most countries during the economic expansion of the 1990s and early 2000s. Once governments begin to cut spending on redistributive measures, as is the case across much of Europe at the time of writing, then inequality is likely to grow rapidly. Rather than relying on social transfers and high levels of public expenditure, the OECD suggests that there should be a greater focus on assisting people into jobs that pay a living wage and offer opportunities for career progression. This view clearly reflects the social integrationist discourse identified by Levitas (2005), which sees work as the source of individual and social empowerment. However, it ignores the problems identified by Bauman (1998), who notes the growth of 'poor jobs', that is, low-skilled and insecure work with poor pay and conditions of employment. The OECD conviction that the route to social inclusion is through work also ignores the socially corrosive effect of the 'redistribution of wealth from the poorest to the richest' that goes on at 'unstoppably accelerating speed' (Bauman, 1998, p 92).

Factors underpinning the growth in inequality

During the immediate post-war period, there was an optimistic assumption across Europe that expanding access to education would more or less automatically lead to a reduction in inequality. However, this has not turned out to be the case (Brown and Lauder, 1996). As noted in Chapter Seven, there has been a rapid expansion in higher education participation, which has coincided with a growth in economic inequality. As illustrated in **Figure 2.3**, in all countries those with higher levels of education are more likely to be in employment and to have access to ongoing education, often delivered in the workplace, while those with low-level qualifications find it difficult to gain a foothold in the labour market. Furthermore, as shown in **Figure 2.4**, in many (but not all) countries those who initially succeed in the education system are more likely than others to participate in education across the life-course, thus amplifying their existing social advantage. In England, Scotland, Belgium, Ireland and Norway the majority of adult participants in formal adult education are already qualified at ISCED levels 5 and 6. By way of contrast, the majority of participants in Slovenia and Austria are qualified at ISCED levels 3 and 4, reflecting the fact that more people have vocational qualifications in these countries and are likely to seek to upgrade their qualifications. In all countries those with lower level qualifications (ISCED levels 1 and 2) are less likely to participate in lifelong learning.

Figure 2.3: Employment rates by educational attainment, 2010 (25–64 years of age)

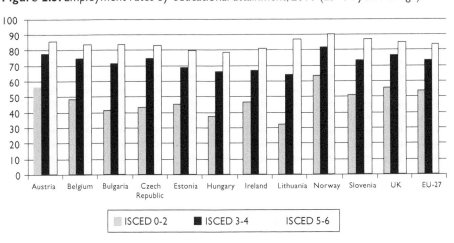

Source: http://epp.eurostat.ec.europa.eu/statistics_explained/index.php/Employment_
statistics#Employment_rates_by_gender.2C_age_and_educational_attainment

Figure 2.4: Highest educational attainment of participants in formal adult education (25–64) for LLL2010 partner countries

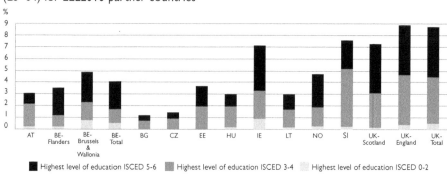

Source: Labour Force Survey ad hoc module on LLL2003; micro dataset, own calculations

Reasons for the growth in inequality

Over the past 30 years in Europe there have been major changes in the composition of the labour market, with the expansion of the service sector and the decline of the manufacturing sector, particularly in the Anglo-Celtic countries. This shift has been accompanied by the growth of skilled as opposed to unskilled jobs (CEC, 2010; Giddens, 2006), described as 'skill biased technical change' (Brakman, 2006). Brakman has argued that production technology has favoured skilled over unskilled labour by increasing its relative productivity, and, therefore, its relative demand. Globalisation clearly plays a part here too, with routine production processes increasingly taking place in less developed countries where labour is cheaper.

The focus on knowledge economy employment has meant that those in highly skilled jobs have captured an increasing share of income at the expense of lower skilled workers. The International Labour Organisation (2008) found that over the past two decades labour's share of output fell in two thirds of countries for which data were available. In countries like the UK, where there has been a particularly marked shift from manufacturing to the service sector, the decline in working-class people's share of wealth has been particularly marked (Lansley, 2011). In the old manufacturing industries that characterised the UK economy until the 1970s, workers had secure jobs and were represented by relatively strong trade unions that were successful in defending wage levels. This led to a period of convergence between working-class and middle-class incomes. As the service sector came to predominate from the 1980s onwards, however, trade union membership declined, wages were lower and conditions of employment became less favourable for those in manual occupations relative to others. In countries such as Germany, Belgium and Sweden, where manufacturing of high-value added products still forms a major part of the economy and trade union membership is higher, the polarisation of skills and income levels has not been as marked as is the case in the UK.

As discussed more fully in later chapters, adults with lower qualifications are much less likely to participate in lifelong learning than more highly qualified individuals. Governments often see participation in lifelong learning as one of the few escape routes from dead-end work. However, it must be recognised that the benefit of such participation may vary greatly, with those who are already highly qualified using additional training to ratchet their incomes even higher. Low-skilled workers, in contrast, are likely to find that they only have access to low-level courses that may have little impact on their labour market position, although such courses may offer other benefits in terms of personal development and social connections. Furthermore, for socially marginalised groups such as people with learning difficulties, adult education is likely to develop bonding rather than bridging networks, offering only limited opportunities for future development (Riddell et al, 2001).

European countries differ greatly in the opportunities to participate in lifelong learning that are available to their citizens. In the following section we consider the way in which countries may be grouped together with regard to the shared characteristics of their lifelong learning systems, which in turn are connected with their wider welfare systems. As noted in Chapter One, a key concept informing this study is that of bounded agency (Rubenson and Desjardins, 2009), according to which individual decisions on whether to participate in adult education are driven not only by personal motivation, but also by the social structures in which individuals are located. The nature of the welfare and lifelong learning regime is critical in terms of opening up or closing down educational opportunities, thus influencing individuals' sense of agency. The data informing this analysis are derived from the review of lifelong learning policies and systems that was conducted by each participating country's national team as part of the LLL2010 project, as well as the review of statistics and secondary analysis of the Adult Education Survey and the Labour Force Survey.

Contrasting approaches to lifelong learning and social welfare

One of the objectives of the LLL2010 project was to develop a typology of lifelong learning systems in the 13 countries of study. Understanding similarities and differences between groups of countries may be useful in terms of viewing critically the variants of the European socioeconomic model that are emerging in the context of globalisation, and, more specifically, the way in which capitalism is evolving internationally (Hall and Soskice, 2004). Lifelong learning is clearly a key aspect of social policy, linking education, social welfare and employment. It is therefore useful to begin with a brief overview of existing typologies of social welfare regimes, considering their applicability to the field of lifelong learning. Most of these typologies have been developed in relation to the EU-15 (EU member countries prior to 1 May 2004 – Austria, Belgium, Denmark, Finland, France, Germany, Greece, Ireland, Italy, Luxembourg, the Netherlands, Portugal, Spain, Sweden and the UK), and one of the major challenges of this project is to begin to understand the directions in which the new member states are moving. In the following paragraphs we briefly review existing typologies of social policy and lifelong learning, before explaining our own grouping of countries.

The best known typology of welfare states is Esping-Andersen's 'three worlds of welfare capitalism' (Esping-Andersen, 1990). This is a theoretically founded typology that divides capitalist welfare states according to welfare regimes as follows:

- the 'liberal' welfare state that has a limited social insurance plan and means tested benefits. The beneficiaries are usually low-income and from a working-class background (for example UK and US);
- the 'conservative-corporatist' regime that aims to retain existing difference in status within the particular society. There is a strong emphasis on social insurance (for example Belgium, Austria);
- the 'social-democratic' regime that aims to promote equality and to provide universal benefits. It normally has a universal insurance scheme but uses some means-testing in provision of benefits (for example Norway).

Esping-Andersen's approach has been criticised on the grounds that even some of the countries for which it was originally developed do not fit neatly into one of the categories.

More recently, following the expansion of the EU, challenges have arisen in terms of incorporating new member states into existing social welfare models. Aiginger and Guger (2006), drawing on the work of Esping-Andersen and others, analysed differences in welfare models across Europe. Writing in 2006, before the advent of the economic crisis of 2007 onwards, they argued that a new European model of welfare was emerging, most notably in Scandinavian countries, characterised by welfare and sustainability on the one hand and efficiency and economic incentives on the other. This model, sometimes described as flexi-curity, differed from the old welfare state model, which emphasised social transfers but placed insufficient emphasis on active labour markets and flexibility through lifelong learning. The new European model differed markedly from the US model, with deregulated labour markets and minimal social protection. Large continental countries (Italy, Germany and France) were less successful than the Nordic countries in developing this new model. Aiginger and Guger (2006) also argued that the education systems and institutions of the knowledge economy were playing an increasingly important role in the new European socioeconomic model, as well as the traditional components of welfare societies such as the social security and taxation system. They suggest that there are three key dimensions – responsibility, regulation and redistribution – that characterise the European socioeconomic model and are reflected in different ways in a variety of European countries. Responsibility refers to the activities that the state undertakes on behalf of its citizens, including providing welfare, health and social care services, housing, education and so on. In some European countries, individuals are expected to accept a greater degree of responsibility for the procurement of social support than in others. Regulation refers to the way in which labour relations are institutionalised and the labour market is regulated, as well as other administrative systems that control social relations. Redistribution refers to the way in which financial support is transferred to those in need and the extent to which social services are available to all. The taxation system is clearly of great importance in determining the extent and nature of distribution that occurs within a society. Overall, the new European socioeconomic model, as interpreted in different nation states, influences and is shaped by every aspect of life, including employment, production, productivity, cultural institutions and behaviour, learning and the creation and diffusion of knowledge.

The typology of countries suggested by Aiginger and Guger, despite emphasising the importance of education and lifelong learning, strongly reflects traditional economic indicators such as annual growth, GDP per capita, employment rate and unemployment rate. It includes the following groupings:

- **The Scandinavian model** (including Denmark, Finland, the Netherlands, Sweden, Norway), which places a great deal of emphasis on redistribution, with social benefits financed by high taxation. Social partnership is also stressed, with employers, trade unions and educationists/trainers contributing to the sustenance of a knowledge society. The model is characterised by active labour market policies and high employment rates.
- **The continental model** (including Germany, France, Italy, Belgium, Austria), which emphasises employment as the basis of social transfers, but places much less emphasis on including those who are outside the labour market or the education system, with little emphasis on redistribution. Industrial relations and wage-bargaining are centralised and education systems are relatively static and hierarchical.
- **The Anglo-Saxon model** (including Ireland, UK), which is economically and socially liberal, emphasising the importance of individuals adopting responsibility for their own education, training and social welfare. Social transfers are smaller, more targeted and means tested. There is less regulation of the labour market and freedom of movement within the education system.
- **The Mediterranean model** (including Greece, Portugal, Spain), within which social transfers are small and the family takes a major responsibility for providing support and care to its members. Employment rates, specifically those of women, are low.
- **The catching-up model** (including Czech Republic, Hungary), which is characterised by deregulated labour markets and low taxes on individuals and companies. New EU member states are relatively much poorer than old member states, and while the old socialist forms of social support have disappeared or diminished, new forms of welfare such as those in the Scandinavian countries have not emerged. Key features of the catching-up model have yet to be

elaborated, and there is clearly a need to investigate existing and emerging differences between these countries.

Green (2006; 2011) has taken the analysis a step further, developing national typologies that allow links to be made between approaches to lifelong learning and social cohesion. The following three regimes identified by Green are characterised by different approaches to lifelong learning and social cohesion:

- the liberal regime (Australia, Ireland, New Zealand, UK, US);
- the social market regime (North–west continental Europe);
- the social democratic regime (Nordic countries).

Within the liberal regime, lifelong learning systems produce unequal skills outcomes that reinforce economic inequality and damage social cohesion. However, problems relating to social cohesion are, at least in part, offset by opportunities for adults to return to formal education, boosting employment, economic competitiveness and social cohesion. Within the social market regime there are less polarised skills distributions, with apprenticeships mitigating the negative effects of skills distribution in some countries, producing less unequal outcomes. However, less participation in adult education reduces employment rates and increases exclusion. In the Nordic regime there are not only less unequal outcomes from school, but also many opportunities for adults to participate in lifelong learning, thus boosting employment rates and diminishing economic and social inequality. Like many other typologies of the social policy and lifelong learning systems of developed countries, Green's typology is partial and Central and Eastern European countries are excluded on the grounds that their systems are currently too embryonic to be clearly defined.

As noted above, an important development in Green's analysis is the demonstration of a correlation between educational inequality and general trust in a range of developed countries, using data from the International Adult Literacy Survey (IALS) and the World Values Survey. Countries with high levels of skills inequality, such as Portugal, the US and the UK, also have low levels of trust, as indicated by the survey question 'Generally speaking, would you say that most people can be trusted or that you can't be too careful in dealing with people?'. Conversely, countries with low levels of skills inequality, such as Norway, Denmark, the Netherlands, Sweden and Finland, have higher levels of social trust. Green's findings indicate that ensuring a greater degree of equality in the level of skills within a population is likely to foster the development of both human and social capital, suggesting that equalising access to lifelong learning may contribute to both social inclusion and economic competitiveness.

Methods used in developing an extended typology of lifelong learning and welfare systems

In developing typologies of countries based on their welfare and lifelong learning systems within the LLL2010 project we considered that the existing typologies were useful as a starting point but had a number of inadequacies, not least because they failed to pay sufficient attention to the new member states in Central and Eastern Europe. In developing our own typology, we drew on the national reports on lifelong learning policies in different countries produced by LLL2010 team members, statistics and policy reviews compiled by bodies such as Eurostat and Eurydice and findings of the various sub-projects. The initial typology was developed at the start of the project, and was subsequently interrogated by data gathered in different elements of the research.

Table 2.1 contains the headline indicators informing the typology. Every effort was made to obtain data from one source for all countries to try and ensure comparability; however, this was not always possible, particularly for the new member states. In addition, it was sometimes difficult to disaggregate figures for Scotland and Flanders from the broader UK and Belgian data. The glossary to the table provides technical information on the meaning of each variable and its source. The indicators reflected key features of the national economy such as GDP and the proportion spent on education and social protection, the employment rate, poverty risk and economic inequality. The organisation of the compulsory education system was noted with regard to whether it might be described as stratified, comprehensive or mixed. The proportion of early school leavers and of young people attaining at least upper secondary education (ISCED 3) were used as broad indicators of the general success of the school system. In relation to the system of lifelong learning, we noted the proportion of 25–64 year olds in formal education and also the proportion of the population with tertiary level qualifications by age group. Clearly the selection of these indicators and not others was somewhat arbitrary; the aim was to include broad indicators that provided some insight into multiple aspects of a county's social welfare and lifelong learning systems without ending up with a set of variables that was too long to be manageable.

Table 2.1: Key characteristics in relation to the economy, labour market and educational achievement of the EU LLL2010 countries

	Norway	Ireland	UK	Belgium	Austria	Slovenia	Bulgaria	Czech Rep	Hungary	Estonia	Lithuania
Country type	Scandinavian social market economy	Anglo-Celtic liberal market economy	Anglo-Celtic liberal market economy	Continental coordinated market economy	Continental coordinated market economy	Central & Eastern European coordinated market economy	Central & Eastern European dependent market economy	Central & Eastern European dependent market economy	Central & Eastern European dependent market economy	Central & Eastern European liberal market economy	Central & Eastern European liberal market economy
GDP[1]	178	127	112	116	124	88	44	82	65	64	55
AIC[1]	190	102	125	107	114	82	46	73	61	56	63
% GDP spent on education[2]	6.6	4.9	5.5	6	5.4	5.7	4.2	4.6	5.4	4.8	4.8
% GDP spent on social protection[3]	22.6	18.2	26.4	30.1	28.5	22.8	15	18.7	22.3	12.4	13.2
At risk of poverty[4]	11.1	15	17.4	14.6	12	11.3	21.8	8.5	12.5	19.6	20.5
Employment rate[5]	79.4	64.2	73.7	68.3	75.3	69.9	64.7	70.8	60.7	69.5	65.9
Unemployment rate[5]	3.5	14.5	7.8	8.0	4.2	7.8	11.3	7.1	11.1	14.3	17.3
Youth (15-24) unemployment rate[5]	8.9	30.3	20.2	21.3	8.0	14.2	25.8	17.2	25.7	25.9	34.2
Gini coefficient of economic inequality[6]	0.276	0.328	0.335	0.271	0.265			0.268	0.291		
Expenditure on public services as proportion of GDP[7]	26.3	16	27.6	27.8	29.1	25.4	27.5	19.9	20.9	14.3	15.2
Organisation of compulsory education system	Comprehensive	Comprehensive	Comprehensive	Stratified	Stratified	Stratified	Comprehensive	Comprehensive	Comprehensive	Comprehensive	Comprehensive
% with upper secondary education[8]	80.9	73.5	76.1	70.5	82.5	83.3	79.4	91.9	81.3	89.2	92

Table 2.1: continued

	Norway	Ireland	UK	Belgium	Austria	Slovenia	Bulgaria	Czech Rep	Hungary	Estonia	Lithuania
Country type	Scandinavian social market economy	Anglo-Celtic liberal market economy	Anglo-Celtic liberal market economy	Continental coordinated market economy	Continental coordinated market economy	Central & Eastern European coordinated market economy	Central & Eastern European dependent market economy	Central & Eastern European dependent market economy	Central & Eastern European dependent market economy	Central & Eastern European liberal market economy	Central & Eastern European liberal market economy
% early school leavers[9]	17.4	10.5	14.9	11.9	8.3	5.0	13.9	4.9	10.5	11.6	8.1
% of population with tertiary education[10] aged 30-34[10]	47.3	49.9	43.0	44.4	23.5	34.8	27.7	20.4	25.7	40.0	43.8
% of population in formal lifelong learning[11]	3.9	5.4	8.6 (Eng) 6.8 (Sco)	3.5 (Flanders)	3.0	7.8	1.2	1.4	2.9	3.7	3.0

Notes:

[1] GDP is a measure of economic activity. GDP for Europe is set at 100 and measures how much countries deviate from the EU average. 2009 AIC, normally the largest component of GDP and therefore strongly correlated with GDP, refers to all goods and services actually consumed by households (http://epp.eurostat.ec.europa.eu/statistics_explained/index.php/GDP_per_capita,_consumption_per_capita_and_comparative_price_levels)

[2] 2006 Eurostat, 2010 (Europe in figures)

[3] 2006 Eurostat news release 80/2009 – 2 June 2009. Social protection refers to out-of-work benefits, disability benefits and pensions

[4] 2009 Eurostat, 2011 (Compact guide). Risk of poverty rate is defined as the proportion of people living in household with less than 60% of median income after social transfers

[5] Q4-2010 Eurostat 2011, Compact guide. Basic figures on the EU, 2nd quarter 2011

[6] The Gini coefficient is an international summary indicator of economic inequalities. Zero indicates perfect equality, with every household or individual having the same amount. A value of one would imply that one household or individual had all of the country's income or wealth

[7] Public services include health, education, pensions and out-of-work benefits (Eurostat, 2002)

[8] Aged 25-64 (http://epp.eurostat.ec.europa.eu/tgm/table.do?tab=table&init=1&language=en&pcode=tps00065&plugin=1)

[9] Aged 18-24 and not in further education or training (http://epp.eurostat.ec.europa.eu/tgm/table.do?tab=table&init=1&language=en&pcode=tsisc060&plugin=1)

[10] 2010 (http://epp.eurostat.ec.europa.eu/tgm/table.do?tab=table&init=1&plugin=1&language=en&pcode=t2020_41)

[11] 2003 Labour Force Survey

Analysis of the data: similarities and differences between European countries

Economic indicators in **Table 2.1** show a clear divide in terms of the wealth of the old and new member states, with Norway the richest as a result of its small population and plentiful natural resources, in particular North Sea oil. At the start of the LLL2010 project (2005), Ireland had a higher GDP per person than the UK, although the Irish economy was particularly adversely affected by the economic crash of 2008, shrinking by 25% between 2007 and 2008. Austria and Flanders have similarly high GDPs per person. The EU-25 average is set at 100 and all the older member states are above this average, while the newer states are all below it. Of the newer states Slovenia is the wealthiest among those included in this study. There is a gap between Bulgaria, which has the lowest GDP per person and is a very recent accession state, and the more established of the new member states. Countries vary in the percentage of GDP spent on education, with Norway, the UK, Belgium, Austria and Slovenia spending more than 5% of GDP on education. Ireland and the new member states of Central and Eastern European countries spend less than 5% of GDP on education. There are also differences in social protection expenditure, with the old member states, with the exception of Ireland, having much stronger redistributive measures than new member states. Estonia and Lithuania, with liberal market economies, have very weak redistributive measures.

Countries differ with regard to the proportion of their working-age population in employment, with Norway having the highest proportion followed by the UK and Austria. Most of the new member states have employment rates of 70% or less, as do Ireland and Belgium. Hungary has the lowest employment rate, standing at 61%. New member states, particularly Bulgaria, have lower employment rates than the old member states, although Slovenia and Ireland are very similar. Employment protection also varies, with the UK and Ireland having less regulated labour markets than all other countries, including the new member states. The risk of poverty is greatest in Bulgaria, Lithuania and Estonia, followed by Ireland and the UK, and lowest in the Czech Republic and Norway. Of the countries for which data are available, inequality is greatest in the UK and Ireland and lowest in Austria. Expenditure on public services as a proportion of GDP is lowest in Estonia, Lithuania and Ireland and highest in Austria, the UK, Belgium, Norway and Bulgaria.

As noted above, the school system is seen as playing an increasingly important role in economic development. Most of the old and new EU states have comprehensive school systems for the compulsory stages of education, although in England the state system is increasingly heterogeneous and selective. Austria and Belgium have stratified systems, where entry to particular sectors is on the basis of academic selection. Belgium, the UK and Ireland have a relatively low proportion of school leavers completing upper secondary education, compared with a much higher proportion in the Czech Republic, Estonia and Lithuania.

With regard to the percentage of the population with tertiary level education, it is evident that, in relation to the 25-29 age group, some countries (Norway, Ireland and Belgium) have already surpassed the EU benchmark participation rate of 40%. By way of contrast, amongst the Austrian 25-29 age group only 16.6% have tertiary level education.

Moving on to consider participation in formal lifelong learning, it is evident that the UK has a relatively high proportion of the adult population in formal education, followed by Norway and Slovenia. In the UK context this is attributable in part to the development of non-traditional routes into further and higher education such as part-time study and distance learning, and open access arrangements so that students without formal qualifications may be admitted to higher level courses. This also reflects the relatively high proportion of young people in the UK who leave school without qualifications and therefore need to seek educational credentials at a later point. Of the old member states, Austria has a relatively low proportion of adults in formal education, with Estonia and Lithuania having higher proportions of adults in formal education. Austria has a particularly rigid system of higher education, with students requiring formal qualifications for course entry and having to follow strictly pre-specified courses with no modularisation. As a result, many undergraduates who go straight from school to university do not graduate until they are nearly 30, and the system is very difficult for adults without formal qualifications to access. Norway does not lead the field on this measure, possibly reflecting its success in helping young people to gain formal qualifications in the compulsory stages of schooling. However, Norway is developing particularly innovative forms of non-formal education, with trade unions and employers working closely with educationists on work-based learning.

We were also interested in the relative emphasis within different countries' lifelong learning policies on the creation of human and social capital and on personal growth. It was clear that policies in all countries reflected the view very strongly that the development of lifelong learning was the key to future economic prosperity. However, the way in which this was done, and the institutions engaged in this enterprise, varied enormously. For example, in the UK and Ireland flexible entry into higher education was prioritised, whereas in Norway there was an emphasis on work-based learning involving partnership arrangements. Austria and Flanders had strong and well-developed (if somewhat rigid) systems of vocational education and training, and in the Nordic and Central and Eastern European countries networks of adult education colleges were involved in the delivery of a variety of forms of lifelong learning. On the other hand, measures to promote social capital and personal growth as ends in themselves were downplayed, although Norwegian policy appeared to place roughly equal value on lifelong learning as a means of developing a knowledge economy, creating socially cohesive communities and encouraging its citizens to engage in personal growth and development. In all countries there was an assumption that the principal means of generating social capital was by upskilling the population and encouraging the development of knowledge economy jobs. In this sense, human capital might be regarded as a meta-value, with social capital generation being seen as a by-product.

Finally, a major aim of the study was to investigate the nature of lifelong learning systems in Central and Eastern European countries, about which little is known. Saar and Ure (2013, forthcoming) suggest that as the economies, welfare regimes and lifelong learning systems of these countries develop in post-socialist times, they increasingly reveal hybrid elements drawing on neoliberal and neocorporatist traditions. Saar and Ure note, for example, a range of influences in initial education systems. These systems are ostensibly comprehensive but also employ forms of tracking that resemble some of the stratified practices that are common in German- and Dutch-speaking countries. Slovenia clearly differs from other Central and Eastern European countries, having a corporatist approach akin to that of Austria, with much training and development taking place in the workplace. Slovenia has high rates of participation in tertiary level education and other forms of lifelong learning, and relatively low rates of poverty and inequality. The Baltic states (Estonia, Lithuania and Latvia), by way of contrast, are developing liberal market regimes along the lines of the Anglo-Celtic model, with relatively low levels of social support and investment in public services, including lifelong learning. This is leading to high levels of poverty and growing levels of inequality. The Visigrad countries[1] (Hungary, Czech Republic, Poland and Slovakia), with large numbers of low-skilled jobs in traditional heavy industries, have tried to develop shared trade links since the early 1990s and are developing a model of embedded neoliberalism (Saar and Ure, 2013, forthcoming). They are described as dependent rather than corporatist market economies because public vocational training takes place outwith the workplace. The emphasis is on the production of semi-standardised goods, for which the existing skills of employees are judged to be adequate. Further investment in workplace training, it is believed, would jeopardise profit margins, and is therefore not encouraged. Finally, Bulgaria and Romania have retained a marked Soviet influence within education, with strong vocational elements within secondary schools. These countries have had particular difficulties in adapting to the new market conditions, with low employment rates, high levels of poverty and little investment in public services or social support.

Typologies of lifelong learning and welfare regimes developed in this study

On the basis of the discussion above, the countries in the study appear to fit, at least to some degree, into the following categories:

• **Scandinavian model:** Norway has high GDP and high investment in all forms of lifelong learning, which are seen as contributing to human capital, social capital and personal growth. Systems are highly flexible and efforts are made to include those at risk of social exclusion, contributing to a relatively low poverty risk. Unlike the Anglo-Saxon model, labour markets are fairly tightly regulated. Norway exemplifies the new European socioeconomic model, combining economic efficiency and effectiveness with strong social inclusion measures, and in both these areas lifelong learning plays a central role.

- **Anglo–Celtic model:**[2] England, Scotland and Ireland fall under this heading, with relatively high GDP, but low employment protection and relatively high risk of poverty, reflecting the wide spread in household income. There is relatively high participation of adults in formal education, and a major stress on lifelong learning as the means of generating economic prosperity for the future. In line with Ireland's traditional emphasis on education, lifelong learning, rather than social transfers, tends to be seen as the means of tackling social exclusion.

- **Continental corporatist model:** Austria and Flanders exemplify the continental corporatist model, with fairly rigid and stratified systems of compulsory and post-compulsory education, highly regulated labour markets but fewer efforts to include socially excluded groups through lifelong learning or social transfers. Slovenia's lifelong learning and welfare system is increasingly coming to resemble that of Austria.

- **Central and Eastern European model:** Within this grouping of countries, there are some similarities, but also very wide variations, as described above. Lifelong learning is valued in terms of its potential contribution to economic growth. There is less emphasis on using lifelong learning to combat social exclusion and the collapse of earlier social protection systems which existed in the Soviet era means that there is high risk of poverty (although the Czech Republic appears to be an exception here). The organisation of compulsory and post-compulsory education in the Central and Eastern European countries still shows some influences from the Soviet legacy, particularly in Bulgaria and Romania, but it is also possible to discern commonalities in education and lifelong learning systems that pre-date the Soviet era. For example, aspects of the education system in Slovenia, Hungary and the Czech Republic have commonalities with the Austrian system, with which there were strong historical links. However, while data are limited, it is clear that the educational systems are changing in these countries. Tertiary education expanded considerably in the 1990s but the expansion was slower in Estonia than in Slovenia and Hungary (Kogan and Unt, 2005). Estonia's education system is now characterised by a high level of standardisation and a medium level of stratification (Saar, 2005).

As noted above, at one end of the spectrum, Slovenia stands out from other Central and Eastern European countries and appears in many ways to be much closer to the old member states in terms of investment in compulsory and post-compulsory education, participation rates in lifelong learning and attention to the needs of groups at risk of social exclusion through access to adult learning opportunities and social transfers. However, it should be noted that the political situation in Slovenia is volatile, with the election of a more right-wing government in 2011 committed to enhancing economic growth and curtailing redistributive measures. This raises the question as to how far, and how fast, governments can reshape education and labour market institutions over relatively short political cycles. At the other end of the spectrum, the Baltic countries in our study (Estonia and Lithuania) are adopting an extreme version of the Anglo-Celtic model, with low levels of redistribution, low expenditure on public services and high rates of poverty. The Visigrad countries are described in **Table 2.1** as dependent market economies in that they are attempting to develop shared trade links as platforms for the production of semi-standardised rather than high-value added goods. Pragmatically, companies focus their efforts on keeping prices down rather than upskilling their workers, so lifelong learning, including workplace learning, is relatively underdeveloped.

Difficulties encountered in developing national typologies

General problems with welfare state typologies

Questions arise as to whether it is feasible to develop a typology that makes assumptions using the nation state as the basic unit of analysis. Clarke (2005), for example, has questioned the validity of assuming that welfare states equate to nation states. In the past, he argues, nation states consisted of people who were united by their residency and culture and were governed by a sovereign state that was responsible for the legislation in that country. This is shifting to more multilevel governance, influenced both by regional and transnational processes. It could be argued that this is particularly evident in some of the new EU member states where independence led to a move away from communist social protection to one that not only had to take account of the capitalist market, but also, after EU accession, had to demonstrate that social protection was in line with EU demands based on the social model (Hantrais, 2002).

Including the new member states

At the start of the LLL2010 research, we noted that existing typologies had significant limitations, in that they generally did not include previously socialist European countries, having been developed prior to or around the period of transition from the communist to capitalist regimes. Cousins (2005) includes the Czech Republic in his analysis of European countries and notes in relation to the Central and Eastern European (CEE) countries that: 'One could not, at this time, argue that the CEE countries make up a coherent world of welfare or even, in any strong sense of the term, a family of nations' (Cousins, 2005, p 123). We have analysed some of the commonalities and differences in the Central and Eastern European countries within our study, noting the similarities between Slovenia and Austria and the tendency of all of these countries to favour liberal market approaches. However, there are significant differences between countries, with Lithuania and Estonia lying at one end of a liberal market continuum, while the

Visigrad countries and Bulgaria continue to reflect elements of the Soviet-era planned economy.

Consistency and reliability of data

Problems of reliability and consistency existed in relation to the European statistics that were gathered as well as the national reports. In relation to the statistics, this was particularly apparent in the context of the measurement of rates of participation in lifelong learning drawn from the 2003 Labour Force Survey. We therefore drew on a range of sources, including the Adult Education Survey, which unfortunately did not include all of the LLL2010 countries. Russia is not included in **Table 2.1** because comparable data were not available. It should also be noted that the economic crisis in Europe has led to a rapid increase in unemployment and a reduction in tax receipts, suggesting that in many countries resources may be diverted from health and education to social security payments.

Conclusion

We began by noting the European trend towards growing inequality over the past two decades, which is particularly marked in Anglo-Celtic countries. Rates of poverty have tended to increase in new member states that are making the transition from planned to market economies. Soviet-era social support systems have not, as yet, been replaced by welfare states, which, despite their recent erosion, still serve redistributive and regulatory functions in old member states in Northern and Western Europe. In all countries lifelong learning is envisaged as playing a major role in the development of the new European socioeconomic model, with its emphasis on economic efficiency and social inclusion. However, despite rhetorical endorsement of this model, there is huge variation across Europe with regard to the extent of economic inequality and investment in public services, including lifelong learning.

A major aim of the LLL2010 project was to understand the impact of welfare and lifelong learning systems on participation in lifelong learning. In this chapter, we outlined the key characteristics of different groups of countries participating in the project, with a particular emphasis on teasing out some of the differences between Central and Eastern European countries, which are still emerging from a period of transition. Representing the Nordic approach, Norway, at one end of the spectrum, combines a regulated labour market with high social transfers and a flexible education system emphasising lifelong learning as a vehicle for economic development, social inclusion and personal growth. Countries within the Anglo-Celtic model have less regulated labour markets and less generous social transfers, and lifelong learning is used to combat social exclusion and promote the growth of a knowledge-based economy. Post-compulsory education is extremely flexible and provides opportunities for individuals to move between employment and education. Countries within the continental model are much less flexible and provide lifelong learning and other forms of protection and welfare to those within the labour market, rather than those who are outside it. The grouping together within earlier typologies of Central and Eastern European countries within a catching-up model was clearly inadequate. Our analysis suggests that Slovenia may be grouped with Austria and Flanders within a corporatist continental tradition. All other countries have adopted some form of neoliberal approach, but there are clear differences between them. The Baltic countries have the most extreme form of neoliberalism, which is mediated within the Visigrad countries by some degree of central planning. Bulgaria, as one of the most recent accession states with relatively low GDP and high levels of poverty, is at an early stage of economic development but also appears to be moving towards a neoliberal rather than corporatist market economy. As we noted above, the Anglo-Celtic group of countries is characterised by their faith in lifelong learning as the means of promoting economic growth and social inclusion. The neoliberal countries of Central and Eastern Europe have not, as yet, been able to make such investments because of limited resources, and it will be interesting to see whether such developments take place in the future. Developing robust welfare and lifelong learning systems will clearly be challenging in the current European socioeconomic context, characterised by relative and absolute economic decline, the crisis of the euro and the implosion of the state in several countries.

Drawing on the typology described above, our analysis in the following chapters explores the development of European lifelong learning policy, the motivations of adult learners at different educational levels and in different types of country and the socioeconomic and demographic factors that impact on participation rates. We also explore the way in which the learning cultures of SMEs in different European countries affects participation in formal adult education and the way in which the expansion of higher education has impacted on social inequality.

Notes

[1] The term derives from a summit meeting of the four head of state that took place in the Hungarian town of Visigrad in 1991 to discuss regional cooperation in politics and commerce. The four countries joined the EU on 1 May 2004.

[2] Note that we prefer to use the term 'Anglo-Celtic' rather than 'Anglo-Saxon' as used by Aiginger and Guger (2006). We suggest that this term describes the three countries included here more accurately.

References

Aiginger, K and Guger, A. (2006) 'The European socioeconomic model', in A. Giddens, P. Diamond and R. Liddle (eds) *Global Europe, social Europe,* Cambridge: Polity Press, pp 124-50.

Bauman, Z. (1998) *Work, consumerism and the new poor,* Buckingham: Open University Press.

Brakman, S. (2006) *Nations and firms in the global economy: an introduction to international economics and business,* Cambridge: Cambridge University Press.

Brown, P. and Lauder, H. (1996) 'Education, globalization and economic development', *Journal of Education Policy,* vol 11, no 1, pp 1-25.

Clarke, J. (2005) 'Welfare states as nation states: some conceptual reflections', *Social Policy and Society,* vol 4, no 4, pp 407-15.

CEC (Commission of the European Communities) (2010) Communication from the Commission 'Europe 2020': a strategy for smart, sustainable and inclusive growth Brussels: CEC.

Cousins, M. (2005) *European welfare states: a comparative perspective,* London: Sage Publications.

Esping-Andersen, G. (1990) *The three worlds of welfare capitalism,* Cambridge: Polity.

Giddens, A. (2006) 'A social model for Europe?', in A. Giddens, P. Diamond and R. Liddle (eds) *Global Europe, social Europe,* Cambridge: Polity Press, pp 14-36.

Green, A. (2006) 'Models of lifelong learning and the 'knowledge society', *Compare,* vol 36, no 3, pp 307-25.

Green, A. (2011) 'Lifelong learning, equality and social cohesion', *European Journal of Education,* vol 46, no 2, part 1, pp 228-43.

Green, A. and Janmaat, J.G. (2011) *Regimes of social cohesion: societies and the crisis of globalization,* Basingstoke: Palgrave Macmillan.

Green, A., Little, A., Kamat, S., Oketch, M. and Vickers, E. (eds) (2007) *Education and development in a global era: strategies for 'successful globalisation',* London: Department for International Development.

Hall, P. and Soskice, D. (2004) *Varieties of capitalism: the institutional foundations of comparative advantage,* Oxford: Oxford University Press.

Hantrais, L. (2002) 'Central and Eastern European states respond to socio-demographic challenges', *Social Policy and Society,* vol 1, part 2, pp 141-50.

Hills, J., Brewer, M., Jenkins, S., Lister, R., Lupton, R., Machin, S., Mills, C., Modood, T., Rees, T. and Riddell, S. (2010) *An anatomy of economic inequality in the UK,* London: London School of Economics.

International Labour Organisation (2008) *World of Work report 2008: income inequalities in the age of financial globalisation,* Geneva: International Labour Office.

Kogan, I. and Unt, M. (2005) 'Transition from school to work in transition economies', *European Societies,* vol 7, no 2, pp 219-53.

Lansley, S. (2011) *Britain's livelihood crisis,* London: Touchstone Pamphlet.

Levitas, R. (2005) *The inclusive society? Social exclusion and New Labour,* 2nd edn, Basingstoke: Palgrave Macmillan.

OECD (2008) *Growing unequal? Income distribution and poverty in OECD countries,* Paris: OECD.

Riddell, S., Baron, S. and Wilson, A. (2001) *The learning society and people with learning difficulties,* Bristol: The Policy Press.

Rubenson, K. and Desjardins, R. (2009) 'The impact of welfare state regimes on barriers to participation in adult education: a bounded agency model', *Adult Education Quarterly,* vol 59, no 3, pp187-207.

Saar, E. (2005) 'The new entrants to the Estonian labour market: a comparison with the EU countries', *European Societies*, vol 7, no 4, pp 547-80.

Saar, E. and Ure, O.B. (2013, forthcoming) 'Lifelong learning systems: overview and extension of different typologies', in E. Saar, O.B. Ure and J. Holford (eds) *Building a European lifelong learning society: the enduring role of national characteristics*, Cheltenham: Edward Elgar.

Wilkinson, R. (1996) *Unhealthy societies: the affliction of inequality*, London: Routledge.

Wilkinson, R. and Pickett, K. (2009) *The spirit level: why more equal societies almost always do better*, London: Allen Lane.

THREE

Neoliberal and inclusive themes in European lifelong learning policy

*John Holford, University of Nottingham and
Vida A. Mohorčič Špolar, Slovenian Institute for Adult Education*

Introduction

When lifelong learning emerged as a key theme of educational policy in the 1990s, international organisations played a decisive role. Some, particularly the Organisation for Economic Cooperation and Development (OECD) and the United Nations' Educational, Scientific and Cultural Organisation (UNESCO), had a 'track record': in the 1970s UNESCO had enthused about 'lifelong education' (Faure et al, 1972), the OECD about 'recurrent education' (OECD 1973). In contrast, the European Union had no such pedigree. Although the Council of Europe had advocated 'permanent education' as early as 1966 (Council of Europe, 1970), the EU itself[1] had been silent. Yet, as Field (2006) suggests, in the 1990s the EU's role was decisive.

Since then, lifelong learning has developed from a policy concept popular among international organisations into a central feature in educational, welfare and labour market policies – and a key element in private and 'third' sector activity – across the 'developed' world. This chapter is concerned with the development and nature of the EU's thinking on lifelong learning, with the part this plays in shaping public policy within member states, and with how the EU interacts with other 'actors' in relation to lifelong learning.

The core of the chapter is an historical account of the evolution of the EU's thinking and practice on lifelong learning. We pursue this chiefly through the continuing tension between two policy themes: education (and training and learning) for productivity, efficiency and competitiveness on the one hand, and education for broader personal development and 'social inclusion' on the other. However, we begin by outlining three areas of debate within the academic literature. The historical account will, we believe, serve to illuminate these debates.

Areas of debate

Economic and social aims

In a much-cited phrase, Boshier described lifelong learning as 'human resource development in drag' (1998, p 4). His point was the contrast between the broad, humanistic approach of the Faure Report and the vocational character of the language used around lifelong learning in the 1990s. The broad thrust of his critique has been widely accepted. As Rizvi and Lingard argue, a 'particular social imaginary of globalization, namely neoliberalism, has underpinned educational policy shifts around the world over the last two decades' (2010, p 184). They see this as linked to attempts to reshape the nature of the individual, quoting approvingly Rose's argument that 'a new set of educational obligations' requires the citizen 'to engage in a ceaseless work of training and retraining, skilling and reskilling …: life is to become a continuous economic capitalization of the self' (Rose, 1999, p 161).

Some (for example Edwards and Boreham, 2003; Edwards, 2004) have seen the European Union's approach through a prism similar to Rose's. The particular approach based on Foucault has been subjected to some theoretical critique (for example Holford 2006); nevertheless, a widespread consensus now exists that the EU's approach to lifelong learning is strongly vocational. As Field writes, lifelong learning is regarded in the European Commission 'primarily as a source of competitive advantage' (2006, p 17; see also Dehmel, 2006; Ertl, 2006).

The EU itself, however, has long stressed that lifelong learning has a range of non-economic justifications. Its 1995 White Paper, for instance, set out five 'general objectives' designed 'to put Europe on the road to the learning society'. These included not only closer links between schools and business, and encouraging investment in training, but also combating exclusion and developing proficiency in three European languages. Lifelong learning was seen in a wider perspective:

> Education and training provide the reference points needed to affirm collective identity, while at the same time permitting further advances in science and technology. The independence they give, if shared by everyone, strengthens the sense of cohesion and anchors the feeling of belonging. Europe's cultural diversity, its long existence and the mobility between different cultures are invaluable assets for adapting to the new world on the horizon. (CEC, 1995, p 54)

The White Paper's recommendations would

> help to show that the future of Europe and its place in the world depend on its ability to give as much room for the personal fulfilment of its citizens, men and women alike, as it has up to now given to economic and monetary issues. (CEC, 1995, p 54)

Subsequent EU statements have continued to emphasise non-economic aims for lifelong learning. The Lisbon strategy set 'a new strategic goal for the next decade [2001-2010]: to become the most competitive and dynamic knowledge-based economy in the world ... with more and better jobs and greater social cohesion' (CEC, 2000). A decade later the Council of the European Union asserted:

> Education and training systems contribute significantly to fostering social cohesion, active citizenship and personal fulfilment in European societies. They have the potential to promote upward social mobility and to break the cycle of poverty, social disadvantage and exclusion. Their role could be further enhanced by adapting them to the diversity of citizens' backgrounds in terms of cultural richness, existing knowledge and competences, and learning needs. (Council of the European Union, 2010a)

Jarring as this does with the academic consensus on the vocational and neoliberal nature of the EU's aims in lifelong learning, the question arises: to what extent are non-economic themes – equity, social inclusion, social cohesion, citizenship, and so forth – genuine priorities in EU lifelong learning policy?

Policy processes and spaces

The second principal area of debate has been over the nature of policy-making in European lifelong learning. Although the EU's policy processes have for many years been a focus of research interest in areas such as Political Science and Social Policy, policy making in education and lifelong learning has seldom been a focus. The fifth edition of the major Oxford University Press textbook on *Policy making in the European Union* (Wallace et al, 2005), for example, has whole chapters on virtually every area of policy (social, agricultural, employment, biotechnology, fisheries, trade, foreign and security, etc), but mentions education only in passing on *one* of its 570 pages; the sixth edition (Wallace et al, 2010) contains passing references to education on four of 597 pages. (Neither the learning society nor lifelong learning is mentioned at all in either edition.) In fact, however, European educational policy had become a focus of attention for a few educational researchers rather before this. Lawn has argued that the notion of a European educational 'space' – a favoured term in some areas of the European Commission – was not only rhetoric, but contained the germ of a new approach to educational governance. In particular, he has argued, it empowered a new range of actors through 'soft governance' by a 'range of particular governing devices (networking, seminars, reviews, expert groups, etc.)' (Lawn, 2006, p 272). Lawn's argument is that in the EU a 'new space for education' now exists within the dominant, market, discourse (Lawn, 2002, p 20). The space is 'fluid, heterogeneous and polymorphic', existing 'within the daily work of teachers and policy-makers, within shared regulations and funded projects, within curriculum networks and pupil assignments, and in city collaborations and university pressure groups'. It represents, he argues, a significantly new approach to policy-making, involving the creation of a 'new cultural space' in which 'new European meanings in education are constructed' (Lawn, 2002, p 5) – though not that it necessarily leads to radically different agendas.

A key question, therefore, is whether a new European space exists for education or lifelong learning in any meaningful sense – and to the extent that it does, what difference this makes. Lawn's initial framing of the argument implied, even where it did not explicitly state, that within this new European educational space, concerns about equity and social agendas could be more effectively asserted – in contrast to the predominantly economic discourse in other educational policy circles. More recently, however, an alternative approach has been promoted, by a group of scholars who acknowledge the EU's role in educational policy, and even accept the existence of an educational space, but question its nature, direction and significance. The principal statement of this position is Dale and Robertson (2009). The root of their argument is that Europeanisation – '"doing" and "making" Europe' (Dale, 2009a, p 8) – should be seen principally as a subspecies of globalisation: that the EU 'is involved in the construction of globalisation and that globalisation frames economic, political, cultural (etc.) possibilities for Europe' (Dale, 2009b, p 25). Globalisation, in their view, comprises considerably more than economic competition, but competitiveness is very much the 'master discourse' (Dale, 2009b, p 26).

They do not see the European project, however, as reducible to globalisation – if that is construed as economic competition: 'there is a distinct "Europe-centred" project whose aim is to "thicken" the discourses and institutions of Europe, irrespective of economic competition' (Dale, 2009b, p 27); the EU is unusual among international organisations 'in having more than economic ambitions, and seeing its project spreading wider and deeper than short-term collective economic benefit' (Dale, 2009b, p 28). So far, this seems to chime with Lawn's view, and the idea of Europe as protector of social rights. But this is not what Dale and Robertson have in mind when they refer to 'thickened' European discourses and institutions. The Lisbon goals were not just about responding to global competition, they were about competing with specific competitors (the US, Japan and so forth). Educational strategies – the European Higher Education Area, the Bologna Process and related projects – are in their view 'ambitious global strategies' (Robertson, 2009a, p 77). The Bologna Process is not simply a mechanism to achieve uniformity within Europe, but a model to transform higher education globally in the European image and the European interest. 'While for a long time Europe has legitimated its activities by presenting itself as a civilising rather than imperialising presence, its more explicit economic and transnational interests open it up to charges of modern-day colonialism and imperialism' (Robertson, 2009a, p 78).

The EU and its member states

The formation of EU thinking on lifelong learning has coincided with the EU's most substantial period of expansion. In 1994, when the white paper *Growth, Competitiveness, Employment* (CEC, 1993) first thrust lifelong learning to the centre of European policy, the Maastricht Treaty was in the recent past; the EU comprised 12 member states with a population of 350 million. By 2007 there were 27 member states, and a population of over 500 million. Many of the new member states had formerly been to the east of the 'iron curtain'; the remainder were principally to the south; their political and economic histories were diverse, encompassing various forms of authoritarian and democratic governments, economic planning and markets. With a population of 38 million, Poland was very much the largest; the remainder had populations below – many well below – 12 million. Perhaps more important, 86 per cent of the EU's GDP in 2010 was generated within the 12 countries which had entered the EU before 1995;[2] the 25 per cent of the population who live within the 'post-1995' countries generate only 14 per cent of EU GDP. After 1995, therefore, EU institutions (and in particular the Commission) were grappling with major challenges of development and cohesion within an increasingly diverse polity.[3]

In this light, European lifelong learning policies appear as mechanisms not for the social and economic development of a stable geographical region (analogous to a national government's formulating policy for its regions and local governments), but similar in many respects to the challenges facing the government of a nascent imperial power (see also Holford, 2006). New populations and cultures must be incorporated; new colonial leaders (and their established political institutions) engaged with; a new imperial economy created – while at the same time the new polity and economy engage with the challenges of a turbulent external environment. The parallel is not, of course, exact: the EU's member states have legal national sovereignty and participate on a basis formally equivalent to other member states in the EU's decision-making processes. It is, however, instructive.

The work of Dale and Robertson relates to this. There is, they argue, a 'hegemonic project' of 'constructing Europe, economically, politically, culturally'. This involves, *inter alia*, an extensive project of reconstructing governance, and it is in this context that developments in European education policy are to be understood. 'Europe', in their view, is a willing collaborator in the processes of neoliberal globalisation. Neoliberal globalisation involves 'harnessing the apparatuses of the state to its own purposes in place of the decommodifying and "market-taming" role the state had under social democracy' (Dale, 2009b, p 29). They see the EU not only as a *location* in which this process plays out, but as a *mechanism* by which nation-states within the EU are educated or disciplined to this end: the open method of coordination, fundamental to the Lisbon Process, for instance, enables the EU to intervene in and shape national policy agendas. According to this argument, therefore, the EU's role in education is not defensive, a protective rampart for discourses of 'equity' and 'social inclusion', but a division of the neoliberal army.

In relation to this, Dale distinguishes between a European education *space* and European education *policy*. The former, he says, is an 'opportunity structure' framed by treaties, policy frameworks and community history. The latter comes not only from the Commission and its Directorates-General, but also from member states' policies and preferences and from 'existing conceptions of the nature and capacity of "education"' (Dale, 2009b, p 32). European education policy is not, therefore, concerned only with the national level: to understand the growing role of Europe in educational governance, we must, in Dale's view, dispense with 'methodologically nationalist and statist assumptions' (Dale, 2009b, p 32). In this vein, Robertson argues that the 'revamped Lisbon strategy' has strengthened 'neo-liberal language of economic competitiveness' in European higher education policies. Higher education, she suggests, is now 'strategically important' for the EU, playing a key part in 'creating both "minds" and "markets" for the European knowledge-economy' (Robertson, 2008a, p 1). From this perspective, therefore, the EU is closely allied with the interests of private capital: the EU recruits markets in the interests of European business, while business recruits the EU in support of the extension of market opportunities both within the EU (for instance, by weakening the walls between public and private sector in education) and across the globe.

Education and lifelong learning in the EU

Education played a trivial role in the origins of the EU. The EU began in the 1950s as the European Common *Market*; it had a subsequent incarnation as the European *Economic* Community. Its founding treaties and fundamental institutions placed discourses of markets and economic competitiveness at its heart. Discussion of education was 'taboo' in European-level debates until the early 1970s – with very minor exceptions (Blitz, 2003, p 4). The 1970s saw only a few educational toes dipped in the policy pond: in 1971 Education ministers agreed a non-binding resolution 'to provide the population as a whole with the opportunities for general education, vocational training and life-long learning' (Blitz, 2003, p 5); in 1974 – influenced by the first enlargement – ministers encouraged 'co-operation' in various priority sectors, while preserving 'the traditions of each country and the diversity of their respective educational policies and systems' (Pépin, 2006, p 67).

The themes of cooperation and diversity enabled the Commission to advance, albeit slowly, on educational policy, largely avoiding conflict with member states. During the 1970s, EU policy tended to confuse – perhaps deliberately – education as a universal value with the economic requirements of the single market. However, neither Commission nor Community put much emphasis on *lifelong* learning at that stage, in the adult or post-compulsory sense,[4] perhaps because the Common Market's economic focus was so distant from the strongly humanistic framing of lifelong education at that time (see also Faure et al, 1972). During the 1980s, development remained incremental. Two features stand out: European Court of Justice decisions that permitted the Community to develop its educational role, and the establishment within the Commission of a *de facto* directorate responsible for education.[5] However, the focus continued to be narrow – chiefly in support of improved school curricula and quality, and on European content. Concern with *lifelong* learning (*qua* post-compulsory learning) remained limited.[6]

As we have seen, when lifelong learning re-emerged in national and international policies in the 1990s, the emphasis was firmly on supporting economic performance, whether individual or societal (Boshier, 1998; Field, 2006). Arguably, however, within the EU this provided space for expansion of non-economically oriented policies: the form which the renewed lifelong learning agenda took was much closer to the EU's mainstream concerns. At the same time, until 1992 the Community's legal 'competence' in education was restricted, and the principle of subsidiarity meant most educational activities were organised and governed by member states. Any EU attempt to intervene in national educational affairs had to be closely related to its core aims, as expressed in the founding treaties: this meant educational measures had to be specifically justifiable as furthering the common *market*. Vocational education clearly fitted this aim, but wider desires to create a 'people's Europe' had to be 'subservient to economic concerns' (Blitz, 2003, p 9). Action programmes in the 1980s, such as 'Erasmus', were therefore based on the need to strengthen the Community's economic position.

Maastricht gave the EU clear, if limited, 'competence' in education: to make 'a contribution to education and training of quality and to the flowering of the cultures of the Member States' (Treaty of Maastricht, Article G, 1992). This general aim was also subject to the principle of subsidiarity. A number of specific Community aims were also set out (chiefly relating to initial education), such as developing a 'European dimension' in education by strengthening language teaching, encouraging student and teacher mobility and recognition of qualifications, 'promoting cooperation between educational establishments', exchanging 'information and experience' on common educational issues, and encouraging youth exchanges, 'exchanges of socio-educational instructors', and distance education (Article G).

Maastricht did, however, explicitly address lifelong (in the form of post-school or post-initial) education – to a limited degree, and with a clear emphasis on the economic. The Community was to 'implement a vocational training policy' which should:

> facilitate adaptation to industrial changes, in particular through vocational training and retraining; improve initial and continuing vocational training in order to facilitate vocational integration and reintegration into the labour market; facilitate access to vocational training and encourage mobility of instructors and trainees and particularly young people; stimulate cooperation on training between educational or training establishments and firms; develop exchanges of

information and experience on issues common to the training systems of the Member States. (Article G)

From an educational policy perspective Maastricht was both modest and significant. It provided general authority for the EU (and its Commission) to contribute to 'education and training of quality', authorising policy development in areas not specifically itemised – although this general authority was circumscribed by the general principle of subsidiarity. Following Maastricht, therefore, those who sought to develop lifelong learning policy were newly empowered: member states could not object on principle to Commission activity in education. However, clear boundaries were set to activity: initial education or schooling was to the fore, as was the 'European' dimension; and insofar as post-school learning was specified, the focus was vocational.

Given the legal framework, when lifelong learning re-emerged in the early 1990s, the Directorate-General for Education developed policy chiefly in support of economic needs. *Growth, Competitiveness, Employment* (CEC, 1993) emphasised globalisation, information and communication technology, and competition from Asia and the US. The unemployment that would arise if Europe did not achieve and maintain economic growth and competitiveness was also a concern: learning was essential throughout life. Based on the competitiveness white paper, lifelong learning was now central to EU policy (and entirely consistent with the educational objectives of the Maastricht Treaty). The education white paper, *Teaching and Learning: Towards a Learning Society* (CEC, 1995) elaborated within this framework, and played a 'crucial role in establishing lifelong learning as a guiding strategy in EU policies' (Dehmel, 2006, p 53).

From the mid-1990s, the 'primarily utilitarian, economic objectives' that brought lifelong learning to centre stage in international policy debates began to be complemented by 'more integrated policies' involving 'social and cultural objectives' (Dehmel, 2006, p 52). In the 'Socrates' and 'Leonardo da Vinci' programmes, for example, lifelong learning was a strong theme; 1996 was designated the European Year of Lifelong Learning. An implicit theme was building European identity and European citizenship.

The Lisbon Strategy

Adopting the language of Rizvi and Lingard (2010), the Lisbon Strategy, launched in 2000, was predicated on 'imaginaries' of neoliberal globalisation and the knowledge economy. The EU set itself 'a new strategic goal for the next decade: to become the most competitive and dynamic knowledge-based economy in the world capable of sustainable economic growth ...'. It was not, however, simply about the economy and competition: innovation, competition and growth were to deliver 'more and better jobs and greater social cohesion' (CEC, 2000). This aim included 'modernising' the European social model and building an 'active welfare state'.

So far as education and training was concerned, this meant Europe's systems must 'adapt both to the demands of the knowledge society and to the need for an improved level and quality of employment'. Within this, adults were given a central role: in particular, 'unemployed adults' and employed people 'at risk of seeing their skills overtaken by rapid change' (CEC, 2000). Other objectives, such as increased 'investment in human resources', a European lifelong learning framework for IT skills, foreign languages, entrepreneurship, social skills and the like, better mechanisms for student, teacher and researcher mobility, and greater transparency and recognition of qualifications, were also very much in the spirit of Maastricht (CEC, 2000).

The Lisbon Strategy also brought a key change in policy: the Open Method of Coordination (OMC), a product of employment policy in the 1990s (Hantrais, 2007), was applied in education. Subsidiarity remained important, but the OMC emphasised agreed timetables and goals, indicators and benchmarks, 'monitoring, evaluation and peer review' (CEC, 2000). This meant – despite subsidiarity – increased intervention by the EU in member states. By 'setting specific targets and adopting measures', European guidelines would be 'translated' into national and regional policies and supported by the 'mutual learning processes' of monitoring, evaluation and peer review (CEC, 2000). As part of the Lisbon process, as we shall see, the volume and detail of education and lifelong learning policy has increased markedly, and formulating and elaborating 'benchmarks' and 'indicators' to measure progress in lifelong learning (and education and training) consistently across member states has become a major Commission activity.

Lisbon in crisis

By 2003 it was clear that the EU would fall short of the Lisbon goals. This was clear in education: all European countries were making 'efforts' to adapt their education and training systems to 'the knowledge-driven society and economy', but the reforms were clearly insufficient and the pace of change too slow to enable the EU to attain the Lisbon objectives (CEC, 2004, p 3). But education's problems were part of a wider malaise. A High Level Group, appointed in 2004 jointly by the European Commission and Council (and chaired by Wim Kok), suggested that Europe's 'growth gap with North America and Asia' had widened (High Level Group, 2004, p 6):

> if we are to deliver the Lisbon goals of growth and employment then we must all take action. To achieve them ... means more delivery from the European institutions and Member States through greater political commitment, broader and deeper engagement of Europe's citizens, and a recognition that by working together Europe's nations benefit all their citizens.

In Robertson's view, Kok helped construct a 'crisis discourse' and, from around 2005, to the EU's forming

> a set of globally-oriented 'education' policies and programmes shaped by a new set of ideas about the production of a European knowledge economy. Together, these policies and programmes mark a significant shift away from a social market/'fortress Europe' as the means to create a knowledge-based economy toward a newer vision; a more open, globally-oriented, freer market Europe. (Robertson, 2008b, p 90)

Neoliberal though its 'imaginary' may have been, the Kok report retained some 'social Europe' rhetoric. It was 'sustaining Europe's social model', which required 'higher growth and increased employment' and 'far more emphasis ... on involving European social partners and engaging Europe's citizens' (High Level Group, 2004, p 7). The emphasis on 'delivery from the European institutions and member states' (p 6) remained – so the OMC and indicators continued to be central. Quantitative measurement of outcomes against targets has therefore strengthened.

Indicators and politics

From around 2004 – roughly coincident with the Kok report – regular measurement and reporting of progress against Lisbon benchmarks began. Probably this has privileged economically related outcomes: by and large, indicators related to vocational learning and participation are better developed than those related to 'softer' aims. However, although measurement tends to privilege the economic, it is not the end of the matter. Within the Commission, and more broadly within the European 'educational space', there have been political processes as well as political outcomes. As early as 2001, very shortly after Lisbon, elements within DG-EAC took advantage of the OMC to establish objectives for European education and training. In an important paper, a key Commission civil servant argued that Lisbon's call for ministers of education to 'undertake a general reflection on the concrete future objectives of education systems, focusing on common concerns and priorities while respecting national diversity' (Council of the European Union, 2001, p 4) in the light of the Lisbon goals was 'revolutionary' (Hingel, 2001, p 15). This gave the EU a 'mandate to develop a "common interest approach" in education going beyond national diversities' increasing 'the European dimension of national educational policies' and extending the 'community dimension to education policy co-operation between the Member States'. Mechanisms to measure progress and ensure compliance could only be based on a high degree of consensus in the setting of objectives and targets.

This led to a set of 'concrete future objectives of education and training systems' being adopted by the EU Council in 2001. These covered improving education and training for teachers and trainers, developing skills for the knowledge society, increasing the recruitment to scientific and technical studies, making the best use of resources, open learning environment, making learning attractive, improving foreign language learning, and increasing mobility and exchange. In 2002, DG-EAC set up a Standing Group on Indicators and Benchmarks (SGIB). This issued a 'final list of indicators' for education and training in July 2003: 29 were proposed, spread across the eight Lisbon objectives (an average of 3.6 per objective; one objective had a single indicator, one had six) (DG-EAC, 2003). Identifying and developing indicators proved both technically and politically challenging. In 2004, Council and Commission emphasised 'the need to improve the quality and comparability of existing indicators'. A 'lack of relevant and comparable data' caused difficulties (Council of the European Union, 2004, p 32). Gradually, however, a range of indicators was established. Those for 'increasing mobility and exchange' are typical:

- inward and outward mobility of teachers and trainers within the Socrates (Erasmus, Comenius, Lingua and Grundtvig) and Leonardo da Vinci programmes;
- inward and outward mobility of Erasmus students and Leonardo da Vinci trainees;
- foreign students enrolled in tertiary education (ISCED 5 and 6) as a percentage of all students enrolled in the country of destination, by nationality (European country or other countries);
- percentage of students (ISCED 5-6) of the country of origin enrolled abroad (in a European country or other countries). (DG-EAC, 2003)

Neither Kok nor the 'crisis of Lisbon' brought an end to political struggles within the European educational space. Holford (2008) has shown how 'policy actors' took advantage of the OMC, attempting to ensure that citizenship remained on the EU's policy agenda. Key policy documents in lifelong learning in the years after Kok continued to give emphasis to discourses of equity. *Efficiency and Equity in European Education and Training Systems* (CEC, 2006a) argued that in vocational education and training the less well-qualified 'are least likely to participate in further learning and so to improve their employment prospects' (p 9). Courses for 'the unemployed and those who have not succeeded in the compulsory education system' were therefore seen as 'important' in 'equity terms'. *Adult Learning: it is never too late to learn* (CEC, 2006b) addressed the increasingly diverse range of member states, stressing that to achieve the Lisbon benchmarks four million additional adults would have to participate in lifelong learning. It posed adult learning as relevant not only to competitiveness, but also to demographic change (ageing and migration), and social inclusion. Barriers to participation had to be lowered; member states were called upon to invest in improved quality of provision, including for older people and migrants; 'validation and recognition of non-formal and informal learning' (within the European Qualifications Framework) and data for indicators and benchmarks should be improved. *Key Competences for Lifelong Learning: European Reference Framework* (DG-EAC, 2007), a technical document designed to 'provide a European-level reference tool for policy-makers, education providers, employers, and learners themselves to facilitate national- and European-level efforts towards commonly agreed objectives' (p 3), specified knowledge, skills and attitudes across eight areas: communication in mother tongue and foreign languages, mathematical and digital competence, learning to learn and sense of initiative and entrepreneurship, social and civic competences and cultural awareness and expression. Not all of these are transparently elements of a 'neoliberal imaginary' of competitiveness and globalisation.

And indeed, more evidence of sustained efforts to bolster non-economic purposes in lifelong learning is to be found in the Council of the European Union's 2010 Conclusions 'on the social dimension of education and training'. This began by rehearsing 11 policy statements (decisions of the EU Council, the European Parliament, and EU government representatives), beginning with the Council conclusions on 'equity and efficiency in education and training' in November 2006, which in various ways emphasised the social importance of education and training. It gave 'particular regard' to:

> The Council conclusions of 12 May 2009 on a strategic framework for European cooperation in education and training (ET 2020), which identified the promotion of equity, social cohesion and active citizenship as one of its four strategic objectives and which defined five reference levels of European average performance (European benchmarks) that also place a strong emphasis on achieving equity. (Council of the European Union, 2010a)

In the context of the intensifying economic crisis, restating existing policies is not without value. But the 2010 Council Conclusions on education's social dimension did not do this alone. It made a number of statements of principle. For instance:

> Education and training systems contribute significantly to fostering social cohesion, active citizenship and personal fulfilment in European societies. They have the potential to promote upward social mobility and to break the cycle of poverty, social disadvantage and exclusion. Their role could be further enhanced by adapting them to the diversity of citizens' backgrounds in terms of cultural richness, existing knowledge and competences, and learning needs. (Council of the European Union, 2010a)

And:

> As the social effects of the economic crisis continue to unfold — and in the context of the European Year for Combating Poverty and Social Exclusion (2010) ... – it is clear that the downturn has hit hard the most disadvantaged, while at the same time jeopardising budgetary

efforts which target these groups. (Council of the European Union, 2010a)

In addition, it made various recommendations, some of which have specific application in relation to adult learning. 'Expanding access to adult education,' it asserted, 'can create new possibilities for active inclusion and enhanced social participation, especially for the low-skilled, the unemployed, adults with special needs, the elderly, and migrants' (Council of the European Union, 2010a). Inter-generational learning was 'a means of sharing knowledge and expertise, and of encouraging communication and solidarity between … generations, bridging the growing digital divide and reducing social isolation' (Council of the European Union, 2010a). It called on ('invited') member states to widen access to higher education, and to promote 'specific programmes for adult students and other non-traditional learners' within the higher education (HE) sector (Council of the European Union, 2010a). In relation to adult education, it called on them to:

> Strengthen policies to enable the low-skilled, unemployed adults and, where appropriate, citizens with a migrant background to gain a qualification or take their skills a step further (one step up), and broaden the provision of second chance education for young adults. (Council of the European Union, 2010a)

It argued for 'collection of data on outcomes, drop-out rates and on learners' socio-economic backgrounds, particularly in vocational education and training, higher education and adult education' (Council of the European Union, 2010a) and it 'invited' member states and the Commission to:

> Pursue cooperation on the strategic priority of promoting equity, social cohesion and active citizenship, by actively using the open method of coordination within the context of the strategic framework for European cooperation in education and training (ET 2020) and by implementing the social dimension of the Bologna and Copenhagen processes and adopting measures in line with the 2008 Council conclusions on adult learning. (Council of the European Union, 2010a)

These excerpts give only a flavour of the Council Conclusions 'on the social dimension of education and training'. They range over all levels of education, seeking to 'promote the role of education and training as key instruments for the achievement of the objectives of the social inclusion and social protection process'. (Council of the European Union, 2010a). They are testament to the continuing presence, within the European educational 'space', of influential political actors, and of their effectiveness in sustaining discourses of social purpose.

Lifelong learning in 'Europe 2020'

Education is, of course, only one aspect of the EU's policy concern. If the Kok report spoke to (and about) a 'crisis' of the Lisbon strategy, the years since 2008 have seen a far more profound and general economic and political crisis in Europe. In the words of *Europe 2020: A strategy for smart, sustainable and inclusive growth*:

> The recent economic crisis has no precedent in our generation. The steady gains in economic growth and job creation witnessed over the last decade have been wiped out – our GDP fell by 4% in 2009, our industrial production dropped back to the levels of the 1990s and 23 million people – or 10% of our active population – are now unemployed. The crisis has been a huge shock for millions of citizens and it has exposed some fundamental weaknesses of our economy. (CEC, 2010, p 5)

The economic crisis coincided with the closing years of the Lisbon strategy; at a technical level, therefore we see in the EU's responses both the impact of immediate pressures and the outcomes of evaluation of the Lisbon years. The heart of the Commission's proposed solution to the unprecedented crisis was 'growth':

- smart growth – developing an economy based on knowledge and innovation.
- sustainable growth – promoting a more resource efficient, greener and more competitive economy.
- inclusive growth – fostering a high-employment economy delivering economic, social and territorial cohesion. (CEC, 2010, p 8)

Education and training were to play a part in achieving this; but it was far from the leading role. *Europe 2020: A Strategy for Smart, Sustainable and Inclusive Growth* focuses on strategies for the financial sector, for competition and innovation, for investment, employment and the single market. At its heart are six 'flagship initiatives'. In terms of specific aims for education, it repeated well-established prescriptions. The Commission should

> give a strong impetus to the strategic framework for cooperation in education and training involving all stakeholders. This should notably result in the implementation of life-long learning principles (in cooperation with Member States, social partners, experts) including through flexible learning pathways between different education and training sectors and levels and by reinforcing the attractiveness of vocational education and training (CEC, 2010, p 17),

while member states were encouraged to work hard to establish national qualifications frameworks (linked to the European Qualifications Framework), and to ensure more widespread acquisition and recognition of 'the competences required to engage in further learning and the labour market' (CEC, 2010, p 17). Not surprisingly, in a document focusing on economic crisis and growth, the emphasis is firmly on skills and vocational learning.

There is, however, a further – and vital – dimension to *Europe 2020:* 'stronger governance' – but in very much the spirit of the Lisbon strategy. To achieve the 'transformational change' required in the EU's economy, the Europe 2020 strategy would need 'more focus, clear goals and transparent benchmarks for assessing progress' (CEC, 2010, p 25). Indicators and benchmarks would still be central, but there would be a 'thematic approach', focusing 'in particular' on the delivery of five 'headline targets' (p 25). This would be accompanied by 'country reporting'. This was described chiefly in economic terms ('helping Member States define and implement exit strategies, to restore macroeconomic stability, identify national bottlenecks and return their economies to sustainable growth and public finances' (p 25)), but it clearly represented a shift in policy development and implementation methodology toward greater focus and integration.

This more focused approach would seem to imply that the emphasis on skills and vocational training would be carried through more centrally across EU lifelong learning policy. There is some evidence of this in the first major education policy statement made in the light of *Europe 2020*, 'Council [of the EU] conclusions on the role of education and training in the implementation of the "Europe 2020" strategy' (Council of the European Union, 2011). This began by

> UNDERLINING [*sic*] its full readiness to put the Council's expertise on education and training policies at the service of the European Council and actively to contribute to the successful implementation of the 'Europe 2020' strategy for jobs and growth and the European Semester[7] …. (Council of the European Union, 2011)

It proceeded to make a number of rather predictable assertions: education and training, and especially vocational education and training, had a 'fundamental role' in 'achieving the "Europe 2020" objectives of smart, sustainable and inclusive growth'; the Council was committed to ensuring that 'issues such as policy measures and reforms in the field of education and training, their contribution to the European targets and the exchange of good policy and practice are fully addressed'. Education and training had 'special relevance' to the 'flagship initiatives' (particularly 'youth on the move' and 'agenda for new skills and jobs'). But among these confessions of loyalty to the new regime, we find reassertions, perhaps *sotto voce*, of long-held commitments. Thus there was a reference to – though no quotation of – 'the "ET 2020" framework and its four strategic objectives', which continued to 'constitute a solid foundation for European cooperation in the field of education and training', and could 'thus make a significant contribution towards achieving the "Europe 2020" objectives' (Council of the European Union, 2011). One of the four strategic objectives was, of course, 'Promoting equity, social cohesion and active citizenship' (Council of the European Union, 2009). And within the parameters of *Europe 2020* concerns, we find such concerns stated: 'the situation of young women and young men who face exceptional difficulties in entering the labour market due to the severity of the crisis' should be addressed 'as a matter of urgency'; education and training systems must provide 'the right mix of skills and competences … to promote sustainable development and active citizenship'; strengthening 'lifelong learning opportunities for all and at every level of education and training is essential, notably by improving the attractiveness and relevance of VET and by increasing the participation in, and the relevance of, adult learning' (Council of the European Union, 2011).

Efforts to maintain an 'inclusion' theme within the new *Europe 2020* order seem clear; and some success in this, albeit partial, should be acknowledged. However, the neoliberal, 'competitiveness' agenda dominates, and appears to be reinforced by the new OMC 'architecture'. In particular, the 'Council conclusions on the role of education and training in the implementation of the "Europe 2020" strategy' focus attention not on the Lisbon benchmarks, though these remain, but on

> increased efforts … to achieve the two EU headline targets in education and training – i.e. reducing the share of early school leavers to less than 10 %, and increasing the proportion of 30-34 year olds having completed tertiary or equivalent education to at least 40 % – [which] will have a positive effect on jobs and growth. Moreover, measures taken in the education and training sector will contribute to achieving the targets in other areas, such as increasing employment rates, promoting research and development, and reducing poverty. (Council of the European Union, 2011)

The new focus on 'headline targets' is now clear. To this end, member states are encouraged to adopt 'National Reform Programmes (NRPs) which are targeted and action-based, and which will contribute to achieving the objectives of the "Europe 2020" strategy, including the EU headline targets', and to take 'policy actions in line with national targets' (Council of the European Union, 2011). The Commission, in turn, is asked to

> Further strengthen – in full agreement with the Member States – links between the implementation arrangements for the 'ET 2020' strategic framework and those for the 'Europe 2020' Strategy, notably as regards work cycles, reporting and objective setting. Particular account should be taken of the headline targets and of appropriate measures taken under the 'Youth on the Move' and 'Agenda for New Skills and Jobs' initiatives, when proposing the mid-term priorities for the next cycle of 'ET 2020'. (Council of the European Union, 2011)

Various other policy-coordination measures are proposed. On the whole, these are focused on the *Europe 2020* targets. However, some space for wider objectives remains. For example, 'as the basis for an exchange of views in Council in the course of each European Semester' the Commission is to provide 'a thorough analysis of the progress made' not only 'towards the headline targets', but also toward 'the "ET 2020" benchmarks' (Council of the European Union, 2011) – that is, towards the broader range of targets developed for education and training, which encompass non-economic objectives.

The extent to which 'neoliberal' and 'inclusive' purposes will be reflected in the practice of *Europe 2020* remains to be seen – though a renewed emphasis on the former seems likely. There remains clear evidence of efforts, within the European educational space, to sustain citizenship and social cohesion concerns. However, EU education policy has always been principally vocational – to a large degree because competition and the free market were central to its founding treaties.

Conclusion: Europe's educational policy and the contours of its educational space

During the 1960s and 1970s, many on the British Left regarded the (then) European Common Market as a 'capitalist club'. To join would 'prevent a Labour government delivering a Socialist manifesto' (Forster, 2002, p 135); 'public ownership', Tony Benn believed, 'is ruled out by the Rome Treaty' (quoted by Mullen, 2005, p 129). Though such attitudes now seem dated – 'social Europe' proved decidedly preferable to unfettered 'Thatcherism' – the European Union *has* deeply capitalist roots. It is a truism, but an important one, that the single market has set the boundaries for European educational policy since the 1950s. A more 'inclusive' agenda – equity, social inclusion and cohesion, active citizenship – was progressively developed during the 1980s and 1990s, allied with the pursuit of the 'European ideal'; they have been defended since with some success; but they have always operated within parameters set by the centrality of the single market in the EU's founding treaties.

At this point, we can usefully return to Dale's (2009b) distinction between a European education *space* (the opportunity structure framed by treaties, policy frameworks, history, etc.) and European education *policy* (the policies of the EU and its member states). From this perspective, in order to understand the direction of educational development in Europe, we should consider not only the policies of the EU, but also those of member states. But we also need to attend to the changing nature of the educational space itself, to the actors within it, the ideological frameworks within which they operate, and on which they draw, and their relative capacity to exercise power – whether economic, political or normative. In this sense, the educational space in Europe has changed significantly over the decade of the Lisbon Strategy. In particular, it has been opened to a wider range of actors drawn from the private sector, and often from substantial international corporations; it has seen a significant expansion of the role of the market in the provision of education and related services; it has seen an erosion of discourses of education, and a strengthening of language related to learning and training. We see the growth of qualifications frameworks, indicators, benchmarks and so forth. While some of these changes may appear technical, there seems little doubt that they are generally biased in favour of neoliberal, rather than inclusive, approaches.

Robertson (2009b) explores this in relation to higher education and public–private partnerships. The impact of *Europe 2020* seems likely to strengthen the neoliberalisation of the European education space. *Europe 2020* calls for 'well-functioning and well-connected markets where competition and consumer access stimulate growth and innovation' and an 'open single market for services' (CEC, 2010, p 19). This seems likely to encourage further the breaking down of 'barriers' to the involvement of private corporations in educational provision and services. Arguably we can see the impact of this already in the Council 'conclusions on the role of education and training in the implementation of the "Europe 2020" strategy'. For example, member states are encouraged to promote 'reinforced cooperation between higher education institutions, research institutes and enterprises', while there is a general call for incentives 'to establish … partnerships with businesses and research' (Council of the European Union, 2011). But this is no more than arguable: with respect to its 'competitive' language, this key education policy document is little different from the EU mainstream.

The invasion of education by private sector actors is a world-wide phenomenon. What sets Europe apart within this global trend is the architecture of EU governance and policy making: partly how this architecture mediates between global pressures and the activities of national governments (to both inclusive and neoliberal ends); partly the number and range of actors involved in educational processes (and the diversity of their cultural and institutional experiences); partly the sheer multiplicity of national and sub-national governments engaged in educational policy formation and implementation both within their own borders and at an EU level. This does not make the EU exempt from the forces of neoliberal globalisation. As Dale, Robertson and others have argued, in some respects the EU is actively complicit in furthering them. But the EU's impact on European education is to be measured not only by advocacy of neoliberalism. The EU is also both a vast organisation and a major institution, 'the most successful example of institutionalised international policy co-ordination in the modern world' developed through 'a series of celebrated intergovernmental bargains' (Moravcsik, 1993, p 473). Institutions and organisations demand sociological analysis. In the work of Dale and Robertson, we see the value of one such perspective: Marxism's emphasis on relations of domination. But the sociology of organisation and bureaucracy is not written in the language of Marx alone. Weber's emphasis on the dynamics of conflict and 'party' within organisations, and on the informal as well as the formal, matters too. So does Durkheim's exploration of 'the links between social practices, symbolic representations and institutional forms, and the methods for analysing them that his students developed through ethnography' (Jenson and Mérand, 2010, p 75):

just as greater attention to social relations of power can enrich the analysis of the EU's institutional development, the study of social practices draws a more compelling picture of how symbolic representations, norms and ideas are instantiated in European dynamics, and in turn shape patterns of behaviour. (Jenson and Mérand, 2010, pp 85-6)

Notes

[1] The term 'European Union' is also used in this chapter to encompass its predecessors under the Treaty of Rome.

[2] Calculated from IMF World Economic Outlook Database (http://www.imf.org/external/pubs/ft/weo/2010/02/weodata/index.aspx), accessed 8 May 2011.

[3] Viewed through a different lens, nearly half of EU member states (12 out of 27) now have populations smaller than its largest city's (London: 7.75m in 2010) (http://data.london.gov.uk/datastore/applications/focus-london-population-and-migration)

[4] Two limited exceptions concerned education for migrant workers and transitions from school to working life – both of which clearly related to the single market.

[5] The Task Force on Human Resources, Education, Training and Youth (TFRH), established under Jacques Delors's Presidency of the Commission in March 1989. During the 1980s, education had fallen under the Directorate-General for Employment and Social Affairs. The TFRH was formally transformed into Directorate-General XXII (Education, training and youth) in January 1995, and reformed (incorporating culture and audiovisual policy) as the Directorate-General for Education and Culture (DG-EAC) in September 1999 (Pépin, 2006).

[6] According to Dehmel, the low profile given to 'lifelong' or adult concerns in Community education policy in the 1980s was mirrored in attitudes of most international organisations: from the mid-1970s to the early 1990s, international and inter-governmental bodies 'said relatively little' about lifelong learning; and the notion of lifelong education as formulated in the early 1970s (Faure. 1972) 'almost disappeared' from policy agendas (Dehmel, 2006, p 51). Lee et al (2008), however, argue that although scholarly debates on lifelong learning diminished during the 1980s, within international policy communities 'international discourse on lifelong learning was still ongoing during this period, albeit in a new neoliberal context', and that this was 'an important formative period out of which emerged a neo-liberal discourse on lifelong learning' (p 448).

[7] 'The so-called European semester is one of the first initiatives to emerge from a task force on economic governance set up at the request of the European Council in March [2010] and chaired by the President of the European Council, Herman Van Rompuy. The aim is to boost coordination of the member states' economic policies on the basis of expected results. ... The new six-month cycle will start each year in March when, on the basis of a report from the Commission, the European Council will identify the

main economic challenges and give strategic advice on policies. Taking this advice into account, in April the member states will review their medium-term budgetary strategies and at the same time draw up national reform programmes setting out the action they will undertake in areas such as employment and social inclusion. In June and July, the European Council and the Council will provide policy advice before the member states finalise their budgets for the following year.' (Council of the European Union, 2010b)

References

Blitz, B. (2003) 'From Monnet to Delors: educational co-operation in the European Union', *Contemporary European History*, vol 12, no 2, pp 1-16.

Boshier, R. (1998) 'Edgar Faure after 25 years: down but not out', in J. Holford, P. Jarvis and C. Griffin (eds) *International perspectives on lifelong learning*, London: Kogan Page, pp 3-20.

CEC (Commission of the European Communities) (1993) *Growth, competitiveness, employment: the challenges and ways forward into the 21st century – white paper*, Luxembourg: Office for Official Publications of the European Communities.

CEC (Commission of the European Communities) (1995) *Teaching and learning: towards a learning society*, Luxembourg: Office for Official Publications of the European Communities.

CEC (Commission of the European Communities) (2000) Lisbon European Council 23 and 24 March 2000,. Presidency Conclusions (available at http://www.europarl.europa.eu/summits/lis1_en.htm#a), accessed 19 July 2011.

CEC (Commission of the European Communities) (2001) *Making a European area of lifelong learning a reality*, Communication from the Commission, COM(2001) 678 Brussels, 21.11.01, final (available at http://www.bologna-berlin2003.de/pdf/MitteilungEng.pdf), accessed 19 July 2011.

CEC (Commission of the European Communities) (2004) *Progress towards the common objectives in education and training: indicators and benchmarks*, staff working paper SEC(2004)73.

CEC (Commission of the European Communities) (2006a) *Efficiency and equity in European education and training systems,* Communication from the Commission, COM(2006) 481, final, Brussels, 8 September.

CEC (Commission of the European Communities) (2006b) *Adult learning: it is never too late to learn*, Communication from the Commission, COM(2006) 614, final, Brussels, 23 October.

CEC (Commission of the European Communities) (2010) *Europe 2020 – a strategy for smart, sustainable and inclusive growth*, Communication from the Commission, COM(2010 2020, Brussels, 3 March.

Council of Europe (1970) *Permanent education*, Strasbourg: Council of Europe.

Council of the European Union (2001) Report from the Education Council to the European Council on the concrete future objectives of education and training systems (5980/01), Brussels, 14 February.

Council of the European Union (2004) *'Education and training 2010': the success of the Lisbon Strategy hinges on urgent reforms*, Joint interim report of the Council and the Commission on the implementation of the detailed work programme on the follow-up of the objectives of education and training systems in Europe (6905/04), Brussels, 3 March.

Council of the European Union (2010a) 'Council conclusions of 11 May 2010 on the social dimension of education and training', *Official Journal of the European Union* (2010/C 135/02), 26 May.

Council of the European Union (2010b) Press Release, 3030th Council meeting, Economic and Financial Affairs, Brussels, 7 September 2010 (13161/10 PRESSE 229 PR CO 14).

Council of the European Union (2011) 'Council conclusions on the role of education and training in the implementation of the 'Europe 2020' strategy (2011/C 70/01)', *Official Journal of the European Union* C 70/1, 4 March.

Dale, R. (2009a) 'Introduction', in R. Dale and S. Robertson (eds) *Globalisation and Europeanisation in education*, Didcot, Oxfordshire: Symposium Books, pp 7-19.

Dale, R. (2009b) 'Contexts, constraints and resources in the development of European education space and European education policy', in R. Dale and S. Robertson (eds) *Globalisation and Europeanisation in education*, Didcot, Oxfordshire: Symposium Books, pp 23-43.

Dale, R. and Robertson, S. (eds) (2009) *Globalisation and Europeanisation in education*, Didcot, Oxfordshire: Symposium Books.

Dehmel, A. (2006) 'Making a European area of lifelong learning a reality? Some critical reflections on the European Union's lifelong learning policies', *Comparative Education*, vol 42, no 1, pp 49-62.

DG-EAC (Directorate-General for Education and Culture) (2003) *Standing Group on Indicators and Benchmarks final list of indicators to support the implementation of the work programme on the future objectives of the education and training systems*, Results of the Consultation of the Working Groups, July.

DG-EAC (Directorate-General for Education and Culture) (2007) *Key competences for lifelong learning: European reference framework*, Luxembourg, Office for Official Publications of the European Communities.

Edwards, R. (2004) 'Mobilising concepts: intellectual technologies in the ordering of learning societies', *Pedagogy, Culture and Society*, vol 12, no 3, pp 433-48.

Edwards, R. and Boreham, N. (2003) 'The centre cannot hold': complexity and difference in European Union policy towards a learning society', *Journal of Education Policy*, vol 18, no 4, pp 407-21.

Ertl, H. (2006) 'European Union policies in education and training: the Lisbon agenda as a turning point?', *Comparative Education*, vol 42, no 1, pp 5-27.

Faure, E. (1972) 'Education and the destiny of man', *The UNESCO Courier*, November 1972, pp 6-10 (available at http://www.unesco.org/new/en/unesco/resources/online-materials/publications/unesdoc-database/), accessed 19 July 2011.

Faure, E., Herrera, F., Kaddoura, A.R., Lopes, H., Petrovsky, A.V., Rahnema, M., Champion Ward, F. (1972) *Learning to be: The world of education today and tomorrow,* Paris: UNESCO.

Field, J. (2006) *Lifelong learning and the new educational order,* 2nd edn, Stoke on Trent: Trentham Books.

Forster, A. (2002) *Euroscepticism in contemporary British politics: opposition to Europe in the British Conservative and Labour parties since 1945,* London: Routledge.

Hantrais, L. (2007) *Social policy in the European Union,* 3rd edn, Basingstoke, Palgrave Macmillan.

High Level Group (2004) *Facing the challenge: the Lisbon strategy for growth and employment, report from the High Level Group chaired by Wim Kok,* Luxembourg, Office for Official Publications of the European Communities.

Hingel, A.J. (2001) 'Education policies and European governance': contribution to the Interservice Groups on European Governance DG-EAC/A/1 (March), unpublished paper.

Holford, J. (2006) 'The role of lifelong learning in building citizenship: European Union approaches in the light of British and colonial experience', *International Journal of Lifelong Education,* vol 25, no 3, pp 321-32

Holford, J. (2008) 'Hard measures for soft stuff: citizenship indicators and educational policy under the Lisbon Strategy', *European Educational Research Journal,* vol 7, no 3, pp 331-43.

Jenson, J. and Mérand, F. (2010) 'Sociology, institutionalism and the European Union', *Comparative European Politics,* vol 8, no 1, pp 74-92.

Lawn, M. (2002) 'Introduction', in A. Novoa and M. Lawn (eds) *Fabricating Europe: the formation of an education space,* Hingham, MA: Kluwer, pp 1-14.

Lawn, M. (2006) 'Soft governance and the learning spaces of Europe', *Comparative European Politics,* vol 4, pp 272-88.

Lee, M., Thayer, T. and Madyun, N. (2008) 'The evolution of the European Union's lifelong learning policies: an institutional learning perspective', *Comparative Education,* vol 44, no 4, pp 445-63.

Mullen, A. (2005) 'The British Left's 'great debate' on Europe: the political economy of the British Left and European integration, 1945-2004', unpublished PhD thesis, University of Bradford.

Moravcsik, A. (1993) 'Preferences and power in the European Community: a liberal intergovernmentalist approach, *Journal of Common Market Studies,* vol 31, no 4, pp 473-524.

OECD (Organisation for Economic Cooperation and Development) (1973) *Recurrent education: a strategy for lifelong learning,* Paris: OECD.

Pépin, L. (2006) *The history of European cooperation in education and training. Europe in the Making – an example,* Luxembourg: Office of Official Publications of the European Communities.

Rizvi, F. and Lingard, B. (2010) *Globalizing education policy,* London: Routledge.

Robertson, S.L. (2008a) 'The Bologna Process goes global: a model, market, mobility, brain power or state building strategy?' Invitational paper to ANPED's annual conference, October 2008, Brazil (available at http://www.bris.ac.uk/education/people/academicStaff/edslr/publications/31slr), accessed 19 July 2011.

Robertson, S. (2008b) 'Embracing the global: crisis and the creation of a new semiotic order to secure Europe's knowledge-based economy', in N. Fairclough, R. Wodak and B. Jessop (eds) *Education and the knowledge-based economy in Europe*, Rotterdam: Sense Publishers, pp 89-108.

Robertson, S.L. (2009a) 'Europe, competitiveness and higher education: an evolving project', in R. Dale and S. Robertson (eds) *Globalisation and Europeanisation in education*, Didcot, Oxfordshire: Symposium Books, pp 65-83.

Robertson, S.L. (2009b) 'Unravelling the politics of public private partnerships in Europe', in R. Dale and S. Robertson (2009) *Globalisation and Europeanisation in education*, Didcot, Oxfordshire: Symposium Books, pp 101-119.

Rose, N. (1999) *Powers of freedom: reframing political thought*, Cambridge: Cambridge University Press.

Treaty of Maastricht, Article G (1992) Provisions amending the Treaty establishing the European Economic Community with a view to establishing the European Community (available at http://www.eurotreaties.com/maastrichtec.pdf).

Wallace, H., Pollack, M.A. and Young (eds) (2010) *Policy-making in the European Union*, 6th edn, Oxford: Oxford University Press.

Wallace, H., Wallace, W. and Pollack, M.A. (eds) (2005) *Policy-making in the European Union*, 5th edn, Oxford: Oxford University Press.

FOUR

Formal adult education in the spotlight: profiles, motivations and experiences of participants in 12 European countries

Ellen Boeren and Ides Nicaise, KU Leuven
Eve-Liis Roosmaa and Ellu Saar, Institute for International and Social Studies,
Tallinn University

Introduction

According to EU policy documents, lifelong learning serves the following four purposes: enhancing or maintaining employability, promoting personal development, fostering social cohesion and developing active citizenship (European Commission, 2010). It is generally believed that – nowadays and in contrast to the humanistic approach of the Faure report in the 1970s – labour market requirements such as employability account for more than 80% of all learning activities, and lifelong learning is therefore often discussed in terms of 'human resource development in drag' (Boshier, 1998; see also Chapter Three). Whereas this may apply to learning as a whole, we find that the reasons for participation in formal adult learning are far more diverse and go beyond vocational aspects, while national systems differ widely with regard to the scope of courses on offer.

This chapter reports on a survey of adult learners participating in formal adult education. A precise definition and full account of the data collection procedure are found in the technical annex to this chapter (see pp 163-9). The survey aimed to collect data from 13,000 adult learners in the 13 European countries/ regions involved in the LLL2010 project; however, because of problems with data collection in one country, only 12 countries/regions were included in the comparative analysis. In this chapter we sketch a comparative picture of the profile of these participants in formal adult education.[1] We explore questions such as: Who are these learners? What do national adult education systems offer them? Why do they learn? How responsive are national systems to adults' learning needs? The main reason for exploring these questions is the fact that adult learning is seen as key to the achievement of a 'competitive and dynamic knowledge based society' as stated in the Lisbon goals (see Chapter Three). Increasing overall participation rates is clearly an important concern for policymakers; however, it is also important to work with motivated and satisfied adult learners in order to achieve successful learning outcomes (Keller, 1987). Two key questions are addressed in this chapter. First, we examine differences in reasons for participation by level of the current course and country and consider whether the outcomes confirm some old stereotypes, for example with regard to the greater extrinsic motivation of people with lower qualifications – and the more intrinsic motivation of highly educated learners. Needless to say, knowledge about the patterns of motivation is crucial for policies that aim to boost participation in lifelong learning, especially among disadvantaged groups. Second, we examine which factors determine the motivation to learn. Determinants at individual, school and system level are included in the analysis, and we analyse what influence the quality of the courses (looking at elements such as the characteristics of the learning environment and the learning process) exerts on learner satisfaction and thus motivation. Lessons can be drawn from this analysis with regard to the key determinants of quality in (formal) adult education.

We start this chapter with a theoretical section on issues related to conducting comparative research on adult education participation and on motivational psychology. The empirical sections of this chapter will build on these theories.

Theoretical framework

Bounded agency model

Participation rates in lifelong learning in Europe differ widely and we can recognise certain general patterns, such as the strong performance of the Scandinavian countries and the weak performance of the Southern regions (Boateng, 2009). Attempts to interpret these national differences are often based on welfare state typologies, such as the one presented by Esping-Andersen (1989) (Rubenson and Desjardins, 2009). However, as shown in Chapter Two, the inclusion of Central and Eastern European countries in such typologies has been problematic. Previous research by Desmedt et al (2006) revealed that the innovation and employment rates in national economies are the main factors boosting participation in lifelong learning. The workplace itself is an important provider of training opportunities and high levels of innovation encourage individuals to update their knowledge and skills over their lifetime. However, in market-centred societies, the impact of markets on participation and on inequality in participation is more important than the output of the education system (Roosmaa and Saar, 2010).

In this chapter, we draw on the bounded agency model of Rubenson and Desjardins (2009) (see **Figure 4.1**). When examining barriers preventing participation across a range of European countries, they found that barriers to adult education were present in all countries, but that some countries were more successful in tackling these problems, especially the Scandinavian countries. Therefore, they concluded that decisions to take part in adult learning activities are affected by government measures and initiatives as well as by individual choice.

Studies of participation, they argued, needed to use a bounded agency approach and include the role of various agents in society. Policy measures and structured support – such as monitoring, evaluation and peer review of the lifelong learning process, which is a dominant approach since the Lisbon Strategy (see Chapter Three) should try to overcome structural and institutional barriers (see left-hand column of **Figure 4.1**) and individuals should be informed about the learning opportunities available in their region (indicated by the rightward arrow). These individuals, in turn, need to identify their own learning needs so that their feedback can be used to refine the educational provision and support (visualised by the leftward arrow). The bottom of **Figure 4.1** shows that the final decision to participate results from the interaction between these different 'agents' and thus goes beyond the individual responsibility of the adult. This recognises a concern expressed by Rubenson and Schuetze (2000) that not all adults have the competencies required to find their own way in the adult education system. If participation is to increase among all strata of the population, governments need to offer guidance and information about learning opportunities and to develop relevant educational provision. Rubenson and Schuetze (2000) comment: 'If a strategy's point of departure is the notion that adults are completely self-directed individuals in possession of the tools necessary to seize on adult education opportunities, then that strategy is doomed to widen, not narrow, the educational and cultural gaps in society'.

Figure 4.1: Bounded agency model (Rubenson and Desjardins, 2009)

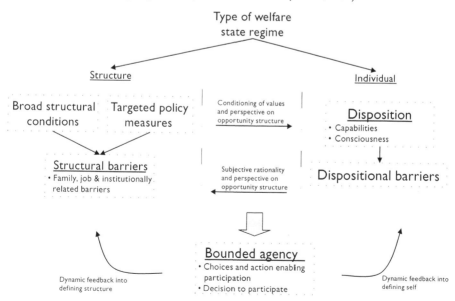

Source: Rubenson and Desjardins, 2009

Attitude, relevance, confidence and satisfaction (ARCS) model of motivation

This chapter analyses the motivation of adult learners to engage in a formal adult education programme. Our understanding of motivation is based on the expectancy value theory of Vroom (1964), further developed into the ARCS model of Keller (1987). While motivational studies often reflect a strong psychological tradition, we incorporate a socioeconomic dimension in our research and relate the psychology of learning to issues such as social class and social inequality (Jung and Cervero, 2002).

In Vroom's view, motivation is the product of the expectancy (that is, probability of success) and the value attached to a certain task one wants to undertake (in our case participation in a formal learning activity). Value refers to the experience that participation in the activity is meaningful for one's personal life and that it will fulfil one's needs (for example the need to increase knowledge or the need to meet new people). A negative assessment of the value of the activity will decrease a participant's motivation, prevent him/her from enrolling, lead to dropping out or poor performance. Moreover, the participant will make an estimation of the probability of success when undertaking the activity – for example obtaining a degree or finding a better job – and will continuously evaluate whether these expectancies are being fulfilled. Keller based his ARCS model on expectancy value theory, with ARCS standing for attitude, relevance, confidence and satisfaction. Attitude and relevance refer to the extent to which people value the course they are undertaking, while confidence and satisfaction refer to expectancy – what people hope to achieve and the extent to which they feel satisfied with the experience. The ARCS model is a sequential model. It identifies that a positive attitude towards participation is the first step towards engaging in learning. Second, the relevance of the course needs to be apparent to any potential learner. Expectancy relates to the adult learner's confidence in his/her ability to complete a course successfully. The last step in the sequential model is the experience of satisfaction. Keller states that satisfaction is the most important step in his cycle, as adult learners with a positive attitude, who understand the relevance of their participation, who have confidence in their own abilities, but are dissatisfied, may drop out and experience lower levels of wellbeing or achieve poorer learning results. This relation between satisfaction, learners' performance, retention and achievement has been found in many studies, both in compulsory and post-compulsory learning, and in the US, Australia and Europe (Bean, 1985; Tinto, 1993; Baily and Lagdana, 1997; Kuh, 2001; Wolf and Fraser, 2008).

Methodology

Our analysis uses data from a new survey among learners in formal adult education in 12 European countries/regions. All country teams participating in the LLL2010 project committed themselves to collect at least 1,000 completed adult learner questionnaires. The national samples were stratified by ISCED (International

Standard Classification of Education) level of the (adult) courses, which means that the results are comparable across countries only by ISCED level. Note also that in some countries the survey was not conducted in the whole country but in one or two regions, for instance because education is regionalised (the UK or Belgium), or because the country is very big (Russia).

The main added value of the survey is its particular focus on formal adult education. Results of the Eurostat (2007) Adult Education Survey show that – on average – only 5% of all adults between 25 and 64 participate in formal adult education (Eurostat, 2009). This means that data on the experiences and outcomes of this group of learners are limited and are overshadowed by the larger sample groups. At the same time, it must be borne in mind that our findings cannot be extrapolated to all types of adult learning. Further details about the sampling procedure, the interview method and the questionnaire can be found in the technical annex to this chapter (see pp 163-9).

Having presented the theoretical framework and the methodology, we now examine the findings of the survey.

Reasons for participation in formal education

The relevance component in Keller's (1987) ARCS model (already described) sets out the prerequisites for successful participation in adult education. In the literature, most research about reasons for participation in adult education is based on the Houle's (1961) typology, which distinguishes between three types of adult learners: (1) activity-oriented learners, who participate because of social contacts and the pleasure of participation; (2) goal-oriented learners, who participate because of a certain indirect benefit – such as a degree or a better job; and (3) learning-oriented learners, who are driven by some intrinsic interest in their study subjects. In adult learning surveys (such as Eurostat's Adult Education Survey), on the other hand, reasons for participation are often split up into job related and personal reasons. For the present research, we used parts of the Education Participation Scale developed by Boshier (1977, 1991) to measure reasons for participation. In our questionnaire, we included items on competency-related curiosity, interpersonal relations, community service, escape from routine, professional advancement and compliance with external influence (Garst and Ried, 1999). Based on this 18 items scale, we conducted factor analysis and ended up with two dimensions: 'intrinsic and social' and 'extrinsic' (or 'instrumental') reasons for participation. In the pooled database (including data from all 12 countries/regions), these new components are standardised with a mean value of 0 with a standard deviation of 1. These two dimensions partly overlap with the different 'areas of debate' in lifelong learning policy, between economic and social objectives (see Chapter Three). Contemporary lifelong learning policy is believed to be biased towards controlled economic approaches, rather than, for example, social inclusive ones. The first purpose of our analysis was to examine whether the adult learners in this survey expressed intrinsic/social or extrinsic motives for participation.

Table 4.1 shows how the specific questionnaire items fit into either the intrinsic or the extrinsic motivation dimensions. Intrinsic reasons for participation focus on the learning content but also on social reasons for participation such as meeting new people. Extrinsic reasons include job related reasons for participation as well as external pressure to participate.

Table 4.1: The motivational dimensions based on the Education Participation Scale

Intrinsic and social	Extrinsic
To learn more on a subject that interests me.	To earn more.
To participate in group activities.	Because my employer required me to enrol.
To contribute more to my community.	To do my job better.
To gain awareness of myself and others.	Because someone advised me to do this.
To get a break from the routine of home and work.	To start up my own business.
	Because I was bored.
To learn knowledge/skills useful in my daily life.	Because I was obliged to do it.
	To get a job.
To contribute more as a citizen.	To be less likely to lose my current job.
To meet new people.	To obtain certificate.

Figure 4.2 shows the different levels of intrinsic and extrinsic motivation according to the ISCED level of the current course. The score 0 indicates the average so ISCED level courses above 0 have an above average score; those below 0 are below average. As can be seen, learners on ISCED 1 and 2 courses have the highest average score on both the extrinsic dimension and the intrinsic dimension. These results indicate that although learners at the lowest levels may be motivated to study to get or retain a job, or may be compelled to study, they also value the social aspects of learning. In contrast, ISCED level 5 learners have the lowest extrinsic motivation for learning; those at ISCED 3 have the lowest intrinsic motivation and ISCED level 4 learners have a similar level of intrinsic motivation to those at levels 1 and 2. Note that although the differences between the averages by ISCED level are statistically significant, they fall within a limited range (up to 0.1 or –0.15 standard deviation).[2]

Differences in motivation patterns between countries

Figure 4.3 shows the differences between extrinsic and intrinsic motivation for each of the countries, which are ranked by order of 'average extrinsic motivation'. Actually, the averages are somewhat artificially 're-weighted' across ISCED levels as if participants were equally spread across levels. In other words, the country averages are 'corrected' for differences in the composition of the target population by level of education.

The differences between countries were statistically significant, particularly in relation to the extrinsic dimension, with Western European countries scoring below the mean (M=0) for extrinsic motives and Eastern European countries

Figure 4.2: Intrinsic versus extrinsic reasons for participation by ISCED level of current course

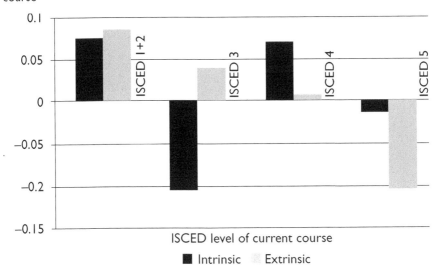

Source: LLL2010 adult learners' survey (2007)

scoring above the mean. Flemish learners score very low on the extrinsic dimension, while Bulgarian learners score very high. There was less evidence of country differences in relation to intrinsic and social motivation; however Scotland and Ireland are the positive outliers here, while the Czech Republic and Austria have the lowest scores. These results, in general, point to a strong influence of the policy priorities in different countries (Boeren and Holford, 2010). The countries that score highest on extrinsic reasons for participation, such as Bulgaria and Lithuania, are countries with the lowest standards of living based on GDP, although these differences may also relate to special requirements for some occupational groups in post-socialist countries. By contrast, the countries that score highest on intrinsic and social motivation (especially Ireland and Scotland) are typically those where government policy on lifelong learning emphasises the social as well as the economic dimension (Holford et al, 2008).

An additional (related) explanation for the observed country differences in motivation patterns can be found in the age distribution of participants (Hefler, 2010). With the exception of Austria and the Czech Republic, the Western European samples include significantly more adults aged over 45 – and fewer young people - than Eastern European samples (see **Figure 4.4**). It is not surprising that older adults indicate fewer job-related reasons for participation, as the 'return period' for investment in training gets shorter for them. In addition, compared to younger adults, most of them have secured their position in the labour market and tend to see learning as a means of self-fulfilment and social capital development rather than a way of enhancing their employability.

Figure 4.3: Intrinsic versus extrinsic reasons for participation by country/region

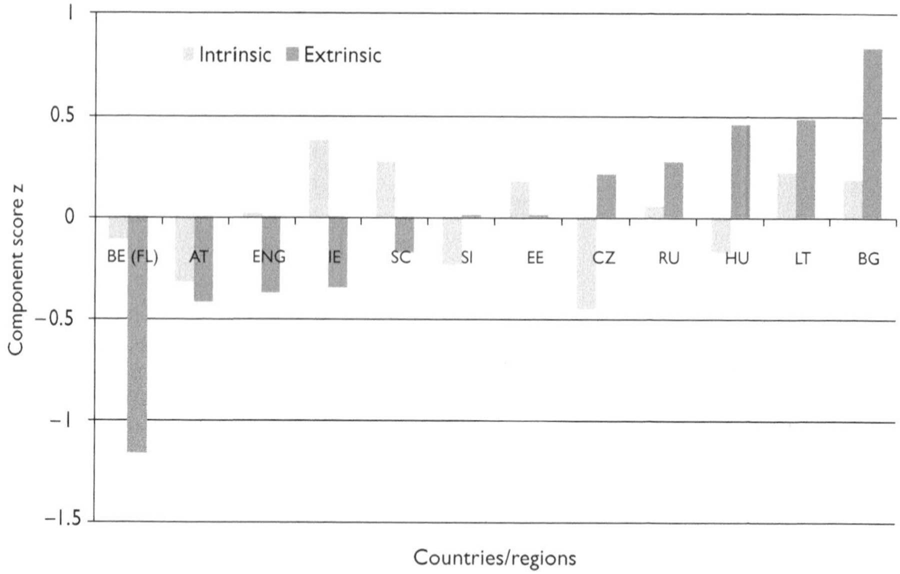

Key: AT = Austria, BE (FL) = Belgium (Flanders), BG = Bulgaria, CZ = Czech Republic, ENG = England, EE = Estonia, IE = Ireland, HU = Hungary, LT = Lithuania, SC = Scotland, SI = Slovenia, RU = Russia

Source: LLL2010 adult learners' survey (2007)

Figure 4.4 shows that the sample included large numbers of young adult learners in some countries. In Austria, Estonia and Russia half the sample was below 25 years of age. Our criterion for inclusion in the sample was that an adult learner was someone who had left the initial education system at least two years prior to the survey. This suggests that, at least in these countries, returning to formal education often occurs at a relatively young age. It also raises questions about the sampling strategy of the Eurostat Adult Education Survey, where adults younger than 25 are excluded.

Looking at the differences in initial educational attainment of participants between the countries/regions in our sample (see **Figure 4.5**), we notice that adult learners in the Western European countries, with the exception of Austria, have a larger proportion of adults with tertiary education than Central and Eastern European countries. This may go some way towards explaining the lower extrinsic pressure felt by participants in the Western European countries: as they are often employed in more knowledge intensive jobs, the benefits of their learning activities are more obvious. For lower educated adults, the benefits may be more uncertain because they often do not have a (permanent) job or are employed in rather monotonous jobs. Participation in a learning activity can possibly help them to secure their position in the labour market and/or find a more interesting job. Furthermore, the difference in educational attainment among adult learners might be related to other aspects, such as the actual courses available to adults, with

Figure 4.4: Age distribution of adult learners by country/region

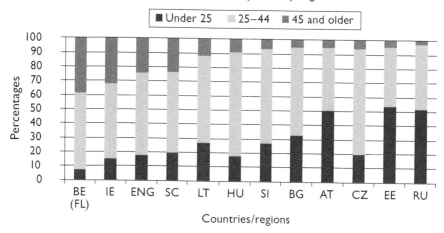

Key: AT = Austria, BE (FL) = Belgium (Flanders), BG = Bulgaria, CZ = Czech Republic, ENG = England, EE = Estonia, IE = Ireland, HU = Hungary, LT = Lithuania, SC = Scotland, SI = Slovenia, RU = Russia

Source: LLL2010 adult learners' survey (2007)

Figure 4.5: Initial educational attainment of adult learners by country/region*

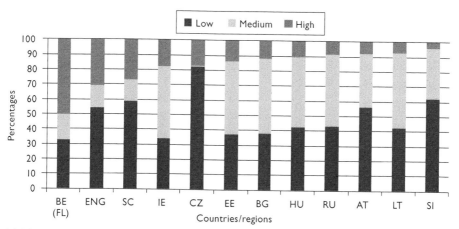

*Adults were classified as low, medium and highly educated. *Low* refers to those with lower secondary education or below, *medium* is upper secondary, and *high* refers to those with a tertiary qualification.

Key: AT = Austria, BE (FL) = Belgium (Flanders), BG = Bulgaria, CZ = Czech Republic, ENG = England, EE = Estonia, IE = Ireland, HU = Hungary, LT = Lithuania, SC = Scotland, SI = Slovenia, RU = Russia

Source: LLL2010 adult learners' survey (2007)

those in Western European countries focusing more on leisure-oriented aspects instead of labour market aspects, and it also reflects the fact that there were more younger school drop-outs in Eastern European samples.

Characteristics of the institutions and the courses

The extent to which schools can affect the performance of their pupils has been discussed extensively. Around 50 years ago, Coleman et al (1966) argued that the main influence on the outcomes for pupils was their socioeconomic and sociocultural background. Later research demonstrated that schools were capable of having an impact and that they could reduce inequalities between pupils, although the socioeconomic background of the pupils remained a powerful determinant of their future educational progress and outcomes (Mortimore et al, 1988).

In the LLL2010 research, we were also interested in the characteristics of adult education institutions and how these are related to the motivation of learners. In this section, we start by identifying some key characteristics based on an international comparative study by Schuetze and Slowey (2002), who argued that (adult) education systems have evolved in recent decades from rather fixed to more flexible systems with the following characteristics:

- *new contents*: more relevant courses;
- *institutional differentiation*: for example horizontal and vertical differentiation, articulation and transfer routes, greater student choice and better information, less dead-end routes, more equivalence between general and vocational routes, coordination between different sectors/programmes;
- *institutional governance*: greater institutional autonomy and flexibility;
- *access*: for example specific policies and outreach strategies for lifelong learners, open or flexible access, recognition of work and life experience, special entry routes, financial and other support, appropriate scheduling, involvement in regional development/service for the community;
- *modes of study*: for example modular courses and credit transfer, part-time programmes, distance learning, independent study.

Although Schuetze and Slowey focused on higher education, it is clear that there has been considerable diversification of institutions at tertiary level (OECD, 2008). The OECD report also notes changes in course provision and links to the external world as well as a stronger emphasis on social and geographical access to tertiary education (OECD, 2008). In the next sections, we examine (as far as possible) to what extent these trends have permeated adult education systems in the LLL2010 countries. First, we explore some main differences in characteristics of the adult education system by ISCED level, and then explore differences by country/region.

Differences in institutional structures by ISCED level

Admission requirements obviously differed by ISCED level (see **Figure 4.6**): certificates of prior qualification as well as admission tests were more common at higher ISCED levels, typically reflecting the 'ladder' structure of formal education.

Nevertheless, even at the lowest levels, learners often had to demonstrate that they had the appropriate level of skills and knowledge to attend the course (for example a certificate of primary education to enrol for an ISCED level 2 course). This mechanism is positive and negative: on the one hand, a skills assessment enables providers to respond accurately to each learner's specific needs, even at the lowest levels; on the other hand, it may in some cases deter adults from entering a course at an appropriate level because they are lacking the correct qualification. Nowadays, institutions are working towards more open access. In the UK the Open University requires no qualifications for enrolling on a higher level course; in Flanders the Open University offers accreditation of prior life experiences outside education. Moreover, National Qualification Frameworks have been, or are, in the process of development. These frameworks are intended to enable recognition of all competencies obtained within and outside educational settings, in order to widen access to further learning arrangements (see chapter Three). However, open access has not yet been achieved in most countries (for example in Bulgaria and many other post-socialist countries). In these countries completion of the previous level is a precondition for climbing the educational ladder, and in the Czech Republic there are no procedures for recognition of prior life experiences outside education.

Figure 4.6: Admission requirements by ISCED level of current course

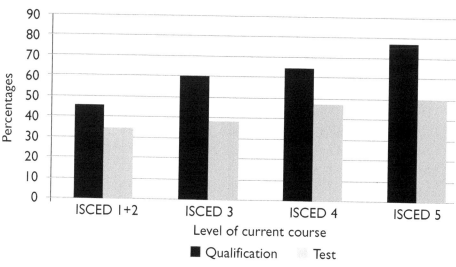

Source: LLL2010 adult learners' survey (2007)

Another general pattern across ISCED levels relates to course organisation (**see Figure 4.7**). Whereas classical linear year systems were the rule in the past, more and more institutions now provide modular courses. This flexible mode of organisation makes it possible to enrol in separate modules without having to commit to completion of the overall qualification. The credits granted after the successful completion of each module can be accumulated over time to obtain a full qualification.

Our survey showed that modular systems were already fairly common at the highest levels of adult education systems. Whereas most courses at ISCED levels 1 and 2 appear to have kept their linear structure, the higher education system in particular has undergone significant transformations in the period following the Bologna agreement. However, a different explanation for a seeming lack of modularisation at the lower level is that these programmes are of a very short duration. This is the case in the UK, where a course in basic literacies may consist of 20 to 30 hours over a period of three months. Although there is modularisation in universities, the requirements of the overall final award, for example a bachelor award, is such that full-time students are likely to enrol for the entire academic year and their course could be seen as part of a linear structure.

Figure 4.7: Modular system by ISCED level of current course

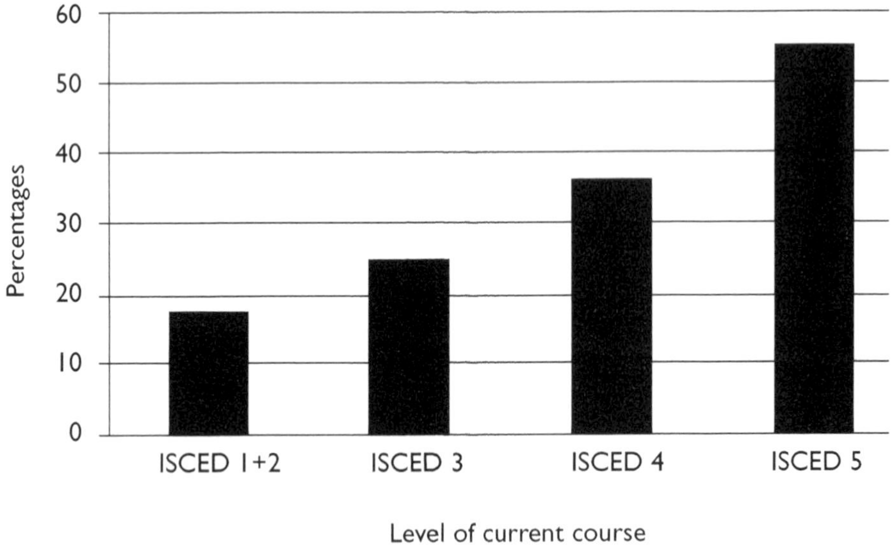

Source: LLL2010 adult learners' survey (2007)

An analysis of class sizes by ISCED level showed that classes were generally smaller at level 1 and 2 courses than in higher education (see **Figure 4.8**). At the lower levels class sizes are comparable to those in initial education, allowing teachers to closely monitor the progress of individual participants. Further analyses of teaching methods used during the course revealed that students on the lowest ISCED level courses got more opportunities for one-on-one guidance from the adult educator compared with students on higher level courses.

Figure 4.8: Class sizes of 21 and over by ISCED level of current course

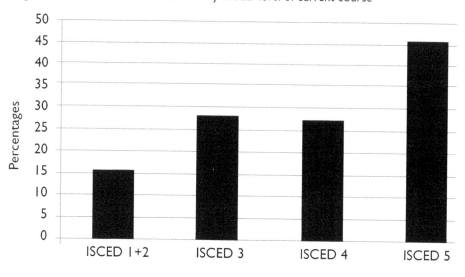

Source: LLL2010 adult learners' survey (2007)

Differences in institutional characteristics between countries

Apart from general patterns by ISCED level, our survey also revealed differences
in characteristics of adult education settings between countries. In the Central and
Eastern European countries, the adult education system is much more embedded
in the initial education system. The provision of daytime education is very similar
to primary or secondary compulsory education. In contrast, in Western European
countries/regions, the formal adult education provision is typically organised in
different institutions. This suggests that the Western systems are more flexible.
One example of this is the frequency of classes. Particularly in Flanders, England
and Scotland, adult learners generally have to attend the institution fewer than
three times per week. In contrast, in all the Eastern European countries except
the Czech Republic, learners have more frequent classes. In countries such as
Bulgaria and Lithuania, the programmes are particularly intensive and class-based.
This difference is partly explained by the presence in the sample from these two
countries of many rather young early school leavers who want to gain their upper
secondary certificate.

An examination of barriers hindering participation shows that adult learners
in Flanders, England and Scotland experienced fewer barriers than those in most
Central and Eastern European countries. Adult learners in Austria differed from
those in other Western European countries because they experienced more
barriers. The barriers mentioned most frequently were too little time for studying,
financial difficulties, transportation problems, lack of preparation for the current
course, and inconvenient time scheduling. There were also differences between
the countries in relation to the perception of the classroom environment. Previous

research has indicated that learners feel better and perform better if they are academically and socially involved, and if they feel connected to each other, the adult educator and the educational institution (Tinto, 1998; New England Adult Research Network, 1999; English, 2005).

In our survey, the classroom environment was measured using the Adult Classroom Environment Scale of Darkenwald and Valentine (1986). O'Fathaigh (1997) used this scale in his research and extracted the following sub-dimensions of classroom environment:

- *affiliation*: the extent to which students like each other and interact positively with each other;
- *teacher support*: the extent of help, encouragement, concern and friendship experienced from teachers;
- *task orientation*: the extent to which students and teachers maintain focus on task and value achievement;
- *personal goal attainment*: the extent to which the teaching process is flexible, providing opportunities for adults to pursue their individual interests;
- *organisation and clarity*: the extent to which activities are clear and well organised;
- *student influence*: the extent to which the teaching is learner centred and allows for student influence in course planning decisions;
- *involvement*: the extent to which students participate actively and attentively.

Factor analysis on our dataset revealed that it is possible to synthesise these items into a single reliable 'classroom environment' variable. **Figure 4.9** shows the average factor scores for each country/region (standardised around mean=0, standard deviation=1). The figure shows that the perception of the classroom environment is generally more positive in Western than in Eastern European countries (F=86,349; df=11; p=0.000). The highest scores are found in the Anglo-Celtic countries, and the lowest ones in the Czech Republic and Slovenia. However, it could be argued that the differences between Russia, Belgium (Flanders), Estonia, Bulgaria and Lithuania are marginal as they are all close to 0. These differences could to some extent be explained by the different courses attended by these learners. The type of institutions providing formal adult education, as well as the content and length of the course, varies greatly between European countries. Overall, courses in Eastern Europe were more focused on providing a qualification, whereas in England and Belgium the courses were more leisure oriented. Hence formal adult education has a 'wider' definition in most of Western European countries studied here compared with the Eastern European countries. In the following section, we explore the extent to which the classroom environment affects the motivation of the participants.

Figure 4.9: Perception of the classroom environment by country/region

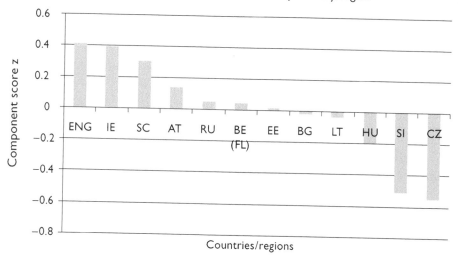

Key: AT = Austria, BE (FL) = Belgium (Flanders), BG = Bulgaria, CZ = Czech Republic, ENG = England, EE = Estonia, IE = Ireland, HU = Hungary, LT = Lithuania, SC = Scotland, SI = Slovenia, RU = Russia

Source: LLL2010 adult learners' survey (2007)

Learner satisfaction

Whereas in the previous section our attention was focused on different quality characteristics of formal adult education, as perceived by the participants, we now examine the link between quality of provision and student motivation. An important limitation of this analysis is that our dataset included only those that were participating in learning. This could result in bias as it would be expected that only the more motivated learners actually enrol in courses and stay on. However, only participants will have sufficient knowledge to enable them to make a reliable assessment of the quality of programmes. However, it is clear that word of mouth from current learners may influence non-learners.

Looking at Keller's (1987) ARCS model of motivation, survey participants have in most cases reached the last stage of the chain of motivation: satisfaction. Whereas none of them would have participated without sufficient commitment, sense of the course's relevance and confidence in their ability to complete it, it seems plausible to assume that there may still be some variation in their level of satisfaction with the learning experience. We therefore suggest that it is possible to examine whether there is a meaningful relationship between learner satisfaction and the characteristics of the courses already discussed.

Level of satisfaction with the learning experience

In the questionnaire, satisfaction with the learning process was measured by four different topics: general progress through the study programme, overall learning climate in the educational institution, satisfaction with the practical organisation, and, satisfaction with the learning outcomes. This last item consisted of two sub-questions: 'What you have learned so far thanks to the course?' and 'What can you go on to do after completion of this course?'. These provided five items that were used in a factor analysis to produce a new standardised component measuring level of satisfaction overall. The component score has a mean of 0 with a standard deviation of 1; countries above the mean of 0 have an above average score; those below 0 have a score that is below the overall average.

Again, like the results on reasons for participation, there is a difference in levels of satisfaction between Western European and Eastern European countries (see **Figure 4.10**). The Western European countries scored above average, and the Eastern European countries, with the exception of Russia, scored below average. However, the differences between Russia, Belgium (Flanders), Lithuania, Bulgaria and Estonia were not significant.

Figure 4.10: Experience of satisfaction by country/region

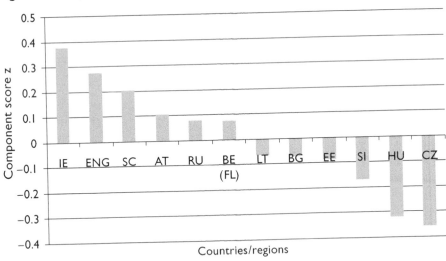

Key: AT = Austria, BE (FL) = Belgium (Flanders), BG = Bulgaria, CZ = Czech Republic, ENG = England, EE = Estonia, IE = Ireland, HU = Hungary, LT = Lithuania, SC = Scotland, SI = Slovenia, RU = Russia

Source: LLL2010 adult learners' survey (2007)

Determinants of learner satisfaction

In order to examine the determinants of learner satisfaction we used a stepwise multiple regression analysis as this allows us to examine the impact of a number of potential factors. The 'stepwise' approach means that we identified four sets of variables that can help explain why some participants are more satisfied than others. These four sets of variables were:

- those relating to personal characteristics of the adult learners, such as gender, age, educational attainment and activity status, as well as the ISCED level of the current course;
- barriers that may hinder the learning process. These barriers relate to time pressure, lack of financial resources, health problems, etc;
- individuals' perceptions of the classroom environment (as already discussed and shown in **Figure 4.10**). These included the relationship between learners; learner engagement in the learning process and ability to pursue their own interest; and teacher support, organisation of the learning and task focus;
- the characteristics of the course and institution, such as the frequency of classes, the type of teaching method and modular versus linear organisation.

These variables were entered into the multiple regression analysis in a stepwise manner that allowed us to determine which ones held greater explanatory power compared with the other variables. As we were also interested in exploring this in relation to causal relations between subsets of countries, we ran separate analyses for the following three clusters of countries: Austria and Belgium (Flanders), representing a continental/corporatist welfare regime; England, Ireland and Scotland, representing a liberal/Anglo-Celtic regime; and the Central and Eastern European countries, representing a transition regime.

Figure 4.11 shows the results of this four-step analysis.[3] Step 1 shows the impact the personal characteristics of the learner; step 2 indicates the influence of barriers on overall satisfaction; step 3 highlights the impact of the classroom environment; and step 4 shows the impact of the characteristics of the course and the institution. It can be seen that the classroom environment is by far the largest influence on learner satisfaction in all of the country clusters. Separate regression analyses for each country confirmed that this was also the case in individual countries. Barriers to participation were more in evidence in the continental countries and least in the Central and Eastern European countries. The characteristics of the course and the institutions featured to a very limited extent in all clusters. However, as already mentioned, we can conclude that the perception of the classroom environment is highly important in fostering the motivation of adult learners. This seems to be the case irrespective of the macro-context of the country under consideration. In other words, our survey suggests that the generally lower level of satisfaction of adult learners in Central and Eastern European countries is not due to macro level influences, but is likely to be caused to a large extent by a poorer classroom environment in those countries.

Figure 4.11: Variation in satisfaction by country clusters

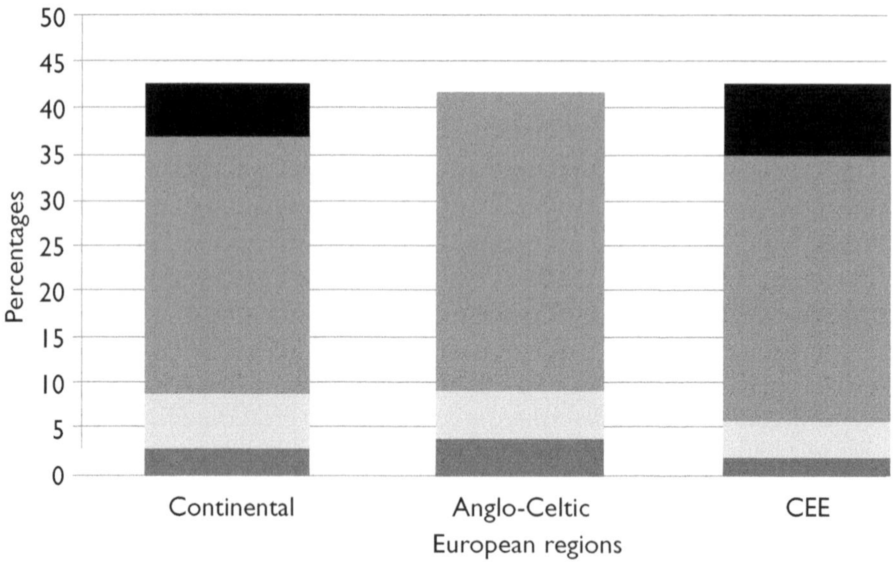

CEE=Central and Eastern European

Source: LLL2010 adult learners' survey (2007)

Conclusion

The main aim of this chapter was to analyse the profile, motivation, perceptions and experiences of adult learners in the formal adult education system across European countries/regions. The target group was defined as adults of any age re-entering the education system after having left the initial education for at least two years.

The characteristics of the adult education systems differ widely between countries, and these differences are reflected in the national profiles of adult learners. In Belgium (Flanders), England and Scotland, adult learners have a higher average age and a higher proportion of adults with tertiary qualifications. In most Central and Eastern European countries, the adult education system is intertwined with the initial education system, which results in less flexible modes of learning (Hefler, 2010). Overall, our findings show that the perception of the classroom environment and the overall satisfaction with various aspects of the course is significantly lower in these Central and Eastern European countries.[4]

We began with an analysis of why adult learners engage in learning, looking at the distinction between intrinsic and extrinsic reasons for enrolling in formal adult education. While intrinsic reasons for participation are present in all countries/regions, the extrinsic reasons differ more across countries and tend to be more prevalent in Central and Eastern European countries. Overall, these findings may be considered as encouraging. In motivational psychology, extrinsic motivation often has a rather negative connotation, associated with poorer performance and a lower level of wellbeing (Deci and Ryan, 2000). Our results suggest that extrinsic and intrinsic reasons for participation can go hand in hand. For example, newly arrived immigrants may be obliged to undertake an introductory course into the language and culture of the host country, but they can also be intrinsically motivated because of their interest in the new country and their wish to integrate in an effective way. Similarly, the stronger economic pressure felt by adult learners in Central and Eastern European countries does not mean that they are necessarily less intrinsically motivated. We also found that participants in courses at ISCED levels 1 and 2 show stronger intrinsic and social motivation than those at level 3, 'despite' the fact that they are also more extrinsically motivated. This contradicts popular stereotypes that adults with low qualifications are generally 'not motivated' and shows that mandatory measures are not always needed to make them participate in lifelong learning. It is also possible that motivation that was initially extrinsic can lead to intrinsic motivation at a later stage. A longitudinal study might enable this hypothesis to be confirmed in future research.

We have also demonstrated that the motivation of the adult learners can be further boosted by creating a positive classroom environment – the second point of attention in this chapter. In all countries/regions, adult learners reported higher levels of satisfaction when they were actively involved in the learning process, enjoyed support and respect from the teacher and where the study programme was well organised and had a clear sense of direction. These results point to the importance of a careful match between adult learners and adult educators so that learners can enjoy learning more.

What lessons can be drawn for education policy and practice from these results, and what issues should be considered for further research? First, the striking country differences in the extent of participation (see Boateng, 2009) and reasons for participation in (formal) adult education raise questions about the feasibility of a one-size-fits-all EU policy with specific targets and policy measures (Dehmel, 2006). There is no doubt that a European approach is needed to guarantee competitiveness and innovation, but based on macro indicators and study of the social, economic and cultural development of separate countries, we have to conclude that a differentiated strategy is desirable (Holford et al, 2008). Adult learners in Eastern European countries in our sample were generally younger, had lower levels of qualifications (in comparison with England, Scotland or Flanders) and were therefore more likely to be focused on gaining qualifications and improving their labour market prospects. It is important to note, however, that the labour market, educational and family structures are very different across countries. It is therefore essential that national governments design their own strategies rather than adhere uncritically to the EU policy agenda.

Second, we need to stress the limited character of a single survey. Without longitudinal data, we cannot know whether dissatisfied adult learners left their course, nor whether adults saw their initial expectations – such as finding a new job – fulfilled after completion of the course. Because of this limited exercise, it is difficult to draw conclusions about the effectiveness of the adult education system. A longitudinal survey would obviously be expensive and complex, but nevertheless, it would be of great value to the adult education field. Because participation is a process, it would be useful to undertake qualitative research to understand the process of adult learning. This should include gathering information about how learners found out about the course, their experiences at various stages during the course and following up on the outcomes of learning. It would also be of interest to follow up dropouts and gather information about their reasons for leaving the course.

Third, as classroom environment variables explain a great deal of learners' satisfaction – and as teachers have a determining impact on the classroom environment – additional research on the role and competence profiles of teachers in adult education becomes a logical next step. Little is known about this key profession. In many countries, specific training for adult educators does not even exist. Jogi and Gross (2009) found that the professionalisation of adult educators is just starting in some Eastern European countries such as the Baltic States. In Flanders, teacher training focuses mainly on compulsory education, and not all adult educators have a teaching qualification (Boeren, 2011). In contrast, as mentioned above, teaching qualifications for staff in tertiary education have been the focus of attention in the UK. In Scotland around 90% of full-time teachers in further education colleges hold a teaching qualification specifically for teaching adults. (Most of the Scottish learners in the LLL2010 survey were located in further education colleges.) Royce (1999) stated in her research that high-quality learning environments only emerge when adult educators are well-trained and high-functioning professionals and that educational institutions should offer them secure employment contracts. In addition to expertise in their teaching subject, adult educators must have strong social and pedagogical skills and be able to monitor the needs, talents and ambitions of each individual adult learner.

Research into the profile of adult educators is highly recommended. In many countries there is little information about who they are, what qualifications they hold, what previous teaching experience they have and whether they are active in other segments of the labour market. While several authors have focused on the needs and psychology of the adult learners, we do not know whether these European adult educators master the competencies to take these needs of the learners into account (Tennant, 2006; Brookfield, 2006). Overall, our research suggests that there is an urgent need to analyse the professional profile of adult educators in greater detail.

Notes

[1] Unfortunately, Norway had to be deleted from the analyses because the data collection method in that country deviated from the common guidelines.

[2] Goodness of fit statistics for intrinsic motivation: $F=18.669$; df$=3$; $p=0.000$. For extrinsic motivation: $F=17.705$; df$=3$; $p=0.000$.

[3] Further details about the regression analysis can be found in the technical annex to this chapter (see p 163), or in Roosmaa et al (2011).

[4] Nevertheless, on the original five-point item scales for sub-items relating to satisfaction and classroom environment, average scores per country exceeded three in most cases.

References

Bailey, J.R. and Langdana, R.K. (1997) 'A factor analytic study of teaching methods that influence retention among MBA alumni', *Journal of Education for Business*, vol 72, no 5, pp 297-303.

Bean, J. (1985). 'Interaction effects based on class level in an explanatory model of college student dropout syndrome', *American Educational Research Journal*, vol 22, no 1, pp. 35-64.

Blunt, A. and Yang, B. (1995) *An examination of the validity of the Education Participation Scale (EPS) and the Adult Attitudes Towards Continuing Education Scale (AACES)*, Proceedings of the Adult Education Research Conference (AERC), University of Alberta.

Boateng, S.K. (2009) 'Significant country differences in adult learning', *Eurostat: Statistics in Focus* 44/2009.

Boeren, E. (2011) 'Participation in adult education: a bounded agency approach', PhD thesis in Educational Sciences, Leuven: Centre for Research on Professional Learning and Development, Corporate Training and Lifelong Learning, KU Leuven.

Boeren, E. and Holford, J. (2010). 'Common values and culture or competitiveness and individualism? Purpose, motivation and content in European lifelong learning', paper presented at ECER conference, Helsinki 2010.

Boshier, R. (1977) 'Motivational orientations re-visited: life-space reasons for participation and the education participations scale', *Adult Education*, vol 27, pp 89-115.

Boshier, R. (1991) 'Psychometric properties of the alternative form of the education participation scale', *Adult Education Quarterly*, vol 41, pp 150-69.

Boshier, R. (1998) 'Edgar Faure after 25 years: down but not out', in J. Holford, P. Jarvis and C. Griffin (eds), *International perspectives on lifelong learning*, London: Kogan Page, pp 3-20.

Brookfield, S. (2006) *The skilful teacher: on technique, trust and responsiveness in the classroom,* San Francisco: Jossey-Bass.

Coleman, J.S., Campbell, E., Hobson, C., McPartland, J., Mood, A., Weinefeld, F. and York, R. (1966) *Equality of educational opportunity*, Washington DC: Government Printing Office.

Darkenwald, G.G., and Valentine, T. (1986) 'Measuring the social environment of adult education classrooms', Paper presented at the Adult Education Research Conference, Syracuse, NY.

Deci, E. and Ryan, R. (2000) 'The "what" and "why" of goal pursuit: human needs and the self-determination of behaviour', *Psychological Inquiry*, vol 11, pp 227-68.

Dehmel, A. (2006) 'Making a European area of lifelong learning a reality? Some critical reflections on the European Union's lifelong learning policies', *Comparative Education*, vol 42, no 1, pp 46-62.

Desjardins, R., Rubenson, K. and Milana, M. (2006) *Unequal chances to participate in adult learning: international perspectives,* Paris: UNESCO.

Desmedt, E., Groenez, S. and Van den Broeck, G. (2006) *Onderzoek naar de systeemkenmerken die de participatie aan levenslang leren in de EU-15 beïnvloeden,* Leuven: HIVA.

English, L.M. (2005) *International encyclopedia of adult education,* New York: Palgrave Macmillan.

Esping-Andersen, G. (1989) *The three worlds of welfare capitalism,* Cambridge: Polity Press.

European Commission (2010) *An agenda for new skills and jobs: a European contribution towards full employment.* Communication from the Commission to the European Parliament, the Council, the European Economic and Social Committee and the Committee of the Regions, COM(2010) 682 final, Strasbourg, 23 November.

Eurostat (2007) *Task force report on Adult Education Survey,* Luxembourg: Eurostat.

Eurostat (2009) *Task force report on Adult Education Survey* (available at http://epp.eurostat.ec.europa.eu/portal/page/portal/microdata/adult_education_survey)

Garst, W.C. and Ried, D. (1999) 'Motivational orientations: evaluation of the Education Participation Scale in a nontraditional Doctor of Pharmacy program', *American Journal of Pharmaceutical Education,* vol 63, pp 300-4.

Hefler, G. (2010) *The qualification-supporting company – the significance of formal adult education in small and medium organisations. Comparative report – subproject 4 LLL2010,* Krems: Danube University Krems.

Holford, J., Riddell, S., Weedon, E., Litjens, J. and Hannan, G. (2008) *Patterns of lifelong learning, policy and practice in an expanding Europe,* Wien: LIT Verlag.

Houle, C. (1961) *The inquiring Mind,* Madison, WI: University of Wisconsin Press.

Jogi, L. and Gross, M. (2009) 'The professionalisation of adult educators in the Baltic states', *European Journal of Education,* vol 44, no 2, pp 221-42.

Jung, J.C., and Cervero, R.M. (2002) 'The social, economic and political contexts of adults' participation in undergraduate programmes: a state-level analysis', *International Journal of Lifelong Education,* vol 21, no 4, pp 305-20.

Keller, J.M. (1987) 'Strategies for stimulating the motivation to learn', *Performance and instruction,* vol 26, pp 1-7.

Kuh, G. (2001) 'Organizational culture and student persistence: prospects and puzzles', *Journal of College Student Retention,* vol 3, no 1, pp 23-39.

Mortelmans, D. and Dehertogh, B. (2008) *Factoranalyse,* Leuven/Voorburg: Acco.

Mortimore, P., Sammons, P., Stoll, L., Lewis, D. and Ecob, R. (1988) *School matters: the junior years,* London: Open Books

New England Adult Research Network (1999) *Factors influencing adult student persistence in undergraduate degree programs,* Amherst, MA: University of Massachusetts.

OECD (2008) *Tertiary education* for the *knowledge society: OECD thematic review* of tertiary *education: synthesis report overview* (available at www.oecd.org/edu/tertiary/review).

O'Fathaigh, M. (1997) 'Irish adult learners' perceptions of classroom environment: some empirical findings', *International Journal of University Adult Education,* vol 36, pp 9-22.

Roosmaa, E.-L. and Saar, E. (2010) 'Participation in non-formal learning in EU-15 and EU-8 Countries: demand and supply side factors', *Sotsiologitseski problemi,* vol 17, nos 1-2, pp 175-200.

Roosmaa, E.-L., Boeren, E., Nicaise, I. and Saar, E. (2011) *'Adult learners in formal adult education: experiences and perceptions. Subproject 3 comparative report',* Leuven: HIVA/Tallinn: Tallinn University.

Royce, S. (1999) *The adult teacher competencies study. Final report A 353 special demonstration project,* Harrisburg, PA: Penn State University.

Rubenson, K. and Desjardins, R. (2009) 'The impact of welfare state regimes on constraints to participation in adult education: a bounded agency model', *Adult Education Quarterly,* vol 59, no 3, pp 187-207.

Rubenson, K. and Schuetze, H.G. (2000) *Transition to the knowledge society policies and strategies for individual participation and learning,* Vancouver: University of British Columbia Centre for European Studies.

Schuetze, H.G. and Slowey, M. (2002) 'Participation and exclusion: a comparative analysis of non-traditional students and lifelong learners in higher education, *Higher Education,* vol 44, pp 309-27.

Tennant, M. (2006) *Psychology and adult learning,* Oxford: Routledge.

Tinto, V. (1993) *Leaving college: rethinking the causes and cures of student attrition,* Chicago: The University of Chicago Press.

Tinto, V. (1998) 'Colleges as communities: taking research on student persistence seriously', *The Review of Higher Education,* vol 21, no 2, pp 167-77.

Vroom, V.H. (1964) *Work and motivation,* New York: Wiley.

Wolf, S.J. and Fraser, B.J. (2008) 'Learning environment, attitudes and achievement among middle-school science students using inquiry-based laboratory activities', *Research in Science Education,* vol 38, pp 321-41.

FIVE

The sociodemographic obstacles to participating in lifelong learning across Europe

Péter Róbert, TARKI Social Research Institute, Hungary

Introduction

This chapter analyses the barriers that potential participants in lifelong learning face when they consider returning to education. There are considerable differences between people in relation to the extent to which they participate in learning after their initial compulsory education. Some engage in learning to improve their opportunities in the labour market, while others do it for personal fulfilment or for social and civic reasons. Some people do not re-enter the education system after their experience of initial education. As mentioned in Chapter One, the need for ongoing engagement in education has become a central focus for policymakers through the lifelong learning agenda. Lifelong learning is seen as a means of enhancing the human capital of the workforce but also as a vehicle for promoting social inclusion by providing individuals with the relevant skills to participate in the labour market. Identifying reasons for non-participation and barriers to participation in learning is therefore of great importance. This chapter examines barriers to participation by comparing a target group of *learners* and a control group of *non-learners*. The aim is to identify the structural features that may deter individuals from obtaining additional qualifications, and how these features vary in relation to particular countries and groups of countries. Of prime interest is the way in which social structures shape a person's capability to participate.

Conceptual framework

Rubenson and Desjardins (2009), in their review of the comparative literature on barriers to participation, note that most analysts draw on the classification of barriers developed by Cross (1981). The types of barrier identified by Cross are situational (that is, relating to job, family or household), dispositional or institutional. According to Rubenson and Desjardins, the main problem with the raft of studies on barriers to participation is that they tend to overemphasise individual factors and underemphasise the salience of structural factors, such as an individual's position in the socioeconomic hierarchy and the way this affects all aspects of their world view. Drawing on the work of Bourdieu (1990) and his notion of habitus, they argue that structural factors are centrally involved in individual motivation, since a person's sense of their ability to actively construct their life is shaped by the social, economic and cultural resources that they are able to mobilise. People living in socially disadvantaged circumstances are less likely to engage in lifelong learning, in part because they lack the financial resources to fund their studies and believe that there will be few economic benefits. In addition, their life experiences may have reinforced a sense of powerlessness and inability to control risk. This interaction of structure and agency is described as a bounded agency model. Rubenson and Desjardins maintain that the type of welfare regime within a particular country is likely to make a significant difference to an individual's chance of returning to education, particularly for those experiencing social disadvantage. Drawing on 2003 Eurobarometer data, they note the success of the Nordic model in achieving more equal rates of participation in adult education across the social spectrum, largely because of the financial and familial support provided for groups who would not otherwise participate. This chapter examines the social characteristics of participants in adult education in different countries and groups of countries. It identifies the barriers encountered in relation to selected demographic variables (gender, family status – in terms of having young children – and place of residence) and socioeconomic variables (low level of initial education, being out of the labour market, part-time work, temporary work and manual work). The chapter concludes by analysing the interaction of these factors in particular countries and groups of countries, drawing on the typology outlined in Chapter Two.

Data sources

This chapter mainly draws on the Eurostat Adult Education Survey (AES), which was carried out in 29 countries during the period 2005 to 2008 (Boateng, 2009). It was the first such survey and was considered a pilot. It was based on a representative sample of those aged 25 to 64 and included not only EU countries but also EFTA and candidate countries. (see http://epp.eurostat.ec.europa.eu/portal/page/portal/microdata/adult_education_survey). The dataset provided by Eurostat to researchers included only 24 countries, and the analysis here is based on these 24 countries wherever possible. Ireland, one of the LLL2010 countries, did not participate, and the UK survey only covered some of the questions, so is not included in all of the analyses. The net sample size for the 24 countries was around 170,000. The questionnaire covered areas such as information about the household, individual demographic data, participation and non-participation in different types of learning, labour market status, use of ICT and language skills, participation in cultural and social activities and attitudes towards learning. With regard to demographic variables, the survey identified respondents' gender, age, family status and place of residence, but did not ask questions relating to race, religion/belief or disability. In relation to socioeconomic variables, questions were asked about highest level of qualification and work status. The question on participation in adult education asked respondents if they had taken part in formal education as a student or an apprentice in the past 12 months. The emphasis was on formal education that led to a qualification (European Commission, 2007).

Participation in lifelong learning and labour market status

This section describes patterns of participation in lifelong learning, drawing on the AES question on participation in formal education. This variable is explored in relation to highest level of qualification, labour market status and time that has elapsed between leaving initial education and returning to formal education. Data on participation in formal adult education by gender are also presented.

Figure 5.1 strongly supports the existence of the Matthew effect ('To those that have shall be given') in all of the countries, in that those who already do well within the initial education system have further advantage conferred on them through participation in adult education. Respondents with only ISCED level 1-2 qualifications participate significantly less than those with a higher level of qualifications. In Finland and to a lesser extent Portugal, there is very little difference between those with ISCED 3-4 and those with ISCED 5-6 qualifications. In Sweden there is a considerable gap between those with the highest and lowest qualification: 25% of those with tertiary qualifications had participated in formal education, but only around 6% with lowest level of qualifications. In spite of this, those with the lowest level of qualifications are still relatively better off in terms of participation in Sweden than in all other countries except for the UK and Belgium. In countries with lower overall levels of participation, only around

Figure 5.1: Participation in formal adult learning by level of initial education

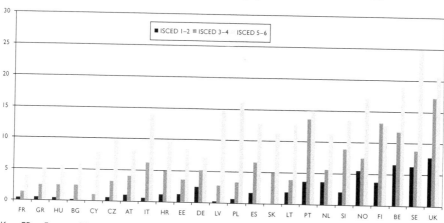

Key: FR = France, GR = Greece, HU = Hungary, BG = Bulgaria, CY = Cyprus, CZ = Czech Republic, AT = Austria, IT = Italy, HR = Croatia, EE = Estonia, DE = Germany, LV = Latvia, PL = Poland, ES = Spain, SK = Slovakia, LT = Lithuania, PT = Portugal, NL = Netherlands, SI = Slovenia, NO = Norway, FI = Finland, BE = Belgium, SE = Sweden, UK = United Kingdom

Source: Eurostat AES

1-2% of the early school leavers return to formal education. In these countries only about 10% of graduates participate in further education.

The results presented in **Figure 5.1** are based on a comparison of two variables: level of initial education and rate of participation in formal education as an adult. Further analysis including a number of variables was also carried out but is not included here. This analysis revealed that the odds of returning to lifelong learning are significantly higher for those with tertiary qualifications, further confirming the presence of the Matthew effect (for further details see Merton, 1968; Hefler et al, 2011). There were no significant differences between those at the two lower levels of qualifications. Thus, the relationship between initial level of schooling and the probability of returning to formal adult learning is not linear: tertiary levels of qualification confer a definite advantage and lower levels of schooling act as barriers. The same pattern appears at the level of the individual countries, though the pattern does not persist when time elapsed between leaving the initial education system and returning to formal education is taken into account.

Figure 5.2 examines participation in formal learning according to the following variables: in work, unemployed, retired and temporarily out of the labour force. It shows that in a large number of countries it is those who are temporarily out of work who have the highest participation rate. This category includes students, so it is not surprising that it contains a large proportion of those who have engaged in formal education. As the data cover the age group 25 to 64, it is likely that the countries which have the highest rates include students who are still in tertiary education following their initial education. Earlier Labour Force Survey data show a wide variation in average age of leaving continuous education or training, ranging from 18 to 24, with students in Sweden being the oldest to leave continuous education (Eurostat, 2003). The participation rate shown for Sweden for the temporarily out of the labour force category may include students who are in the process of completing or have just completed their tertiary level qualifications; this would account for the high rate in this country. In contrast, the UK shows a different pattern to many countries. Here participation in formal learning is similar between those in work, the unemployed and those temporarily out of the labour force.

The multivariate regression analysis showed significant negative effects in relation to unemployment and self-employment in some countries. It is in the countries with generous income protection linked to a strongly developed active labour market policy where we see the highest rate of participation among those temporarily out of the labour market and also, in Sweden, Norway and Belgium, relatively high participation among those that are unemployed.

Figure 5.3 further points towards the highest participation rate among those weakly integrated in the labour market, with the exception of the UK, Belgium and the Netherlands. In all countries, self-employed people are least likely to be involved in formal learning. Although participation rates among self-employed individuals are high in some nations, such as Belgium, the UK and Croatia

(**Figure 5.3**), these estimates are insignificant in the country-level multivariate regression models (although the UK was not included in this analysis) (Hefler et al, 2011).

Figure 5.2: Participation in formal adult learning by labour force status

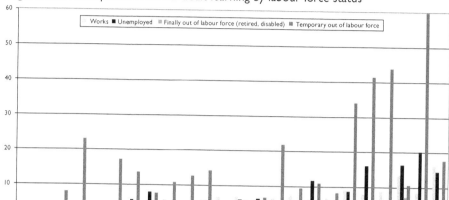

Key: FR = France, GR = Greece, HU = Hungary, BG = Bulgaria, CY = Cyprus, CZ = Czech Republic, AT = Austria, IT = Italy, HR = Croatia, EE = Estonia, DE = Germany, LV = Latvia, PL = Poland, ES = Spain, SK = Slovakia, LT = Lithuania, PT = Portugal, NL = Netherlands, SI = Slovenia, NO = Norway, FI = Finland, BE = Belgium, SE = Sweden, UK = United Kingdom

Source: Eurostat AES

Figure 5.3: Participation in formal adult learning by labour market integration

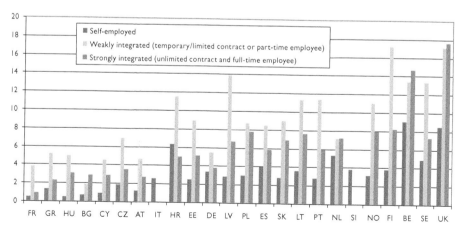

Key: FR = France, GR = Greece, HU = Hungary, BG = Bulgaria, CY = Cyprus, CZ = Czech Republic, AT = Austria, IT = Italy, HR = Croatia, EE = Estonia, DE = Germany, LV = Latvia, PL = Poland, ES = Spain, SK = Slovakia, LT = Lithuania, PT = Portugal, NL = Netherlands, SI = Slovenia, NO = Norway, FI = Finland, BE = Belgium, SE = Sweden, UK = United Kingdom

Source: Eurostat AES

In **Figure 5.4** the impact of time elapsed since the completion of initial education on rates of participation can be seen. Examination of the AES data shows that the length of time that has elapsed between leaving continuous education and returning to formal education has a significant impact on rates of participation. The rate decreases with an increase in the number of years that have elapsed, as can be seen in **Figure 5.4**. It is clear that the age of leaving initial education is a crucial variable, since this is closely linked to the level of education attained. In most cases, the lower the level of initial education, the younger the age will be on leaving initial education. The other crucial variable is the age at which someone returned to education. Participation rates for those that return to education within five years of leaving the initial education system are generally higher than those who stay away from learning for longer. **Figure 5.4** shows that in around half of the countries, the rate for those returning within five years was around or above 30%. However, in countries such as France, Greece, Hungary, Bulgaria and Cyprus, where participation is generally low, as well as in Austria, Estonia and the Netherlands, the participation rate for this group is lower. In contrast, for those who are out of the education system for 11 to 20 years, the rate was never above 15%, and in most countries it was considerably lower. Finland and Slovenia differ from the rest, since the participation rate in lifelong learning in these two countries is the highest for those who have been out of the system for six to 10 years.

The multivariate regression analysis which was conducted demonstrated the importance of passage of time and the likelihood of someone returning to formal learning. Those who had left the initial education system and not returned to learning within five years were far less likely to return to formal education. This relationship was particularly evident in countries where overall participation rates

Figure 5.4: Participation in formal adult learning by interruption of studies

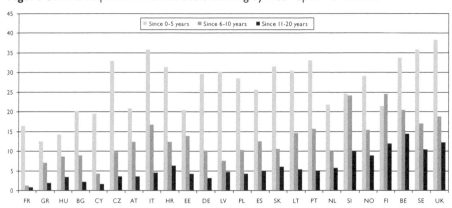

Key: FR = France, GR = Greece, HU = Hungary, BG = Bulgaria, CY = Cyprus, CZ = Czech Republic, AT = Austria, IT = Italy, HR = Croatia, EE = Estonia, DE = Germany, LV = Latvia, PL = Poland, ES = Spain, SK = Slovakia, LT = Lithuania, PT = Portugal, NL = Netherlands, SI = Slovenia, NO = Norway, FI = Finland, BE = Belgium, SE = Sweden, UK = United Kingdom

Source: Eurostat AES

in lifelong learning are low (Hefler et al, 2011). This suggests that if the impact of early school leaving is to be addressed through lifelong learning, any intervention should focus on engaging this group at the earliest opportunity.

Figure 5.5 shows that in almost all countries women are more likely than men to participate in adult education, the exceptions being Cyprus, Austria, Hungary, Germany and the Netherlands. The relationship between gender and other demographic variables is explored further in the next section.

Figure 5.5: Rates in participation in formal adult education by gender

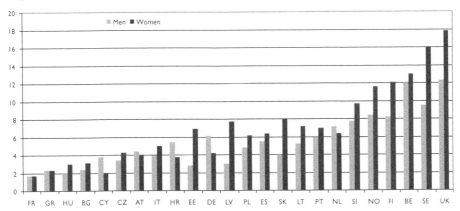

Key: FR = France, GR = Greece, HU = Hungary, BG = Bulgaria, CY = Cyprus, CZ = Czech Republic, AT = Austria, IT = Italy, HR = Croatia, EE = Estonia, DE = Germany, LV = Latvia, PL = Poland, ES = Spain, SK = Slovakia, LT = Lithuania, PT = Portugal, NL = Netherlands, SI = Slovenia, NO = Norway, FI = Finland, BE = Belgium, SE = Sweden, UK = United Kingdom

Source: Eurostat AES

Obstacles to participating in lifelong learning: country patterns

This section explores country patterns associated with demographic and socioeconomic obstacles to participation in formal learning for learners and non-learners. This analysis draws on a smaller number of countries than the earlier analysis because of missing data in some of the country AES datasets. As noted earlier, Ireland did not participate in the Adult Education Survey at all, and because the UK used only a limited suite of questions it is not included in this analysis.

It is clear that there may be a range of factors that can impact on an individual's ability to engage in formal education. In this analysis, demographic barriers include being a woman (although, as noted earlier, men are in general less likely to participate), being over 45, having young child/ren and living in a rural area. Socioeconomic barriers include low level of initial education, being out of education for a longer period of time, being weakly attached to the labour market and being a manual worker.

The initial statistical analysis for both sets of variables (demographic and socioeconomic) identified clusters of countries. In some of these the barriers were strongly present, while in others they did not constitute a barrier. In other words there was considerable country variation. **Table 5.1** presents the analysis for the demographic variables and shading is used to indicate the four clusters of countries that were identified. The plus signs (++, +) are used to indicate that there were no obstacles in returning to adult formal education in that particular country. The negative signs (--, -) are used to show that these obstacles are likely to hinder participation in formal education. In the countries where these barriers are in existence, individuals affected by them will be underrepresented among those participating in formal learning. The table is arranged to show countries with a high level of barriers to the left and those with no or limited barriers to the right.

Table 5.1 shows that in the first group of countries, which includes Bulgaria, France, Cyprus and Hungary, the rate of participation in formal adult education is low and the demographic barriers significantly impact on participation rates. Some of these barriers may also work in an additive manner; for example, if you are a woman with young children in a rural setting you may be at a particular disadvantage in these countries. The next group includes the two German speaking nations, Austria and Germany, two of the Mediterranean nations, Spain and Portugal, and two of the former socialist countries, the Czech Republic and Croatia. Here the barriers are likely to be a factor influencing participation but to a more limited extent than in the first group. In Spain and Portugal being a woman does not have a negative impact, and in Germany and Spain being over 45 is not a barrier. In Portugal having a young child does not have a negative impact on participation, and in Austria and Portugal living in a rural location does not present a problem. The third cluster contains the three Baltic countries and Slovakia. In this group it is only age – being over 45 – that is likely to be a barrier, and rural residence presents no obstacle. The last five nations form a group where Belgium and Finland are similar as are Norway and Slovenia. Sweden forms part of this group and is the only country where no demographic barriers are present. In Slovenia having a young child presents a limited obstacle, and in Belgium rural residence is a significant barrier. Countries in this last group have the highest overall rates of participation.

The socioeconomic obstacles were also analysed using an initial cluster analysis. However, this yielded a different pattern of country variation to the one for demographic barriers and this was more difficult to interpret (see **Table 5.2**). The first cluster contained a large number of Central and Eastern European countries (the Czech Republic, Slovakia, Estonia, Latvia, Bulgaria, Croatia and Hungary), France and Cyprus. It therefore included all the post-socialist countries except Slovenia. In this cluster, low level of education represented a significant obstacle in all countries except Croatia, where it was a less severe obstacle. Being out of the labour force was a significant obstacle in France, Latvia and Hungary and less of an obstacle in the remaining countries in the cluster. Weak labour force affiliation represented a considerable obstacle in Cyprus, Bulgaria and Hungary and to a

Table 5.1: The occurrence or non-occurrence of the demographic obstacles in 19 AES countries

Barrier	BG	CY	FR	HU	HR	CZ	AT	DE	ES	PT	EE	LT	SK	LV	BE	FI	SI	NO	SE
Being a woman	--	--	--	--	-	-	-	-	Ø	Ø	Ø	Ø	Ø	Ø	+	+	+	+	++
Aged over 45 yrs	--	--	--	--	-	-	-	Ø	Ø	-	-	-	-	Ø	++	+	+	+	++
Dependent child 0–3 yrs	--	-	--	--	-	-	-	-	-	Ø	-	Ø	Ø	Ø	+	+	-	+	++
Dependent child 4–5 yrs	--	--	--	--	-	--	-	-	-	-	Ø	Ø	Ø	Ø	+	+	++	+	++
Rural residence	--	--	--	--	-	-	Ø	--	-	Ø	+	+	+	+	---	Ø	++	++	++

Key: ++ = strong over-representation, no obstacles are present; + = over-representation; Ø = around the mean; - = under-representation; -- = strong under-representation, large obstacles are present

Key to countries: BG = Bulgaria, CY = Cyprus, FR = France, HU = Hungary, HR = Croatia, CZ = Czech Republic, AT = Austria, DE = Germany, ES = Spain, PT = Portugal, EE – Estonia, LT = Lithuania, SK = Slovakia, LV = Latvia, BE = Belgium, FI = Finland, SI = Slovenia, NO = Norway, SE = Sweden

Table 5.2: The occurrence or non-occurrence of the socioeconomic obstacles in the 19 AES countries

Barrier	CY	CZ	FR	SK	BG	LV	EE	HU	HR	AT	DE	LT	SI	ES	NO	PT	FI	BE
Highest level of education ISCED 1–3	--	--	--	--	--	--	--	--	-	--	-	-	-	Ø	+	++	++	+
Not in the labour force	-	-	--	-	-	--	-	--	-	Ø	Ø	-	Ø	Ø	+	Ø	+	+
Temporary/limited work contract	--	--	-	-	-	-	-	--		--	-	--	++	+	Ø	+	++	Ø
Part-time work	--	--	--	--	--	-	--	--	--	Ø	Ø	Ø	--	Ø	+	--	--	++
Manual work	--	-	-	-	-	-	-	-	Ø	-	Ø	+	++	+	+	++	++	++

Key: ++ = strong over-representation, no obstacles are present; + = over-representation; Ø = around the mean; - = under-representation; -- = strong under-representation, large obstacles are present

Key to countries: CY = Cyprus, CZ = Czech Republic, FR = France, SK = Slovakia, BG = Bulgaria, LV = Latvia, EE = Estonia, HU = Hungary, HR = Croatia, AT = Austria, DE = Germany, LT = Lithuania, SI = Slovenia, ES = Spain, NO = Norway, PT = Portugal, FI = Finland, BE = Belgium, SE = Sweden

slightly more limited extent in the other countries. In Cyprus and Slovakia being in manual work represented a significant barrier, but was less of an obstacle in the remaining countries. Croatia was similar to the overall average.

The second cluster included only three countries that were in some respects similar to the first cluster. In Austria and Lithuania having low qualifications and being weakly affiliated to the labour market (on a limited or temporary contract) presented significant obstacles, while in Germany it was only low level of education and being on a temporary contract that presented barriers. This was in contrast to Lithuania, where manual work was not an obstacle. For the remaining variables these countries were close to the average.

The third cluster included the three Scandinavian countries, plus Belgium, Slovenia and the two Mediterranean countries, Spain and Portugal. While these countries appeared in the same cluster, the links between the countries were weaker. Sweden is characterised by the greatest equality in access to formal education with no socioeconomic barriers present. Belgium and Norway, as well as Spain, have few barriers. In Finland, Portugal and Slovenia part-time work constitutes a barrier, and in Slovenia having a low level of education is also an obstacle.

Table 5.3: Demographic and socioeconomic obstacles to participation in formal education

Socioeconomic obstacles**	Demographic obstacles*			
	Low level	Low-middle	High-middle	High level
Low level	Finland, Sweden, Belgium		Portugal	
Low-middle	Norway, Slovenia		Spain	
High-middle		Lithuania	Austria, Germany	
High level		Estonia, Latvia, Slovakia	Czech Republic, Croatia	Hungary, Cyprus, Bulgaria, France

* Expected disadvantage for women, old aged respondents, rural inhabitants, those with small children.

** Expected disadvantage for early school dropouts, those with weak integration in the labour market, manual worker status

Table 5.3 provides an overview of the intersection of demographic and socioeconomic barriers. It is evident that socioeconomic and demographic obstacles are rare in the Scandinavian countries (Finland, Sweden and Norway) as well as in Belgium and Slovenia. This supports the descriptive analysis presented earlier, which showed that these countries have a high level of participation in formal adult education. The cluster analysis does not identify causal relationships. However, the explorative analysis revealed a link between having a low level of sociodemographic obstacles in these societies, suggesting that greater equality in access to adult education leads to a higher frequency of participation for all. At the other end of the spectrum, those four countries with the lowest participation rates in adult learning (France, Hungary, Bulgaria, Cyprus) have significant socioeconomic and demographic obstacles. This, it could be argued, confirms, in an indirect manner, that the greater the inequality in access, the lower the participation rate is likely to be.

The other countries fall in between these two groups of extremes and show bigger variation in relation to socioeconomic and demographic obstacles. It seems that socioeconomic barriers (being an early school leaver, being weakly integrated into the labour market, being a manual worker) have an impact on participation rates, especially in the former post-communist countries as well as in Austria and Germany. Slovenia differs, as it, alongside Norway, has few demographic obstacles and low levels of socioeconomic barriers. Spain and Portugal are relatively high on demographic barriers but relatively low on socioeconomic obstacles, and Lithuania has more socioeconomic than demographic obstacles.

In order to go beyond the explorative results on the country patterns, multivariate techniques were used to shed light on the combined effects of sociodemographic barriers to lifelong learning. Separate logistic regression models were carried out on each of the AES countries. This analysis identified the odds of returning to formal education and found three larger clusters of countries, with a small number of countries that did not fit into any of these.

According to this analysis, the timing of the return to formal education, measured as the duration of time between leaving initial education and returning to formal education, is a crucial determinant of participation, being the main factor that differentiates countries in relation to participation rates. This is shown in **Figure 5.6,** which demonstrates that the odds against returning to formal education

Figure 5.6: The impact of interruption of studies on participation in formal education, based on a gap of less than five years

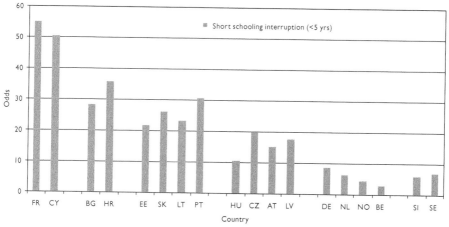

Key: FR = France, CY = Cyprus, BG = Bulgaria, HR = Croatia, EE = Estonia, SK = Slovakia, LT = Lithuania, PT = Portugal, HU = Hungary, CZ = Czech Republic, AT = Austria, LV = Latvia, DE = Germany, NL = Netherlands, NO = Norway, BE = Belgium, SI = Slovenia, SE = Sweden

for those who have been out of education for less than five years are highest in France and Cyprus and lowest in Slovenia and Sweden.

Table 5.4 presents the final overview of the countries in relation to the obstacles to participation in formal adult education based on the AES data. The table shows the countries according to the socioeconomic and demographic obstacles at the observed level as well as in relation to the causal relationships identified by logistic regression models applied to each individual country.

This final picture of the statistical data looks quite consistent in terms of the bivariate and multivariate relationships, on the one hand, and of the participation rates in lifelong learning, on the other. This can clearly be seen in **Table 5.4**. The countries with high participation rates and few obstacles appear in the right-hand 'lower' corner and the countries with low participation rates and a high number of socioeconomic and demographic barriers appear in the left-hand 'upper' corner. Most of the countries appear in the diagonal of the table, but it can be seen that, as overall participation rates increase, the barriers for certain groups decrease.

Table 5.4: Obstacles to participation in formal adult education: observed indicators and casual effects

Observed levels of demographic and socioeconomic barriers	Causal effects of socioeconomic and demographic barriers			
	High impact	High-middle	Low-middle	Low impact
High	Bulgaria, France, Cyprus	Hungary		
High-middle	Croatia	Austria, Czech Republic, Latvia	Portugal	Germany
Low-middle			Estonia, Lithuania, Slovakia	
Low				Sweden, Norway, Belgium, Slovenia

Conclusion

The preceding analyses indicate the mechanisms influencing participation and non-participation in formal adult education and the country groupings that emerge. There is strong empirical support for the Matthew effect, as it has been demonstrated that being an early school leaver with low levels of initial qualifications acts as a strong barrier to engaging with formal education later in life. Similarly, there is also strong empirical support for the effect of length of absence from the education system. As the interval between leaving the initial education system and returning to formal learning increases, the likelihood of participation in formal education decreases. The results also reveal a strong interaction between labour force position, labour market activity and participation in lifelong learning. However, the causal direction in this regard is not entirely clear as there are a number of differences between countries that suggest an impact of country-specific labour markets and educational policies.

Confirming the argument of Rubenson and Desjardins (2009), there appears to be a relationship between the nature of a country's welfare regime, labour market and its education and lifelong learning system. The social market regimes found in Scandinavian countries have fewer inequalities in access to lifelong learning than do the other countries. In the Scandinavian countries the initial education system is comprehensive, there is generous support for adult education and there are more structural opportunities for job mobility. This may contribute to stronger participation in formal adult education programmes.

Countries such as Austria and Germany have a corporatist welfare regime and these two countries are found in the same cluster. Here there are quite substantial educational inequalities and the initial education system is highly stratified. The organisation of the labour market also appears to be of great importance. Maurice et al (1986) and Müller and Shavit (1998) draw a distinction between the Occupational Labour Market (OLM), where vocational qualifications are essential for a wide range of occupations, restricting labour market mobility, and the Internal Labour Market (ILM), which has a less highly regulated labour market in terms of qualifications required to undertake certain jobs, and a higher degree of occupational mobility. Austria and Germany have a strong OLM, supported by employment protection legislation, although the multivariate analysis indicates that the odds of returning to formal education are higher in Germany than in Austria. However, a different picture emerges in Belgium, which has similar institutional structures. Here there is less inequality in relation to participation in lifelong learning than one would expect on the basis of these structures.

The Mediterranean countries present some anomalies. In the explorative analysis of the demographic and socioeconomic obstacles, Spain and Portugal differ from the other two countries within this regime (France and Cyprus). France and Cyprus are classified as having high levels of both types of obstacles. Portugal has low levels of socioeconomic barriers but middle to high demographic barriers and Spain is similar. The data also revealed large inequalities in participation in formal education in France and Cyprus. The Mediterranean countries, not including France, are characterised by a family-orientated welfare regime, so that much caring work is carried out by families rather than the state and investment in public services is consequently lower. However, France fits in with the Mediterranean countries in terms of its skill formation system and labour markets features. It has an ILM that allows for considerable occupational mobility and less strict employment protection legislation.

Ireland was excluded from the analysis because it did not participate in the Adult Education Survey, and therefore the UK, for which only partial data were available, was the only country representing the liberal market regime. The data on participation rates suggest that there are policy measures and practices in relation to lifelong learning participation that make the country an exception to the 'rule' of the linkage between high level of educational inequalities and low level of participation in formal adult learning. Participation rates are high and there is relatively little inequality in access to formal adult education. This may be explained by the strong ILM that is a feature of the UK as well as very low employment protection legislation, both of which encourage movement between occupations and participation in lifelong learning in between career changes.

Among the new EU member states the analyses point towards considerable differences, which confirm that these countries cannot be treated as a homogenous group, as already discussed in Chapter Two. Slovenia stands out as a country with high participation rates and low levels of inequality in educational opportunities for adults to return to formal education.

There are a number of messages from these analyses for policymakers. The evidence points towards a relationship between overall levels of participation and the level of inequalities that exist in access to formal adult education. In countries where overall levels of participation are high, there are fewer socioeconomic and demographic barriers than in countries with overall low levels of participation. This would suggest that policy measures and practices are able to have a positive impact on reducing inequality in adult education participation. However, lifelong learning policies can only form one part of such measures, and labour market and welfare policies are also important. There is strong support for the idea of bounded agency, in which individual biographies, including decisions to return to education, are strongly shaped by the overarching social structures, including the welfare regime within particular countries.

One particular group, early school leavers, deserves particular attention. The analyses have shown that low levels of qualification have a detrimental impact on later participation and that, as time passes, it becomes increasingly unlikely that this group will return to learning. Early school leavers are also likely to avoid engaging in later learning as they may have had negative experiences during their initial schooling. It would seem that measures for members of this group should include both focusing on the type of learning experience that they have while in the initial compulsory phase of education and the development of strategies to re-engage them when they have been out of the education system for some time. It is likely that such measures would need to engage both educational institutions and employers.

References

Boateng, S.K. (2009) 'Significant country differences in adult learning', Eurostat: Statistics in Focus 44/2009.

Bourdieu, J.-P. (1990) *The logic of practice*, Cambridge: Polity Press.

Cross, K.P. (1981) *Adults as learners: increasing participation and facilitating learning*, San Francisco: Jossey-Bass.

European Commission (2007) *Adult Education Survey (2005-2007) Manual, version 24.08.2007*, Brussels: European Commission.

Eurostat (2003) *Young people's social origin, educational attainment and labour market outcomes in Europe*, Statistics in Focus 6/2003, Luxembourg: European Communities.

Hefler, G., Róbert, P., Ringler, P., Sági, M., Rammel, S., Balogh, A. and Markowitsch, J. (2011) 'Formal adult education in context – the view of European Statistics SP 2 – synthesis report', LLL2010 project report.

Maurice, M., Sellier, F. and Silvestre, J.-J. (1986) *The social foundations of industrial power: a comparison of France and Germany*, Cambridge, MA: MIT Press.

Merton, R.K. (1968) 'The Matthew effect in science', *Science*, vol 159, pp 56-63.

Müller, W. and Shavit, Y. (1998) 'The institutional embeddedness of the stratification process: a comparative study of qualifications and occupations in thirteen countries', in: Y. Shavit and W. Müller (eds) *From school to work: a comparative study of educational qualifications and occupational destinations*, Oxford: Clarendon Press, pp 1-48.

Rubenson, K. and Desjardins, R. (2009) 'The impact of welfare state regimes on barriers to participation in adult education', *Adult Education Quarterly*, vol 59 no 3, pp 187-207.

SIX

The qualification-providing enterprise? Support for formal adult education in small and medium-sized enterprises

Günter Hefler and Jörg Markowitsch, 3s Unternehmensberatung GmbH, Vienna

Introduction

Various fields of research deal with formal adult education, but it does not feature prominently in the literature on company training, human resource development (HRD) or adult education. Particularly in countries such as Austria, with strong occupational labour markets, it is expected that formal education will have been completed *before* entering the world of work. In other countries, such as the UK, although an applicant would be expected to have the basic qualifications necessary for the job, undertaking additional qualifications while in post is common.

This chapter seeks to make two contributions. First, we investigate whether formal adult education occupies a separate domain within companies' training activities and human resource management. Managers distinguish between formal and non-formal education and training; however, in some countries, these boundaries are more blurred than in others (Hefler, 2010, Chapter 7). To investigate formal adult education's significance at the company level, an enterprise's practices with regard to formal adult education must be distinguished from its more general approaches to training and HRD. Consequently, we first analyse formal adult education separately from more general patterns of training, so that we can assess whether it shows significant independence. Second, we work towards a comparative framework, by identifying differences in the significance of formal adult education in the European corporate training context. We do this by taking a broad view that reflects statistical and case study evidence for 12 of the 13 LLL2010 project countries.

In corporate training, the organisation initiates and decides on participation, course content and purpose of the training. Employees may be asked for their personal interests in appraisal interviews and organisations may act to motivate their staff to take courses. Enterprises presumably choose the training in line with their particular interests, and employees participate in the training arranged as part of their duties, typically within paid working time and at their employer's expense.

For formal adult education, the praxis is more complex. In many cases, the employee unilaterally decides to participate; the employer must accept and deal with this decision, comparable to other important life events such as parental leave or extended periods of illness. Often participation ranks high among personal values, so that workers may opt to undertake a course even if this involves leaving their present job. Therefore, responding to individuals' educational plans becomes an issue in enterprises' retention policies. Yet formal adult education also provides particular opportunities for enterprises. In contrast to short training sessions, participation in extended, demanding programmes can hardly be made mandatory because learners must be highly motivated, but the knowledge gained will often benefit the firm. Thus enterprises may have reasons to encourage participation in formal adult education, despite some concerns about retaining workers after they complete the formal programme.

Like other contributions to this volume, the present chapter must address the numerous ambiguities of the concept of formal adult education. In the context of company training, 'formal' is often used to refer to 'organised', 'off-the-job' or 'course-like' in opposition to 'work-embedded' or 'informal'. It is important to note that throughout this volume we apply a particular definition of formal adult education (see Chapter One) that closely follows the current statistical definition, including any learning activity leading to a nationally recognised certificate (Eurostat, 2006). Within each country, formal adult education covers a range of clearly distinct types of education, characterised by their particular institutional logics and their relations to current or future employers of graduates (see Chapter 3 in Hefler, 2012, forthcoming). Formal adult education can be firmly institutionalised within organisational or professional career patterns, with space for negotiation between individual employees and their employers (see Chapter 6 in Hefler, 2012, forthcoming). However, the programmes frequently remain outside of any given career trajectories, for example when students simply work to pay living costs before graduation (Wolbers, 2003). Moreover, considerable differences in the concept of formal adult education result from a country's institutional frameworks shaped by the relative dominance of organisational space, skill space or professional space (Fligstein and Byrkjeflot, 1996; Hefler and Markowitsch, 2012, forthcoming) and, in particular, the existence of modularised or credit-based qualifications and/or qualification frameworks.

Consequently, we start with a short overview of *comparative* statistical evidence that underlines the significance of formal adult education *within* the field of corporate training and human resource development. Subsequently, we use case studies from the LLL2010 project to explore the ways small and medium enterprises (SMEs) support formal adult education and present a typology of support patterns. Next, we discuss briefly the concept of 'training cultures' that relates to enterprises' training activities beyond formal adult education and explore the relationship between training cultures and levels of support for formal adult education. Finally, we draw some comparisons between enterprises' approaches to formal adult education in different countries.

No *quantité négligeable* – statistical accounts of formal adult education in enterprises

Comparative statistical accounts of formal adult education of employees are scarce and difficult to interpret. Yet, staff participation in formal education is clearly underestimated in its significance. Among the approximately 11 million adults aged 25–64 years in the EU-25 countries identified as participants in formal adult education in 2003 by the Labour Force Survey (LFS) Module on Lifelong Learning) (Hefler et al, 2011), roughly 60% were found to be working while studying. Results of the Adult Education Survey (AES) (Hefler et al, 2011) point in the same direction and indicate that the majority of the approximately 15 million participants (more than 70%) are employed.[1] Given the importance of gainful work in adult lives, it is no surprise to find that most participants are economically active.

While total participation rates in formal adult education in the 25–64-year-old population range from about 2% in Croatia to about 13% in the UK, we find a much more equal participation in programmes with more than 200 hours of annual course work. In these more intensive programmes, the participation rate ranges from more than 4% in Sweden, Norway and Finland to between 1% and 2% in Croatia, Greece, Hungary, Cyprus and Italy. Participation in more intensive formal programmes in the UK or in Belgium is comparatively low and at the same level as, for example, in Austria, Bulgaria or even Hungary. Participation in longer programmes in the Baltic countries or Slovenia is comparatively high and topped only by the Scandinavian countries, which have extraordinarily high participation rates in adult education. For a detailed analysis of characteristics of learners, institutions, and courses in formal adult education, also differentiated by level of qualification, see Chapter Four.

Enterprise-based surveys, such as the Continuous Vocational Education and Training Survey (CVTS) (Markowitsch and Hefler, 2008; Cedefop, 2010), do not provide information on formal adult education, but the AES allows for calculation of some indicators. However, because of the small sample size (often covering only 100–250 participation cases in formal adult education for countries), these statistics require careful interpretation. Again, participating in formal adult education is *not* a rare event for enterprises. In countries for which formal adult education implies increased participation in multi-year, time-demanding programmes, as in Austria, Bulgaria or Estonia, participation rates are between 2% and 4% for all employees and clearly above that level for younger and mid-career staff. From the standpoint of life-cycle-oriented personnel management (Schein, 1978; Graf, 2002), many workers could be expected to participate in extended formal adult education programmes at some point in their career (although data are missing and estimates available are notoriously vague). Lifetime expectancies for participation are above

20% in all countries (with the lowest in Bulgaria and the highest in Norway, England and Scotland; see Hefler et al, 2011, p 47). Participation rates may be much higher for highly skilled employees and those in strongly institutionalised organisational careers (for example those seeking craft mastership status in Austria or Germany). As a life event, participation in formal adult education is therefore as frequent as parental leave.

AES data on formal adult education do not allow for analysis of significant differences in support for formal adult education for sectors or enterprises of different sizes. However, we know from LFS data (Hefler et al, 2011, p 87) that participation in formal adult education among employees in small enterprises (1–49 employees) is nearly at the same level as in larger enterprises. Referring to the definitions used in the CVTS, formal adult education of staff would count as corporate training when the company either contributes to the costs or allows paid work time to be used for part of a programme's work load. In the 24 countries for which information is available, roughly 3% of all employees are engaged at a given time in company-supported formal adult education and half of all formal learning activities would count as corporate training. The substantial country differences reflect the previously stated differences in the understanding of formal adult education. In Belgium, the UK, the Nordic countries and Croatia, between 4% and 8% of staff participate in corporate-supported formal adult education. At the other end of the spectrum, in 10 countries, less than 2% of staff participate with employer support (see **Figure 6.1**). However, participation rates do not reveal the level of enterprises' support for formal adult education. Some countries with comparatively high participation rates have considerably low support rates such as in Sweden or Slovenia. In some countries with comparatively low participation rates, such as Hungary, Bulgaria or Estonia, enterprises support the vast majority of all reported formal learning activities, which partially reflects statutory employee rights. In some countries (for example Latvia, Norway, Estonia, Finland, Bulgaria, the UK and Hungary), enterprises are more likely to support shorter courses. However, in most countries there is little difference in support for short and extended programmes (+/– 10%).

The AES survey reports that between one and two thirds of all instruction hours are delivered in formal adult education (see Chapter 3.3 in Hefler, 2010). Hours in formal adult education supported by enterprises also make up a considerable amount of all training activities in enterprises However, despite the statistical evidence that indicates the considerable importance of formal adult education for companies' human resource management and training policies, we lack information on some crucial aspects. First, we do not know about the proportion of formal adult education initiated by the enterprise. Second, we have no information on particular organisational career patterns and embedding particular types of formal adult education in careers (Hefler and Markowitsch, 2012, forthcoming). Does formal adult education form an element within organisational careers? If so, what role do occupations or professions play in its institutionalisation?

Figure 6.1: Participation in formal adult education of employed persons and proportion of employees with (some) support from the enterprise

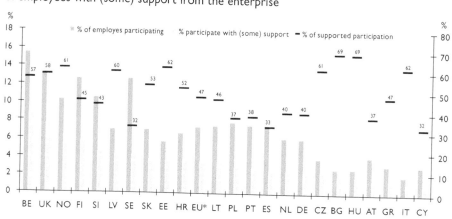

Key: BE = Belgium, UK = United Kingdom, NO = Norway, FI = Finland, SI = Slovenia, LV = Latvia, SE = Sweden, SK = Slovakia, EE = Estonia, HR = Croatia, EU* = European Union (average of participating countries), LT = Lithuania, PL = Poland, PT = Portugal, ES = Spain, NL = Netherlands, DE = Germany, CZ = Czech Republic, BG = Bulgaria, HU = Hungary, AT = Austria, GR – Greece, IT = Italy, CY = Cyprus

Source: First reported formal activity, micro dataset AES 2005–2007; own calculation

Theories of support for formal adult education

Despite weaknesses in the statistical data available, the evidence indicates that enterprises, irrespective of their size, support formal adult education. However, we lack theories explaining the reasons for this support. Available approaches include 'post-Beckerian' variants of economics of education. According to Becker's original position (Becker, 1975), formal adult education provides *general skills*, useful for a broad number of employers, and therefore should instil a skill premium for the individual employee. As the beneficiary of the returns, the participant in formal adult education should cover the training costs, while the enterprise stays neutral. Earlier empirical research explains the importance of employers' engagement in improving deficits in general skills attributable to market imperfections, information asymmetries (between the current and a future employer) or risk aversion (employees not knowing in advance the working conditions with a new employer).

Newer accounts (starting with Bishop, 1988) highlight the value of combining firm-specific experience and general (formal) education and training for the enterprise. By combining firm-specific experience and formal (general) training, firms may unleash their employees' genuine and situated potential that is hard to replicate. This, at least in theory, allows for a market premium high enough to pay wages substantially above market level, thus deterring staff from moving to other firms (for more studies see Bishop and Kang, 1996; Loewenstein and Spletzer, 1997; Acemoglu and Pischke, 1999). However, post-Beckerian approaches explain only why the enterprise may benefit from supporting training in general, rather than formal education more specifically, and, like all research in this tradition, are based on functional-rationalistic assumptions on the productivity-boosting nature of education and training. They have nothing to say about employees' intrinsic motivation to engage in learning.

In a comparable fashion, the literature on rational choice theory at institutional level focuses on ways of overcoming problems of coordination among employers. Enterprises are expected not to invest in formal initial or further vocational education and training, when their competitors may choose to save on training costs and 'free-ride' through poaching other firms' well-trained employees by paying higher wages (Estevez-Abe et al, 2001). Effective coordination between employers may limit free-riding; however, the benefits of training are taken for granted and enterprises are expected to invest as soon as the threats to benefiting from their investments are removed.

Other explanatory frameworks rarely distinguish between formal adult education and non-formal training (with the important exception of Scott and Meyer, 1994; see also discussion in Chapter 2 in Hefler, 2012, forthcoming). Summing up, few specific explanations exist for how and why enterprises should support formal adult education.

Case study methods

To explore support for formal adult education at a company level within the LLL2010 project, case studies on the importance of formal adult education in SMEs were provided by teams from 12 countries (Austria, Belgium (Flanders), Bulgaria, England, Estonia, Hungary, Ireland, Lithuania, Norway, Russia, Scotland and Slovenia). Our analysis builds on these case studies as well as national reports based on the same material and prepared by the various national teams. For the case studies, members of the management and participants in formal adult education within selected SMEs were interviewed. Interviews were conducted by the local research teams in local languages. All interviews were transcribed. The selection of enterprises sought to achieve the greatest variety of meaningful cases. Participants engaged in education at different ISCED levels, representing a wide range of backgrounds (for example age and migration background). The enterprises selected for case studies and participants within each case study are by no means representative of all enterprises or participants in formal adult education in one country or overall. This is mainly because the decision to participate in the study rested with the management, and firms with little education and training activity were generally not interested in participating. This means that a self-selection bias is to be expected, and that organisations taking a clear interest in formal adult education, training and human resource development are over-represented. Employees might partly have withheld opinions that conflicted with their management's point of view. Evidence was available for 86 enterprises and

126 participants in formal adult education. More information on methods applied can be found in Hefler (2010).

Approaches to support for participation in formal adult education

Drawing on our case studies, **Table 6.1** provides an overview of the various ways in which institutions support participation in formal adult education (for more details, see Chapter 7.5 in Hefler, 2010). The typology of support patterns highlights how systematic support is established at an organisational level and the range of such support.

Table 6.1: Types of support for participation in formal adult education of employees in small to medium-sized enterprises

Support offered	Examples of support
Ways in which the enterprise may support an individual's decision to participate in formal education	
Strengthening (existing) motivation	- Consenting to the participation - Acknowledging symbolically individual participation - Declaring explicit support for formal adult education
Easing time constraints	- Providing time flexibility (while work assignment remains unchanged) - Rearrangement of work schedules - Adjusting working time and extension of work (reduction of long hours) - Agreeing to educational leave - Devoting paid working time for participation in formal adult education - Using and granting work assignments within the educational programme for enterprises' purposes
Supporting competence development	- Using business cases/projects from the employer within the educational programmes - Allowing consultation with company's experts - Assigning activities in relation to the educational activities
Reducing individual financial burdens	- Using enterprise's infrastructure for educational purposes - Covering some or all of the fees and costs of educational programmes
Inspiring individual participation by providing advancement options	- Offering increased wages for successful completion - Offering promotion for participation/completion of a programme
Ways in which the enterprise may encourage an individual to enrol for a particular qualification	
Initiating individual participation	- Suggesting that an individual enrol for a particular qualification(in the course of individual career agreements) - Agreeing on participation to support an employee in a new position

Table 6.1: Types of support for participation in formal adult education of employees in small and medium enterprises (*cont*)

Support offered	Examples of support
Initiating participation of groups of employees/ types of positions	- Initiating a programme for staff on a project basis - Long-term cooperation with an education institution - Systematic integration of attendance at formal programmes in strategic personnel development (for example by regularly offering participation to specific groups of employees) - Organising formal programmes on a permanent basis

Source: Hefler (2010, Chapter 7.5)

The following five types of organisational patterns of support for participation in formal adult education were identified: (A) Ignorance, (B) Acceptance, (C) Individualised support, (D) Support in principle and (E) Integrated support. These types build on a double hierarchy running from *less* to *more* support and from *no* to *substantial* organisational activity to initiate formal adult education. **Table 6.2** summarises the dimensions used to identify the patterns, which are illustrated with reference to specific case studies.

Type A: Ignorance

As the base line, the enterprise takes no initiatives to promote participation in formal adult education and shows little support for formal adult education, which plays no role in the enterprise's wider training or HRD policy. If any support exists, it is cursory and without any guarantee for prolongation. Participation in formal adult education takes place without acknowledgement from the employer.

Type B: Acceptance (medium-level support, low level of organisational initiative)

Enterprises within this category take no initiative to promote participation in formal adult education. However, in individual cases the enterprise offers some forms of support, mainly with regard to work schedules and permission to use actual work activities for educational purposes.

Table 6.2: Typology of patterns in supporting formal adult education in enterprises

Types	A Ignorance	B Acceptance	C Individualised support	D Support in principle	E Integrated support
Level of support	Low	Medium	Medium	High	High
Level of organisational initiative	Low	Low	Medium	Medium	High
Requirements					
[I] Acknowledge verbally the individual interest and accept interference	-	√	√	√	√
[II] Regularly support activities of any kind	-	√	√	√	√
[III] Substantial support at least in particular constellations	-	-	√	√	√
[IV] Co-initiate at least in particular situations	-	-	√	√	√
[V] Generally adjust organisation needs and participation requirements	-	-	-	√	√
[VI] Generally offer at least financial support or working time	-	-	-	√	√
[VII] At least one project initiative to increase formal adult education for a group of employees	–	–	–		√

Source: Hefler (2010, Chapter 7.6, with adaptations)

Case study 6.1: Metal production enterprise, Norway

This Norwegian metal production enterprise (20–49 employees) has a strategy built on artisanship and experience to provide reliable quality in a low-tech production regime. The enterprise has an apprenticeship scheme and provides internal courses for staff to develop the specific necessary skills. Their training meets the required standards of their quality management system. Moreover, the enterprise follows a peer-learning approach, where experienced employees personally pass their knowledge and skills to less experienced workers. In principle, the company welcomes any learning activity, including participation in formal adult education, but does not initiate participation. There is no general rule concerning formal adult education. The company provides its workers with informational material on free-of-charge formal education offered to union members. When employees participate in formal training, they individually negotiate a schedule and some time off for educational reasons (Ure and Bjørg, 2008).

Type C: Individualised support (medium-level support, medium level of organisational initiative)

Enterprises of this type support individual participants in formal adult education, but do not initiate projects. Support is mainly agreed with individual employees, can be substantial, and includes financial assistance and/or dedication of some working time to the education programme.

Case study 6.2: Copper production enterprise, England

Copper Products Incorporated (50–99 employees, England) offers individualised support for formal education. The company does not distinguish between formal and non-formal adult education, but compares any form of taught activity to forms of informal workplace learning and on-the-job training. However, the enterprise values the National Vocational Qualification (NVQ) and supports employees willing to take courses leading to an NVQ. The management positively regards NVQ courses for both the individual employees and the enterprises. The enterprise fully funds obligatory courses of great interest to the enterprise. Moreover, the enterprise cooperates with a non-profit provider offering courses leading to NVQ. The enterprise regularly covers tuition fees; however, it only exceptionally grants work-release time. Time off the job for educational purposes is regarded as a major challenge to the organisation and is therefore seldom arranged. Support for formal education is embedded in a supportive HRD culture that adheres to the Investors in People principle (Holford et al, 2008).

Type D: Support in principle (high-level support, medium level of organisational initiative)

This type of enterprise offers support for formal adult education in several ways and its general policy includes financial support and/or devotion of some working time to the programme. At least sometimes, the enterprise initiates formal adult education.

Case study 6.3: Chemical production enterprise, Slovenia

This Slovenian chemical production enterprise (100–249 employees) is strongly expanding its workforce based on a globally leading position in a niche market. The HRD strategy focuses on improving the workforce's skills, in particular in the area of technical education. As a result of shortages in the local labour market, promoting participation in formal adult education in technical fields is important within the personnel development strategy. Employees, who hold a position or are preparing for a certain position, where a particular qualification seems to be favourable, are openly invited by the enterprise to take up formal adult education. A formal education contract is fixed for participation in formal education in line with the organisational requirements. On the basis of an individual study contract, the firm supports the student financially by paying the tuition fee and some compensation for transportation costs, guarantees time off to attend lectures, seminars and exercises when those are delivered during working time and the time for preparation for exams. When education is in line with the firm's HR plan, the workers are promoted after course completion to more demanding work or their existing work is broadened. Support for formal adult education is restricted to programmes also meeting the company's needs. (Mirčeva, 2008).

Type E: Integrated support (high level support, high level of organisational initiative)

Such enterprises offer support for formal adult education in several ways, some of them on a regular basis, including financial support and the devotion of working time. Programmes leading to formal adult education are established for one or more groups of employees.

Case study 6.4: Chemical production enterprise, Austria

This Austrian chemical production enterprise (50–99 employees) faces strong competition for skilled workers in chemical industries in the regional labour market. The company invests substantially in training, which is systematically provided to staff at all levels. One major approach is to hire unskilled workers with a different trade (for example carpenters) and to offer them extended training on and off the job, before they start to work as helpers within the shift-work teams. To become a full member of the organisation and to benefit from the substantially higher wages for skilled chemical workers, unskilled workers are openly invited to prepare for a particular type of apprenticeship examination (*Außerordentliche Lehrabschlussprüfung*) available only for adult learners, which provides a formal qualification at ISCED 3b level. To help workers prepare for this examination, a former trainer provides one lesson per week over an 18-month programme at the work site. The company covers all costs of the courses, which take place mainly during paid working time; the firm also arranges the participants' work schedule to accommodate the course work. After passing the examination, participants become 'skilled chemical workers' and enjoy a statutory pay rise. Furthermore, the company supports the preparation for the master examination (*Meisterprüfung*) in chemical work. The examination is classified at ISCED 5b level. The company supports this step on an individual basis, paying the high course fees. Although there is no specific policy, the company generally offers promotion to white-collar positions, including a considerable pay rise, after the completion of the programme. Further career options within chemical industries involve either attending a higher secondary education evening school (ISCED 4b level) or a university for applied science (ISCED 5b level). Both of these courses take three to four years of study and would be supported by the company. For white-collar employees, programmes in continuing higher education (including MBAs) are supported, based on individual negotiations (two cases are reported) (Hefler and Bacher, 2008).

The cases selected illustrate a wide range of possible forms of support for participation in formal adult education. By defining criteria, it became possible to arrange these forms into patterns of support and to classify these patterns. From our case studies of SMEs, it is clear that a large number have a policy towards formal adult education that clearly goes beyond occasional contingent support of single participants.

Training cultures in enterprises

The support of formal adult education is likely to represent only one line of activity within company HRD. To investigate the relative independent or dependent status of support for formal adult education within enterprises' training policies, we need to classify independently an organisation's approaches to corporate training and HRD.

Enterprises develop comparatively stable training patterns or training cultures, which could be characterised either as (more) reactive, showing little momentum, or (more) expansive, demonstrating a tendency to evolve up to a certain level of training activity. **Table 6.3** presents an overview of these two contrasting cultures. The cultures differ in their overall attitudes towards training, understanding it as a cost factor or an investment, in the level and range of training activities, in the development of the overall use of training, the dependence of environmental factors ('drivers', 'barriers') and the diffusion of training activities in a given workforce. This basic dichotomy – developed in Hefler and Markowitsch, 2008 has been further elaborated elsewhere (Hefler, 2010; see also Chapter 5 in Hefler, 2012, forthcoming). Below, we provide case studies of reactive and expansive training cultures.

Reactive training cultures

Case study 6.5 provides an illustration of a firm with a reactive training culture. Such enterprises use only a minor proportion of their potential for training, and their overall training activity is low over the years. Most training occurs when it is externally enforced, which leads to a dependency on external drivers determining the quantity of training activity. The absolute volume of training activity, however, can be substantial because of legal obligations, requirements of quality-management systems, training required in the course of technological improvements, project-based training activities in the course of process redesign

Table 6.3: Reactive versus expansive training cultures – defining characteristics

Reactive training cultures	Expansive training cultures
Training mainly seen as a cost factor and therefore minimised	Training is understood as an investment with significant value added
The average training activity (over a multi-year period) is comparatively low	The training activity is high and tends to make full use of the potential to support workplace learning
Experiences with and competences about the use of training are restricted to smaller groups of employees	Experiences with and competences about the use of training are widely diffused within the organisation, providing a framework for further improvements
Training mainly reacts to a need; the training volume depends on the increase/decrease of this need	Within an existing potential (Training Potential), the use of training and other opportunities to support learning at the workplace are optimised; changes in external requirements influence only the composition of the range of training activities, not the level of activity
Changes in external factors may lead directly to more/less training	Changes in external factors have little effect on the level of training activities

Source: Adapted from Hefler and Markowitsch (2008, p 40)

and innovation. These and similar training activities lead to a total training volume that already requires some professional management and budgetary foresight. While the *relative* training activity remains low by any standards, training becomes at least a subject on the management's agenda. Overall, company policy reveals a low level of commitment. Sometimes, a more progressive approach towards training is balanced by a list of reservations. Training is still clearly understood as a cost, which most managers seek to limit. The range of experience with training is low. However, significant parts of the workforce are included in some organised learning activity, for example, in health and safety. The general tendency in the use of training is still oriented towards the required minimum.

Case study 6.5: Packaging enterprise, Ireland

This packaging company (20–49 employees) is engaged in a niche market of the printing sector and limits training to that required by regulations and short-term needs in particular workplaces. The HR manager described company policy thus: 'like [in] many small companies, it's as it is or as needs insist'. Nearly all activity around training and workplace learning is informal and not regulated. Training needs analyses are performed in order to meet quality management criteria. Courses are available on computer applications and for newly acquired printing facilities. Training is clearly understood as a cost factor. Even when fees are covered by public funds, the loss of working time is seen as a serious handicap. The management is quite sceptical about the short-range returns of investments in training. Overall training activity is significant, but the use of the assumed training potential is clearly low. Learning on the job is clearly the most favoured way of acquiring new skills. Opportunities for workplace learning are somewhat restricted, given the stable production in a mature niche market. Because of the importance of optimising a given way of production, the workplace-learning regime seems more restrictive. Levels of organisational learning could be regarded as low to medium, but are mainly focused on competing on costs in a mature and shrinking market (EDC/CSHD SP4 Project Team, 2008).

Expansive training cultures

Case study 6.6 provides an example of a firm with a well-developed expansive training culture. Enterprises of this type show an above-average level of training activity. Their engagement in training is much greater than the average of all enterprises in the same industry. Training policy is oriented towards innovating and optimising the training activity, while a further expansion of the training activity is possible only in a rather limited way. Management focuses on deciding between alternatives in training and replacing particular activities with more efficient and appropriate ones. Therefore, while the training activities remain at a very high level over the years, the training portfolios are constantly reformed. Investment in technologies (for example e-learning, blended learning) often reflects a way to gain space for other training activities by improving efficiency. Inevitably formal adult education makes up a very small part of all training activities. Most of the workforce shares experiences through various kinds of training and thus has a common understanding of related issues. Supervisors as well as workers are able to provide advice on using particular types of training and education and they share experiences of what does and does not work. The range of opportunities to use training is very broad and training policy focuses on innovative projects, while constantly improving well-established methods.

Case study 6.6: Chemical research and distribution enterprise, Russia

A+ Pharma Research and Distribution (100–249 employees) is engaged in research and production as well as gross sales for a wide range of products needed by medical laboratories. Three university researchers founded the company in the early days of Russia's new capitalism (1992). The enterprise has experienced rapid growth in recent years, developing from a local supplier to a principal actor in the Russian market. Currently, 85% of the employees are highly qualified and 60 out of 200 employees engage in research and development activities. Nearly 120 employees have obtained higher education degrees (almost one fifth of them have two diplomas of higher education). Relevant fields include medicine, biochemistry and chemical engineering. However, qualifications in management (including project management) and marketing have become increasingly important for trained physicists and chemists. Therefore, while working for the enterprise, many employees, including the founders, attended formal adult education in these fields. The company works in a quickly expanding yet unstable market, subject to external shocks such as quickly changing regulations and tax requirements. Securing 'western' quality at a locally competitive price level is the key to success, requiring continuous innovation, not so much in the field of basic research but in directing and combining processes, finding new ways of balancing advantages and disadvantages of the local market situations. The firm has a HRD manager. All employees have a yearly appraisal interview that includes discussing individual training plans. Workplace learning is supported by regular meetings, collaboration in multidisciplinary project teams, job rotation and regular attendance at seminars and conferences. Nearly all the employees are engaged in in-house training activities. Aside from more regular activities in different fields (for example learning about new products), training includes project-based, targeted programmes (in the year of the interview, a programme for all members of the sales staff). In 2007, about 10% attended external educational programmes, in particular, university-based formal programmes. Even without a formal agreement, the company regularly covers 50-100% of tuition fees and grants days off to attend courses and prepare for examinations. Training costs are about 8-10% of the wage costs and each employee has on average between 5 and 6 days of training a year. Long-term partnerships have been established with various higher education institutions that also provide non-formal educational provision (Khokhlova, 2008).

Assessing the interdependence of support patterns for formal adult education and training cultures

So far, we have seen that formal adult education represents a significant though under-recognised part of training and HRD activity in all the countries studied. As a life event, participation occurs as frequently as parental leave, so companies must consider carefully how to react and whether to support individuals participating in formal adult education. During their working life, a fifth or more of all employees may participate, and even more among particular groups. Between one third and two thirds of all participants undertake courses that are closely linked to the work of the enterprise, are fully or partly funded by the employer and take place at least partly within paid working time. Enterprises not only support formal adult education on an individual basis, but also develop overall patterns or policies towards training, which we have classified into five types. Next, we have argued for the necessity to grasp enterprises' more general cultures in supporting training and development, and have referred to a dichotomy of reactive versus expansive training cultures. Thus, while enterprises undoubtedly support formal adult education, it is unclear to what extent this support results from developed training cultures or from other factors. For an initial approximate answer to this question, we compare the support patterns for formal adult education with the types of training cultures of our available case studies (see **Table 6.4**).

With regard to our six examples, we find limited support for formal adult education within reactive training cultures in **Case studies 6.1** and **6.5**, some support for formal adult education within a reactive training culture in **Case study 6.2** and strong support for formal adult education paired with expansive training cultures in **Case study 6.6**. Unsurprisingly, companies with expansive training cultures are also more likely to adopt more extended support patterns for formal adult education. More than half of all enterprises in our sample are classified as having an *expansive training culture* and also a policy of systematic support for formal adult education. Slightly less than half of enterprises with *reactive training cultures* provide little support for formal adult education of their employees. However, we are more interested in the more unexpected combinations of training culture and support for formal adult education as in **Case study 6.3**, where an organisation is combining a reactive training culture with strong support for formal adult education.

Table 6.4: Cross-tabulation of training cultures and support patterns in case study enterprises

	'Ignorance'/ 'Acceptance'	'Individual support'	'Support in principle'/ 'Integrated support'
Reactive training cultures	44%	30%	26%
Expansive training cultures	13%	33%	54%

Source: LLL2010/SP4 Data, n=74

Among SMEs with reactive training cultures, we find many that openly support formal adult education. We have learnt that in most countries, individual employees of small enterprises are as likely to engage in formal education as employees in larger ones. Thus the issue cannot be ignored by the organisations. Extended, multi-year, formal adult education programmes have the potential to support systematically the development of individual capacities and thus help to overcome the shortcoming of a firm's rudimentary HRD. Individuals' readiness to contribute substantially to the costs of education may help overcome the restrictions of a reactive training culture. Moreover, particular conditions in the organisation's environment can introduce support for formal adult education as an explicit strategy. For example, in **Case study 6.3**, the combination of a lack of formally qualified employees in local labour markets combined with strong regulative enforcement of the use of properly qualified personnel leads to strong support for formal adult education in very specific areas. To sum up, there is evidence that formal adult education could substantially add to the personnel development policies of SMEs. Small enterprises may start with supporting the formal adult education of their employees as a first step to developing more supportive cultures for HRD. When considering existing theory that sees formal adult education mainly as a topic of large corporations (for example 'corporate universities'), this comes as a surprise. More research is needed to explore, confirm or challenge this result. In particular, we have to learn more about the types of formal adult education programmes and their institutional embeddedness within careers. We will return to this point later.

Contrary to our expectations, we also find a high proportion of SMEs that expansively support non-formal training, but provide disappointingly little support for formal adult education and do not go beyond individualised support. A high proportion of working students and legal frameworks reduce the incentive for the employer to pay. For example, tax regulations in Estonia or Bulgaria stipulate that the employee must pay income taxes on the tuition fees paid by the employer. We have some indication that enterprises are less inclined to support formal adult education, where education that leads to individually earned credentials of considerably lower vocational specificity is more clearly distinguished from vocationally oriented and more organisationally specific non-formal training.

However, the relative dependence or independence of policies for formal adult education within enterprises' general training cultures seem to vary with countries' dominant qualification and skill formation systems (see Hefler, 2010; Streeck, 2011; Chapter 7 in Hefler and Markowitsch, 2012, forthcoming). In countries, where vocational qualifications are narrowly defined and where credit-based provision of vocational qualifications is well developed, as in England, Scotland and Ireland, the differences between formal and non-formal adult education (with the exception of higher education) are weak and so are the differences between organisations' policies for formal and non-formal adult education. In countries where vocational qualifications are frequently bound to comparatively broad and legally defined occupational profiles, typically available only by extended and centrally controlled vocational educational programmes, as in Austria, Slovenia and Norway, the differences between formal and non-formal education tend to be clearer and more significant for enterprises. Consequently, more independence between policies for formal and non-formal adult education is in place. More research is clearly needed on the impact of skill formation systems on the interdependence of SMEs' support for formal and non-formal training, as we discuss in our outlook.

Outlook: towards a comparative framework

We have learned that available statistics on formal adult education provide unsafe ground for starting comparative work. Yet differences in the societal meaning of formal adult education cannot be overcome simply by refining statistical concepts. Borrowing from the 'societal effects' school (Maurice and Sorge, 2000) in comparative research, we conclude that only by accepting the paradox of 'comparing the non-comparable' (Maurice, 2000) can we expect to make progress in both our understanding of formal adult education within one country and differences in its significance for companies between countries. This implies standing back from the accepted view of formal adult education in a particular country.

The broadness or narrowness of a country's concept of formal adult education closely connects to the presence or absence of modularised and credit-based qualifications. However, the existence of credit-based qualifications points towards fundamental differences in how education and work interact, what roles they play within the skill-formation systems and, more broadly, the employment systems. This relationship then affects the production and reproduction of social stratification. Expanded credit-based access to qualifications of various types may (or may not) imply a comparatively low institutional value of the credentials achieved as, for example, with some formal vocational qualifications in England and Scotland compared with Austria or Slovenia. Possible trade-offs between a programme's accessibility and its typical entitlements for more open or restricted further career opportunities have to be carefully taken into consideration.

However, for any further analysis, the loosely defined category of formal adult education has to be deconstructed, first into its various institutional components, providing access to the logics behind such distinguished socially hybrid fields such as, for example, second-chance education, retraining or continuing professional education (see Chapter 3 in Hefler, 2012, forthcoming). We expect enterprises to be engaged and this can be demonstrated as being clearly different for the various institutionalised types of formal adult education. Moreover, differences between the countries could be more appropriately grasped as differences between social fields and institutions responsible for particular types of formal adult education (Markowitsch and Hefler, 2012, forthcoming). Higher education and continuing professional education in Scotland, England or Ireland are worlds apart from the corresponding areas in Austria, Slovenia, Bulgaria or Estonia.

Second, to understand the significance and institutionalised qualities of types of formal adult education, we have to observe them within the context of career patterns. While occasionally any idiosyncratic career in lifelong learning may be possible, we should clearly focus on the availability of institutionalised patterns that firmly pre-establish the aims and content of particular programmes, the conditions for individual participation and the support and recognition by the enterprises.

Typically, the most visible of such building blocks constitute the peculiar features of a country's education system. Examples include the preparation for crafts mastership examination in countries with a strong tradition in dual apprenticeship (for example Austria and Germany), the Master of Business Administration (MBA) or other programmes within continuing professional education (for example in the UK or the US). Although we might find programmes such as the MBA nearly everywhere (Mazza et al, 2004), their particular institutionalisation and significance for careers may entirely differ. For example, the very same programme (such as an MBA taken in the UK) may allow for highly different careers for participants aiming at working in various European countries and their particular employment systems. However, the most visible examples for institutionalised programmes in formal adult education may represent only a proportion of all established patterns, which often exist on a more local level, such as within a particular industry.

Types and frequencies of formal adult education as institutionalised building blocks differ between countries and should have a high priority in comparative research. Countries certainly vary with regard to the use of formal adult education in different sectors, such as engineering versus retail, finance versus health, for-profit consultancy services versus public administration. These sectors build on and explore different logics of controlling work and access to more privileged positions within the organisation and thereby in the social space. When considering this context, comparative research would improve our understanding of differences in organisational behaviour towards formal adult education and we could learn about possibilities and restrictions for diffusion of educational and personnel development practices across boundaries of sectors or countries.

Finally, the influence of employer organisations on formal adult education cannot be overestimated, given their dual role in *defining* the demand for and value of qualifications and *providing* support for the acquisition of skills, competencies *and* qualifications. Sociotechnological innovation, global competition and societal transformation towards a knowledge economy within a learning society imply more demand for skills and qualifications. Yet organisational decisions and institutional environments both matter, because, as has been recognised since the days of the *labour process debate* (Marrs, 2009), there is no automatic link between increased technological refinement and more demand for skills. Organisations are political agents of social stratification (Baron, 1984; Stainback et al, 2010), not mere transmitters of technical or economic requirements. Employers provide training and formal education, as outlined by Scott and Meyer (1994), not only for technical reasons or issues of control, but for emerging institutional requirements, reflecting *organisational citizenship rights, professional standards* and *organisational legitimacy* in a world full of contested values. The study of formal adult education within organisations helps to make sense of the *institutional(ised)* sides of corporate training, breaking up its rationalistic myths that merely trumpet its necessity and efficiency.

Note

[1] The steep increase in participation mainly reflects differences in concepts and methodologies for identifying formal adult education.

References

Acemoglu, D. and Pischke, J.-S. (1999) 'Beyond Becker: training in imperfect labour markets', *The Economic Journal,* vol 109, F112-42.

Baron, J.N. (1984) 'Organizational perspectives on stratification', *Annual Review of Sociology*, vol 10, pp 37-69.

Becker, G. St. (1975) *Human capital: A theoretical and empirical analysis, with special reference to education*, New York, National Bureau of Economic Research.

Bishop, J.H. (1988) 'Do employers share the costs and benefits of general training?' *CAHRS Working Paper Series – Paper 429,* Ithaca, NY: Cornell University Center for Advanced Human Resource Studies (CAHRS).

Bishop, J.H. and Kang, S. (1996) 'Do some employers share the costs and benefits of general training?', *CAHRS Working Paper Series – Paper 188,* Ithaca, NY: Cornell University Center for Advanced Human Resource Studies (CAHRS).

Cedefop (2010) *Employer-provided vocational training in Europe – evaluation and interpretation of the third continuing vocational training survey,* Luxembourg: Publications Office of the European Union.

Eurostat (2006) *Classification of learning activities – Manual,* Luxembourg: Office for Official Publications of the European Communities.

EDC/CSHD SP4 Project Team (2008) *LLL2010 – subproject 4, case study 48 – Ireland: SP4, case study 4: print and packaging,* Dublin: St Patrick's College (EDC/CSHD).

Estevez-Abe, M., Iversen, T. and Soskice, D.W. (2001) 'Social protection and the formation of skills: a reinterpretation of the welfare state', in D.W. Soskice and P.A. Hal, (eds) *Varieties of capitalism: The institutional foundations of comparative advantage,* Oxford: Oxford University Press, pp 145-83.

Fligstein, N. and Byrkjeflot, H. (1996) 'The logic of employment systems', in J. Pock, J.N. Baron, D.B. Grusky and D.J. Treiman (eds) *Social differentiation and social inequality: Essays in honor of John Pock,* Boulder, CO: Westview Press, pp 11-35.

Graf, A. (2002) *Lebenszyklusorientierte Personalentwicklung – Ein Ansatz für die Erhaltung und Förderung von Leistungsfähigkeit und -bereitschaft wähend des gesamten betrieblichen Lebenszyklus,* Bern, Stuttgart, Vienna: Verlag Paul Haupt.

Hefler, G. (2010) *The qualification-supporting company – the significance of formal adult education in small and medium organisations – comparative report, subproject 4 LLL2010* (status: version 2.0, 15 February 2010 – further small adaptations till 30 July 2010), Krems: Danube University Krems.

Hefler G. (2012, forthcoming) *Taking steps – formal adult education in private and organisational life: a comparative view,* Vienna: LIT-Verlag.

Hefler, G. and Bacher, D. (2008) *LLL2010 subproject 4, case study 18 – Austria: XY Chemicals Austria: formal adult education as a strategic resource for growth, sector family 1: 50–249 employees,* Krems: Danube University Krems.

Hefler, G. and Markowitsch, J. (2008) 'To train or not to train – explaining differences in average enterprise training performance in Europe – a framework approach', in J. Markowitsch and G. Hefler (eds) *Enterprise training in Europe – comparative studies on cultures, markets and public support initiatives,* Vienna: LIT-Verlag, pp 23-60.

Hefler, G. and Markowitsch, J. (2012, forthcoming) 'Bridging institutional divides: linking education, careers and work in 'organizational space' and 'skill space' dominated employment systems', in R. Brooks, A. Fuller and J. Waters (eds) *New spaces of education: the changing nature of learning in the 21st century,* London: Routledge, pp 160-81.

Hefler, G., Róbert, P., Ringler, P., Sági, M., Rammel, S., Balogh, A. and Markowitsch, J. (2011) *Formal adult education in context – the view of European Statistics – SP 2 – Synthesis Report – LLL2010 project.* Krems: Danube University Krems, TARKI.

Holford, J., Engel, L.C. and Wilson, H.L. (2008) *LLL2010 – subproject 4, case study 36 – England: Copper Products Incorporated, sector family A: 50–99 employees,* Nottingham: University of Nottingham

Khokhlova, A. (2008) *LLL2010 – subproject 4, case study 82 – Russia: research-and-production firm 'A+': formal education as an adaptation strategy and development resource, sector family A: 50–249 employees,* St Petersburg: St Petersburg State University (SPSU).

Loewenstein, M.A. and Spletzer, J.R. (1997) 'Delayed formal on-the-job training', *Industrial and Labor Relations Review,* vol 51, pp 82-99.

Markowitsch, J. and Hefler, G. (eds) (2008) *Enterprise training in Europe – comparative studies on cultures, markets and public support initiatives,* Vienna: LIT-Verlag.

Maurice, M. (2000) 'The paradoxes of societal analysis – a review of the past and prospects of the future', in M. Maurice and A. Sorge (eds) *Embedding organizations – societal analysis of actors, organizations and socio-economic context,* Amsterdam: John Benjamins, pp 13-36.

Maurice, M. and Sorge, A. (eds) (2000) *Embedding organizations – societal analysis of actors, organizations and socio-economic context,* Amsterdam: John Benjamins.

Marrs, K. (2009) 'Herrschaft und Kontrolle in der Arbeit', in F. Böhle, G.G. Voß and G. Wachtler (eds) *Handbuch Arbeitssoziologie,* Münster: VS Verlag für Sozialwissenschaften, pp 331-56.

Mazza, C., Sahlin-Andersson, K. and Pedersen, J.S. (2005) 'European constructions of an American model – developments of four MBA programmes', *Management Learning,* vol 36, pp 471-91

Mirčeva, J. (2008) *LLL2010 – subproject 4, case study 2 – Slovenia: SP 4, case study B: improving the effectiveness of the company's performance through stimulating the employees participation in formal education, NACE: C 25.930; DJ 28.730, sector family 1: 50–250 employees,* Ljubljana: Slovenian Institute for Adult Education (SIAE).

Schein, E.H. (1978) *'Career dynamics: matching individual and organizational needs',* Reading, MA: Addison-Wesley Publishing Company.

Scott, R.W. and Meyer, W.J. (1994) 'The rise of training programs in firms and agencies: an institutional perspective', in R.W. Scott, and W.J. Meyer (eds) *Institutional environments and organizations – structural complexity and individualism,* Thousand Oaks, CA: Sage, pp 228-54.

Stainback, K., Tomaskovic-Devey, D. and Skaggs, S. (2010) 'Organizational approaches to inequality: inertia, relative power, and environments', *Annual Review of Sociology,* vol 36, pp 225-47.

Streeck, W. (2011) 'Skills and politics – general and specific', *MPIfG Discussion Paper 11/g1.* Cologne: Max Planck Institute for the Study of Societies.

Ure, O.B. and Bjørg, E.A. (2008) *LLL2010 – subproject 4, case study 52 – Norway: in-company training is important to secure the quality of the employees: a case study of XY Metals Norway,* Oslo: Fafo, Institute for Labour and Social Research.

Wolbers, M.H.J. (2003) 'Learning and working: double statuses in youth transitions', in W. Müller and M. Gangl (eds) *Transitions from education to work in Europe: the integration of youth into EU labour markets,* Oxford: Oxford University Press, pp 131-55.

SEVEN

Reducing or reinforcing inequality: assessing the impact of European policy on widening access to higher education

Elisabet Weedon and Sheila Riddell, Centre for Research in Education Inclusion and Diversity, University of Edinburgh

Introduction

During the post-war period across Europe, higher education was only available to a small proportion of the population, with an over-representation of men and those from socially advantaged backgrounds. As Europe has sought to transform itself over the last decade into 'the most competitive and dynamic knowledge based economy in the world capable of sustainable economic growth with more and better jobs and greater social cohesion' (CEC, 2000), the importance of higher education has been increasingly recognised. Workers in knowledge economy occupations clearly require higher levels of education, so, from the 1990s onwards, human capital logic suggested that there were strong grounds for equipping a higher proportion of the population with tertiary level qualifications. However, the expansion of higher education was not driven solely by economic concerns, but was also seen as a means of promoting social cohesion by opening the doors of professional and managerial jobs to a wider section of the population. In addition, enabling more people to benefit from a liberal education was seen as a good in itself, producing a more enlightened and cultured society. One of the earliest education targets established by the EU in 2010 was that all countries should aim to achieve a 40% participation rate in higher education by 2020, an extremely challenging target for some.

Of course, widening access policies were not the only, or indeed the major, focus of higher education policy in Europe from the 1990s. As noted by Marginson (2008), throughout this period, universities in the developed world were jostling for position within a global educational market. The establishment of international league tables encouraged universities to compete for research funds and, particularly in English-speaking countries, for the recruitment of international students as a source of revenue. Within some countries, particularly the UK, national league tables intensified competition between institutions for the best staff and students. Increasingly, higher education has been defined as a 'positional good' (Hirsch, 1976) in which some student places are seen to offer better social status and lifetime opportunities than others. Hirsch noted that 'positional competition … is a zero-sum game. What winners win, losers lose' (Hirsch, 1976, p 52). Within any one nation, there is a limit on the number of positional goods at a given level of value. In order for socially advantaged groups to maintain their advantage, they are likely to compete for places in a narrow range of institutions, squeezing out students from poorer backgrounds, who may have lower grades and a greater chance of dropping out. Overall, the marketisation of higher education tends to intensify existing institutional hierarchies, with the less prestigious universities defining their mission in terms of widening access, while the more elite universities focus on research and postgraduate teaching. Therefore, there have been contradictory trends in higher education over the past two decades. The democratisation of higher education has been accompanied by increasing competition by socially advantaged groups for places in the most elite institutions (Osborne, 2003).

While the marketisation of higher education has been particularly marked in the UK, with an intensification of existing divisions between universities (see **Case study 7.1**), this trend is also evident in other European countries, where older universities recruit a disproportionately large number of students from more socially advantaged backgrounds. In Austria, as illustrated in **Table 7.1**, the scientific universities and the universities of fine arts are the most prestigious and they recruit a much higher proportion of students from high socioeconomic backgrounds compared with the universities of applied sciences and teacher training academies.

Table 7.1: Students in Austrian state tertiary educational institutions by socioeconomic status

Type of institution	Low socioeconomic status	Middle socioeconomic status	Upper socioeconomic status	High socioeconomic status
Scientific universities	18.1%	30.2%	33.1%	18.6%
Fine arts universities	15.1%	25.1%	39.8%	19.8%
Applied sciences universities	23.4%	34.8%	31.9%	9.9%
Teacher training academies	20.9%	34.4%	35.6%	9.1%

Source: Unger et al (2010). Data are drawn from a survey of parents of Austrian students conducted in 2009. Social stratum was identified by using vocational position and educational attainment of parents.

As illustrated in **Table 7.2**, in Flanders the majority of students from lower socioeconomic backgrounds do not participate in tertiary education and only 2% attend university, which is the most prestigious form of tertiary education. In contrast, more than 20% of students from a high socioeconomic background attend university.

Table 7.2: Participation in different types of tertiary-level education in Flanders by socioeconomic status, percentages, cohort born 1976[1]

Type of institution	Low socioeconomic status	Middle socioeconomic status	High socioeconomic status	Total
University	2.1	6.8	23.3	9.8
4-year college	1.7	3.8	8.8	4.5
2-year college	13.7	28.2	27.7	24.4
No tertiary education	82.4	61.3	40.1	61.3
Total	100	100	100	100

[1] Figures based on a representative sample of 2,984

Figures based on the SONAR database, with thanks to Heidi Knipprath, HIVA/Policy Research Centre for Study and School Careers, Flanders

SONAR = Studie van de overgang van ONderwijs naar ARbeidsmarkt (Studies of the transition from school to the labour market)

Case study 7.3 provides an example of marketisation in an Eastern European country – Estonia. In that country there has been a considerable growth in the number of private universities and a cap on government-funded university places. However, students who can afford to pay can enter public universities if they meet the minimum entrance requirement and fees are charged for some of the courses, which attract high student numbers.

This chapter begins with a brief review of European policy on higher education, particularly with regard to widening access strategy. Understanding of which groups of students are to count as under-represented varies greatly in different European countries, and we discuss the significance of these distinctions for monitoring and positive action activities. Subsequently, on the basis of a review of statistics, we consider which groups have benefited from higher education expansion in different countries, particularly with regard to gender and social class. Finally, we present case studies of the implementation of widening access policies in five contrasting European countries. In conclusion, we return to the central question addressed in this chapter, which is the following: To what extent have widening access policies resulted in the reduction of social inequalities, and which groups appear to have been the major beneficiaries? We conclude that although all European countries have recognised that diversifying the social profile of higher education students is essential in order to achieve the goals of social justice and economic growth, there has been much greater emphasis on widening access in some countries than in others. The UK, in particular, over a decade and a half developed strong positive action programmes for a range of under-represented groups and used benchmarks to track progress towards established benchmarks. Despite the progress that has undoubtedly been achieved, it is clear that education can only partially compensate for wider economic inequality, and the current financial crisis threatens to derail progressive policies.

The development of European policy on higher education and widening access

Education did not feature in the original Treaty of Rome (1957) that established the European Economic Community (EEC). However, as noted by Hingel (2001), the treaty encouraged cooperation between member states in the field of education. The emphasis was originally on vocational education and the recognition of formal qualifications in order to promote free movement of labour (European Commission, 2006; Keeling, 2006). However, according to Keeling, the definition of vocational education gradually changed to include higher education study, and the influence of the EU increased in the period between 1971 and 1992 through its community action programmes (Hingel, 2001). In higher education, the Erasmus programme, launched in 1987, promoted cooperation through the development of credit transfer and networking across European higher education institutions. The Treaty of Maastricht (1992) further increased the influence of the EU through programmes in the Socrates framework, while at the same time maintaining the concept of subsidiarity in education by noting that higher education was the responsibility of member states (Keeling, 2006, p 204). Although the Bologna Declaration of 1998 and the development of the Bologna Process was based on intergovernmental cooperation and led by ministers of education from nation states, it received strong support from the EU. The declaration was signed by representatives of 29 countries in 1999. By 2010, 46 countries from Europe and the developed world had joined the process. These signatories agreed to the development of a common framework of qualifications based on credit and cycles of study, facilitation of student mobility, the development of a common degree level system at all levels and the development of a 'Europe of Knowledge'. In 2001 it was agreed to increase the emphasis on the lifelong learning and social dimensions of higher education. The lifelong learning dimension focused on alignment of the Bologna Process to national lifelong learning policies, including the recognition of prior learning and the development of generic skills for employability. The social dimension focused on equal access and, while this dimension was included in the Prague Communiqué of 2001, it was recognised in 2007 that insufficient progress had been made in this area. The London Communiqué reaffirmed 'the importance of students being able to complete their studies without obstacles related to their social and economic background' (London Communiqué, 2007: 2.18). This led to a commitment in 2007 to produce national action plans with effective monitoring. In 2009, it was agreed that each country should set measurable targets for widening overall participation and increasing the participation of under-represented social groups in higher education by the end of the next decade (Leuven/Louvain-la Neuve Communiqué, 2009). In 2010, there was further clarification that the aspiration across the EU was that 'the student body entering, participating in and completing higher education at all levels should reflect the diversity of our populations' (EACEA, 2010, pp 27-8). In the 2010 report the following is noted:

- The social dimension of higher education presents the most significant challenge to European cooperation as it is understood so differently from one country to another.
- Very few countries have linked their policy on the social dimension to the Bologna commitment of raising the participation of under-represented groups to the point where the higher education population mirrors the overall societal distribution.
- Very few countries have set specific targets to improve the participation of under-represented groups in higher education, and only about half of the Bologna countries systematically monitor their participation.
- The most common national measures to widen participation are the provision of targeted financial support and the development of alternative access routes and/or admission procedures (EACEA, 2010, p 27).

Recent assessments of the Bologna Process suggest that implementation of its various elements continues to be patchy. While considerable progress has been made in relation to harmonised degree systems, quality assurance, student mobility and the qualifications framework, less progress has been made in harmonising access to higher education for under-represented groups (EACEA, 2010). Particularly in the wake of the economic crisis, it is feared that some countries may reduce investment in widening access initiatives. Lažetić (2010) maintains that the implementation of the Bologna Process relies on 'mutual adjustment'. While policy agendas have been agreed, there has been 'little coherence in terms of implementation at the national and institutional level' (Lažetić, 2010, p 550).

As discussed by Holford and Mohorčič Špolar in Chapter Three, there are different readings of EU policy on higher education. Robertson (2009) interprets efforts by the EU to standardise higher education qualifications across Europe and to encourage free movement of staff and students as part of its wider marketisation agenda. From the 1990s, she argues, higher education was characterised within EU policy discourse as an engine for economic growth, a private rather than a public good and as a new service sector within the economy. Within the globalised competition for international students, Europe wished to compete with the US and Australia, and mechanisms such as the European Qualifications Framework were an essential element of this enterprise. By way of contrast, Holford and Mohorčič Špolar remind us that the emphasis on the social dimension of higher education within EU policy discourse provided space for the development of a range of projects and initiatives promoting widening access and greater social equality. In this chapter, quantitative and qualitative data are used to explore the extent to which higher education in Europe has intensified or reduced social inequalities.

Data drawn upon in this chapter

The statistics presented in the following section are drawn from the report on the social and mobility indicators of the *Bologna Process in Higher Education* report (European Communities and HIS, Hochschul-Informations-System GmbH, 2009) as well as data from the Labour Force Survey. The social indicators used represent a collaboration between Eurostat and Eurostudent III. Eurostat made use of three databases: UNESCO-OECD-Eurostat data collection (UOE), the European Union Labour Force Survey (EU-LFS) and the European Union Statistics on Income and Living Conditions (EU-SILC). Eurostudent data are drawn from the survey carried out in 19 of the member countries as well as three non member countries.

The case studies were conducted by members of national teams in order to illustrate efforts made by particular countries and institutions to widen access for under-represented groups. The case studies are drawn from very different countries – Estonia, Slovenia, Scotland, Belgium (Flanders) and Austria – that reflect different typologies of lifelong learning and welfare regimes. Estonia and Slovenia occupy different positions within the Central and Eastern European group, Flanders and Austria are located together within the continental group and Scotland provides an example of the Anglo-Celtic approach to welfare and lifelong learning. The institutions also range from an ancient and elite university to newer institutions with a much greater focus on attracting non-traditional students. In the following sections, we first note the expansion of higher education that has happened in all European countries over the past two decades, before considering which groups have been the major beneficiaries. We also consider the nature and extent of labour market advantage that accrues from participation in higher education, and whether this advantage is enjoyed equally by different groups.

Cross-country interpretations of under-representation in higher education

As discussed previously, one of the goals of European higher education policy was to encourage a more concerted approach to the inclusion of socially and culturally disadvantaged groups. However, as is evident from **Table 7.3**, there are marked differences between European countries with regard to which groups are regarded as under-represented in higher education. Being recognised as an under-represented group is clearly important, since once a group achieves this status, their participation rate is likely to be monitored and additional support may be provided. The Czech Republic and Norway apparently do not conduct any monitoring of student background, and the reasons behind this would be interesting to explore. Among countries where monitoring is undertaken, the participation rates of students from low socioeconomic backgrounds are monitored in most countries apart from Russia, Slovenia and Estonia. Gender and disability are also frequently monitored, although disability is interpreted differently throughout Europe (Riddell, 2012). Practice with regard to the monitoring of ethnicity and immigrant status varies greatly across countries, but

Table 7.3: Main categories monitored on social dimension in LLL2010 countries as recorded in EACEA (2010)

Country	Category/categories monitored
Austria	Educational background of parents; occupational type of parents; type of HE accession prerequisite; immigrants/migrant status; dependent children; special needs/handicapped
Belgium (Flanders)	Socioeconomic status; migrant background; disability; gender
Bulgaria	Disabled students and students with low socioeconomic background (study free); orphans; people with disabilities; mothers of many children (three or more)
Czech Republic	No monitoring
Estonia	Young people without sufficient knowledge of Estonian; people with physical disabilities; regional background; gender
Hungary	Disabled students; disadvantaged students; students belonging to the Roma ethnic minority; students rearing a small child/family supporters/students with a large family
Ireland	Students from socioeconomically disadvantaged backgrounds, including members of the Travelling Community and refugees; students with a disability; mature students
Lithuania	Students with low socioeconomic background; students with disabilities
Norway	No monitoring
Russia	Disabled people; people from the Chernobyl region; orphans; people without citizenship; migrants from the Commonwealth of independent states; foreign students
Slovenia	Gender; students from underdeveloped regions; Roma students; students with special needs
UK: England, Wales and Northern Ireland	Socioeconomic class; young people in receipt of free school meals (FSM) as a proxy measure of low income; geography (low participation neighbourhoods); gender; ethnicity; disability; type of school attended
UK: Scotland	Socioeconomically disadvantaged; gender; ethnicity; disability; prior participation in higher education by a family member; age

Source: EACEA (2010)

is far from universal. Of course, simply monitoring participation rates does not necessarily lead to affirmative action. For example, in a number of countries data are gathered on the extent to which Gypsy Travellers and the Romany population have access to tertiary education, but participation rates remain very low, and in the UK the education outcomes of Gypsy Travellers is declining over time (Hills et al, 2010). The lack of shared understanding of particular social categories, along with uncertainty about how to improve participation rates of marginalised groups, has undoubtedly hindered progress across Europe in relation to equalising participation in higher education. In the next section we discuss in greater detail patterns of social inequality relating to some of these categories with regard to higher education participation.

The expansion of higher education across Europe

A common trend across Europe since the early 1990s has been the massive expansion in the proportion of the population participating in higher education (see **Figure 7.1**). Based on the assumption that participation in higher education has both social and economic benefits, the EU set a target of 40% participation in tertiary education by 2020. **Figure 7.1** shows that for some countries this target has already been overtaken; for example, Belgium, Estonia, Ireland, Lithuania, Norway and the UK are on or above the target. Slovenia is below the target but if the rate of increase between 2005 and 2010 continues, then it should also reach the 40% target. However, the Czech Republic, Austria and Hungary fall well short of the 40% target, and in Austria there has been a limited increase between 2005 and 2010. While some of these differences reflect generally lower levels of participation, it may also be an artefact of the translation of national qualifications into ISCED levels. For example, in England and Scotland some vocational courses may be regarded as tertiary-level education, whereas in other countries such as Austria they might be regarded as intermediate level.

Figure 7.1 also demonstrates a steady increase in the proportion of 30-34 year olds with tertiary-level qualifications, though in some countries the increases are small. Earlier data show that in all north western European countries (with the exception of the 50-54 age group in Norway) there has been a steady increase in tertiary education qualifications since the 1990s, and it is the youngest generation that is the most highly qualified. The picture is somewhat different for the post-socialist countries. In the Czech Republic and Estonia, it is the 45-49 age group that is most likely to hold a tertiary-level qualification. This suggests that during the Soviet era there were opportunities for gaining qualifications that may have disappeared during the transition period. However, **Figure 7.2** suggests that reforms in these countries are now leading to an expansion of higher education.

Figure 7.1: Proportion of 30–34 year olds with tertiary education, 2005 and 2010

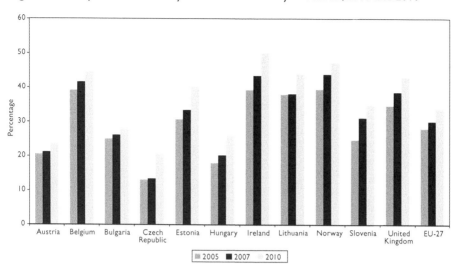

2005 ■ 2007 ░ 2010

Source: http://epp.eurostat.ec.europa.eu/portal/page/portal/europe_2020_indicators/headline_indicators

Figure 7.2: Proportion of the population with tertiary education (ISCED 5–6) by age, 2007

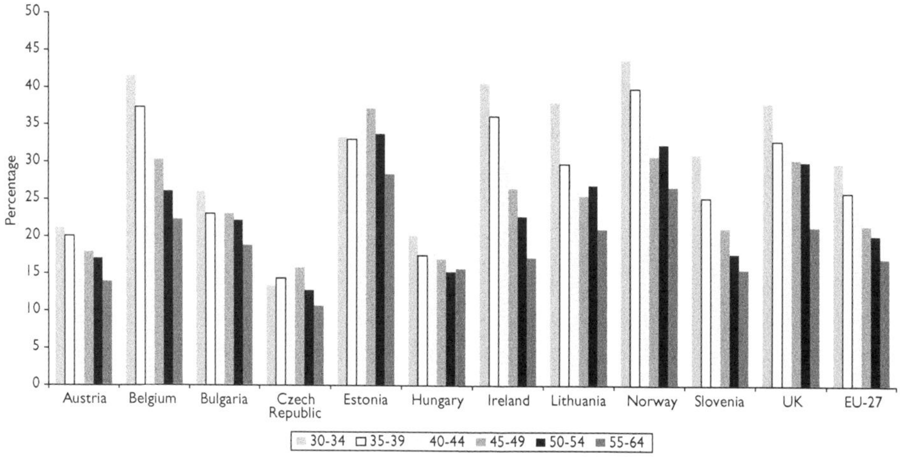

30-34 ☐ 35-39 40-44 ■ 45-49 ■ 50-54 ■ 55-64

Source: Eurostat, LFS

Gender differences in higher education participation

Across Europe, women have been major beneficiaries of higher education expansion, as illustrated by **Figure 7.3**. In all countries, women in the youngest age group outnumber men, and the difference in participation rates is particularly marked in Slovenia, Ireland, Estonia, Lithuania, Bulgaria and Belgium. Among the oldest age groups, the gender balance is more even. Austria and the Czech Republic, both with low overall rates of participation, present atypical examples. This pattern is also evident in Chapter Five in relation to sociodemographic barriers (see **Table 5.3**). In the two older age groups men predominate, and in the youngest age group women are only marginally more likely to have completed tertiary education than men. As previously noted, these differences reflect cultural variations between countries, but also differences in definitions of what counts as a tertiary level qualification.

Figure 7.3: Percentage who have completed tertiary education (ISCED 5–6) by age and gender, 2007

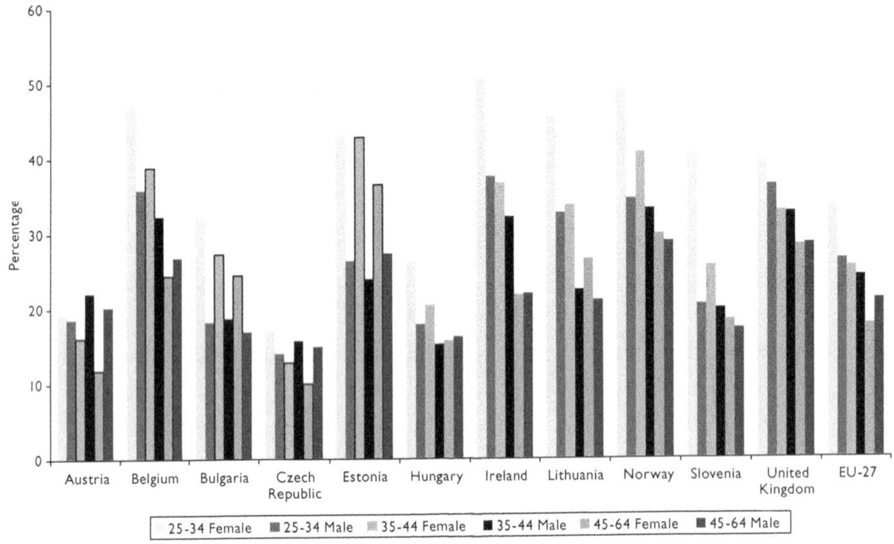

Source: Eurostat, EU-LFS in European Communities and HIS, Hochschul-Informations-System GmbH (2009)

As illustrated in **Table 7.4**, there has also been a change over time in the subjects women are studying in university, with growing representation in science, mathematics and technology subject areas, which are likely to lead to better paid jobs. There are fascinating country differences here, with women making up more than 40% of science, mathematics and technology graduates in Estonia and Bulgaria, but less than a quarter in Austria. This raises questions about the construction of gender identity in different countries, reflected in the position of men and women in higher education, the labour market and the family. Overall, the European-wide decline in manufacturing and the growth of the service sector, particularly in the Anglo-Celtic countries, appears to have boosted women's chances of obtaining higher level qualifications. The emphasis on equal opportunities, particularly in the Scandinavian and Anglo-Celtic countries, has also benefited women.

Table 7.4: Proportion of women graduates in mathematics, science and technology,[1] 2000 and 2005

Country	Graduates per 1,000	Share of female graduates	
		2000	2005
Austria	9.8	19.9	23.3
Belgium	10.9	25	27.3
Bulgaria	8.6	45.6	41.1
Czech Republic	8.2	27	27.4
Estonia	12.1	35.4	43.5
Hungary	5.1	22.6	30
Ireland	24.5	37.9	30.5
Lithuania	18.9	35.9	35.2
Norway	9	26.8	26
Slovenia	9.8	22.8	26.2
United Kingdom	18.4	32.1	30.8
EU-27	13.1	30.8	31.2

[1] This covers the following disciplinary areas: (a) science, mathematics and computing (EF400) and (b) engineering, manufacturing and construction (EF500) (Eurostat, 2011)

Source: Official Journal of the European Union (2008)

Socioeconomic differences in higher education participation

As previously noted, the ambitious goal of the EU has been to erode or remove the link between socioeconomic background and the attainment of higher education qualifications. Parental level of education may be taken as a proxy measure of social class, since those with higher education qualifications are likely to work in professional and managerial occupations and to have higher incomes. While there has been great success in addressing women's under-representation in higher education, the social class gap remains firmly in place (see **Figure 7.4**).

The association between parents' and children's level of education is particularly marked in the old member states, where participation rates have traditionally been higher. Belgium and Ireland appear to have particularly strong links between parents' and children's educational attainment. In all countries children from families with low educational attainment are much less likely to achieve higher education qualifications. This pattern is particularly marked in the Czech Republic, Hungary and Slovenia, where only around 5% of those whose parents have low educational attainment achieve a tertiary level qualification, compared with the UK, where 30% of those whose parents have low educational attainment achieve a higher level qualification. Iannelli (2011), writing in relation to Scotland, suggests that once middle-class participation in higher education has reached saturation point, then additional places are likely to be filled by those from lower socioeconomic backgrounds. Thus higher rates of participation in higher education are likely to lead to a more equal distribution of opportunity. One means of addressing socioeconomic differences in higher education participation advocated within the Bologna Process has been the development of more accessible routes into higher education for non-traditional students, and the success of these efforts is discussed in the following section.

Figure 7.4: Percentage of those aged 25+ who have completed tertiary education (ISCED 5–6) by level of educational background of parents and by gender, 2005

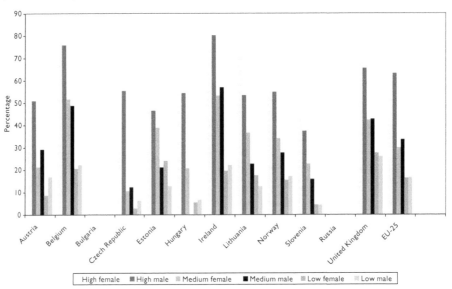

Source: Eurostat, EU-SILC in European Communities and HIS, Hochschul-Informations-System GmbH (2009)

Age differences in higher education participation

The traditional pattern of entering higher education in all European countries is to progress to university on completion of upper secondary education and to study full-time. Clearly this pattern favours those whose economic circumstances allow for continued full-time study. Young people whose parents have not been to university are less likely to take for granted progression from school to university and may regard obtaining employment as more important than gaining a degree. In order to disrupt this pattern, countries within the Bologna Process have adopted a range of measures to encourage first generation and mature students to attend university, including financial support, flexible entry routes with accreditation of prior learning and work experience, and the opportunity to study part-time. However, as can be seen from **Figure 7.5**, younger students still make up the vast majority of the higher education population.

Figure 7.6 shows the proportion of students entering higher education via a non-traditional route, which is defined as gaining admission 'either through validation of prior learning or work experience, with or without an entrance examination' (European Communities and HIS, Hochschul-Informations-System GmbH, 2009, p 59). It can be seen that England and Wales have the highest proportion of non-traditional students, followed by Scotland and Estonia. This reflects the fact that these countries have developed flexible and diverse entry routes, compared with other countries where completion of upper secondary education is still an essential requirement for university entrance. The majority of Central and Eastern European countries, as well as Belgium, fall into the latter group.

Figure 7.5: Net entry rate (%) by age, ISCED 5A, 2006

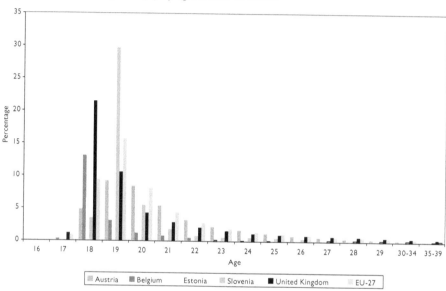

Source: UNESCO-OECD-Eurostat (UOE) data collection in European Communities and HIS, Hochschul-Informations-System GmbH (2009)

Figure 7.6: Percentage of students entering higher education via non-traditional route, 2006

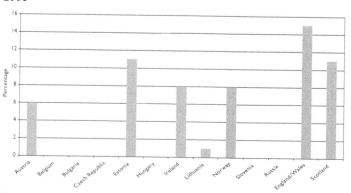

Source: Eurostudent III in European Communities and HIS, Hochschul-Informations-System GmbH (2009)

Non-traditional students are also more likely to be studying part time, defined as studying less than 75% of the week or less than the full academic year (European Communities and HIS, Hochschul-Informations-System GmbH, 2009, p 61). **Figure 7.7** shows that older students are more likely to choose this option, and the rates are highest in Hungary followed by Lithuania, Slovenia, Bulgaria and the UK. In Ireland there is no age breakdown of part-time study, although it is likely to reflect the pattern in other countries. Data were not available for Austria, and in the Czech Republic and Estonia, the rates are relatively low. These country differences point to variations in funding regimes, the extent of modularisation and the existence of regulations that allow students to complete a degree programme over a longer period of time.

Figure 7.7: Percentage of students studying part time by age

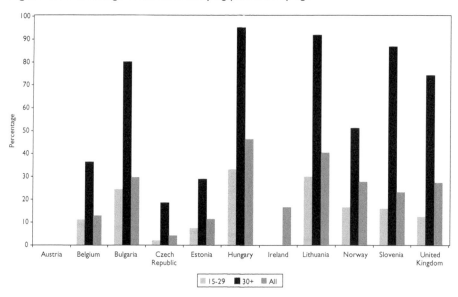

Source: Eurostat UOE in European Communities and HIS, Hochschul-Informations-System GmbH (2009)

Higher education and labour market advantage

While there are country differences in the proportion of the population educated to tertiary level, it is clear that in all countries having a higher education qualification confers advantages in the labour market, although the extent of this advantage varies by country (**Figure 7.8**). Those with the lowest level of qualification in Lithuania and the Czech Republic have extremely low employment rates, in contrast with Norway, where the gap between those with the highest and lowest level qualifications is smaller. Austria has the smallest gap in employment rates between those at ISCED levels 3–4 and levels 5–6, suggesting that having tertiary level education confers fewer benefits in the labour market in this country than it does in many of the other countries, especially Lithuania and the Czech Republic.

Figure 7.8: Employment rates by educational attainment, 2010 (25–64 years of age)

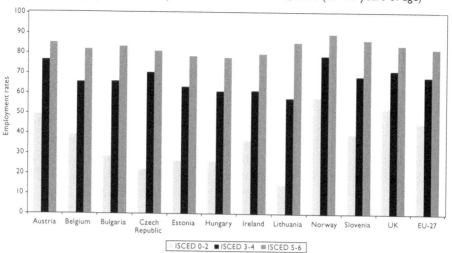

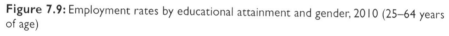

Source: Eurostat, EU-LFS, accessed 10 June 2011

As illustrated by **Figure 7.9**, the negative consequences of leaving school with low qualifications appear to be particularly pronounced for women, who have lower employment rates then men, particularly in countries such as Ireland. In addition, women's advantage in higher education participation does not translate into better labour market outcomes, and social class differences are much greater than, and intersect with, gender differences.

Figure 7.9: Employment rates by educational attainment and gender, 2010 (25–64 years of age)

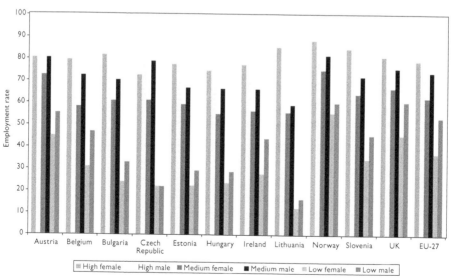

Source: Eurostat, EU-LFS, accessed 10 June 2011

The extent to which higher qualifications lead to graduate level employment is illustrated in **Figure 7.10**. In almost all countries at least half of those with tertiary level education work in professional and managerial occupations. Three quarters of Russians aged 25–34 with tertiary level qualifications are in professional or managerial occupations, a much higher proportion than the EU average of about 50%. In Norway, by way of contrast, those with tertiary level education in this age group are more likely to be found in an intermediate (ISCO 3) job. In Ireland, a high proportion of those with higher qualifications are in non-graduate jobs, suggesting that the graduate labour market has not expanded sufficiently rapidly to absorb the increased number of higher education graduates. Across Europe a slightly higher proportion of male graduates appear to be employed in professional and managerial occupations compared with their female counterparts.

Figure 7.10: Percentage of people with tertiary level education, aged 25–34, by level of occupation and gender, 2007

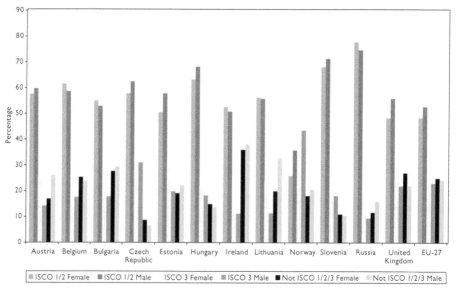

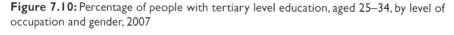

Note: ISCO = International Standard Classification of Occupation. ISCO 1 and 2 refers to legislators, senior officials, managers and professionals; ISCO 3 includes technicians and associate professionals

Source: Eurostat, EU-LFS in European Communities and HIS, Hochschul-Informations-System GmbH (2009)

To summarise, there has been a rapid expansion of higher education in all European countries, and women graduates tend to outnumber men. However, social class differences continue to be very significant. About 60% of those with tertiary level qualifications have a parent with higher level qualifications, most people with higher level qualifications appear to have followed a traditional route from school to university without a break and most countries have a low proportion of part-time and mature students. Only a minority of countries appear to have made progress in developing flexible entry routes to higher education based on the recognition of prior experience or work-based learning. The value of a tertiary level qualification is clear in relation to an individual's ability to obtain employment, and the majority of graduates are working in professional and managerial occupations. Across Europe less than half of those with lower qualifications are in work, compared with more than 80% of those with graduate-level qualifications. The next section looks in more detail at the way that five of the LLL2010 countries have dealt with widening access to higher education.

Widening access to higher education: institutional case studies

This section presents case studies of five higher education institutions in LLL2010 partner countries to explore the measures in place to facilitate the participation of non-traditional students. The case studies were conducted as part of sub-project 5, which examined strategies to promote social inclusion through lifelong learning.

Case study 7.1: An elite Scottish university

The university is described as 'research-intensive' and is located in a large Scottish city. It has around 29,000 students and offers a wide range of courses at undergraduate and postgraduate level with the majority of students studying humanities or social science subjects. It attracts a high proportion of middle-class students with around a third coming from the fee-paying independent school sector, which caters for only 5% of Scottish pupils. It also caters for a high proportion of students who normally live in England and international students.

Over the past two decades, encouraged by the Scottish Funding Council, the university has developed a range of widening participation initiatives including the following:

- Student recruitment and admissions (SRA) outreach activity has been developed. University staff and students visit local schools with low participation rates to encourage pupils to apply.
- Access courses have been run under the auspices of the Scottish Widening Access Programme (SWAP). These provide a route to higher education for mature learners.
- Access courses for adult learners have been developed. These tend to be part-time and geared towards the needs of adults returning to education. Study skills courses for adults wishing to return to higher education are also provided.
- Learning support tutors are employed to help students with difficulties such as dyslexia following admission.
- Students from poorer backgrounds are admitted to courses with lower examination grades than those from more affluent backgrounds.
- The institution publishes an annual report evaluating admissions and examination outcomes with regard to social class and other equality strands including race, disability and age.

- Funding has been provided for a number of research projects exploring the experiences of non-traditional students in the institution, especially in relation to transitions and employment outcomes.

Despite these efforts, the university has continued to recruit a disproportionate number of students from socially advantaged backgrounds. Although there was an increase in the number of students from state schools during the period 2004–08, the proportion of students from more socially advantaged backgrounds remained high. Furthermore, the proportion of students from low-participation neighbourhoods fell to 8%, against a benchmark of 11%. Having emphasised widening access for more than two decades, the Scottish Funding Council is currently placing greater emphasis on the differential mission of a range of institutions, with less pressure on elite institutions to alter their student profile. Admission criteria are set by individual institutions and are not subject to government regulation. There are currently strong financial incentives to recruit more English and international students, who may be charged fees of up to £9,000 per annum to study on undergraduate programmes, whereas Scottish and EU students do not pay fees to study in Scottish institutions. Fee-paying international postgraduate students are also prioritised in terms of recruitment. Overall, the university is increasingly seeking to recruit overseas students from affluent backgrounds rather than the local Scottish population.

The university has also prioritised the recruitment of disabled students and has been successful in this regard. Those who have a medically recognised condition are entitled to the nationally administered Disabled Students Allowance (DSA), which is claimed by 3.5% of the student population in this university. A further 7.5% of students receive support from the Disabled Students' Office. Students entitled to DSA are able to use the additional funding for a range of purposes such as purchasing a laptop, additional tuition, personal assistance, services of a sign-language interpreter and accommodation adaptations. Efforts have also been made across the university to make the curriculum and assessment more accessible. Despite these positive measures, it is evident that the majority of disabled students are from more affluent backgrounds and often have a diagnosis of dyslexia rather than more significant impairments

Case study 7.2: A Slovenian university

The university is located in the northern part of Slovenia. In 2003–04 the institution had a total of 5,741 students and 3,818 of those were mature students who were part-time and fee-paying. As part of the LLL2010 project, interviews were conducted within the business faculty, where the case study interviews were also conducted. The interviews revealed that the institution had special regulations for disabled students, but no other groups were recognised as in need of additional support. However, there were very few disabled students in the business faculty. During the year of 2008–09 the faculty believed that only two disabled students were enrolled, representing around 0.03% of the student population. Interviewees did not mention any other groups who were defined as under-represented and they confirmed that they did not have any social inclusion, access or lifelong learning committee at institutional level.

As in other Slovenian institutions, there were no reserved places, scholarships, grants or fee reduction schemes for students from disadvantaged backgrounds. The institution's ability to offer any such support was curtailed by nationally controlled funding mechanisms. However, fee-paying students were offered the opportunity to pay by instalment. There were plans to introduce student loans, and interviewees expected that demographic changes might lead to the development of scholarships and other measures.

The interviews also revealed that in the business faculty there was an even gender balance, and among the adult students 19% were younger than 24 years and 21% were from the 30-40 year age group. Around 10% were over 40 years old. Interviewees suggested that there were very few students from under-represented groups such as Roma and students with special needs. Virtually all students were Slovenian nationals with a small number from other ex-Yugoslavian republics and only very few from other countries.

In Slovenia, students from lower socioeconomic groups are not identified as a target group for widening access initiatives. The institution did not have any measures in place for monitoring the composition of the student population, but staff interviewed felt that they were inclusive since their promotional activities reached around 75% of the Slovenian population and they believed that there was a good social class mix in the faculty: "I can say at least for full-time studies that in our faculty you can find a student whose parents are top managers and a student whose parents are unskilled workers or farmers" (Dean of Faculty). However, this statement was not backed up by any evidence.

The institution did not have any preparatory or foundation courses or systems for prior non-formal learning and work experience. One of the respondents mentioned that, according to the Bologna Process, students may have non-formal learning recognised, but the institution had no experience of managing this. As a result, only formal qualifications attained in other schools or programme were recognised. According to the Dean, there was no system for the recognition of prior non-formal learning and work experience.

The faculty did not have any support services such as counselling or learning support. All students with problems took their queries to the central students' office and the staff would direct them to an external institution if they could not deal with the problem.

Case study 7.3: An Estonian research-intensive public university

There has been a significant expansion and marketisation of the higher education system in Estonia. The case study institution, a research-intensive public university, is one of the largest and oldest in Estonia. Students are either self-funded or are awarded a state-sponsored scholarship. Interviews revealed that the university had an above average rate of state-commissioned study places, so there were more students with limited economic means. Despite that, some state-commissioned study places, such as in sciences, were not filled because most students tended to prefer 'softer' courses, such as business administration, which were mainly provided for a fee. To encourage *potential students*, the following initiatives were reported:

- The university has for more than 50 years offered preparatory courses, now administered by the Open University. There is a fee for these courses and they focus on the state examination subjects: physics, maths, chemistry and Estonian language (grammar and essay writing skills). These are particularly useful for mature students, who have been away from studies for a while, and for students from disadvantaged backgrounds. The university also organises courses, summer schools and workshops for upper secondary students, and is actively recruiting highly motivated young people, including those from disadvantaged backgrounds. Since 2005, special programmes have existed for them, and the university currently participates in a joint project consisting of larger state universities in Estonia to ensure sustainability of science and technical education.
- The selection board can also admit up to five students with a disability, raised in an orphanage, or living in a shelter, who do not have to pay fees, regardless of their academic performance in admission tests.
- Each year the university admits 100–150 vocational school graduates, who make up about 10% of first year students. If they continue in the same field they studied in vocational school, they are granted extra credits on admission. Although the general knowledge of these students is poorer than that of traditional students, they are seen as highly motivated and able to catch up with the other students.
- The university has also established a college in North-Eastern Estonia, an area where Russian-speaking minorities are over-represented. In this college three courses are taught in Russian; however, Russian students study some general subjects in Estonian. The college, financially supported by the Ministry of Education, enables these students to obtain a higher education degree closer to their home, which minimises their transport and subsistence costs.

To support *enrolled students,* a number of support mechanisms were reported, including:

- Financial support is available to the highest-performing students if they are experiencing financial difficulties (1-2% of the total). Travel fare concessions are available to all students upon presentation of a student identification card.
- As some students from disadvantaged backgrounds have problems with basic skills in sciences, all students can participate in catch-up courses following the US model. These involve studying secondary school maths and physics for 1.5 months.
- Russian is the first language for more than 40% of students in the university, and to help them cope with studies in Estonian, some of the first-year courses are taught in Russian and students learn Estonian in parallel to their main studies. Starting from the second year, the courses are taught in Estonian. Estonian language courses are financed by the state, so they are free of charge to all students.

Case study 7.4: An Austrian university of applied sciences

The tertiary education institution is a university of applied sciences. It has four different locations in a region that has a strong industrial tradition. The institution is publicly financed at national and regional level. Its main focus is on degree courses in the technical field (engineering and technology) and 75% of courses are in classical technical areas.

One of the aims of the introduction of universities of applied sciences in Austria in 1994 was to make tertiary education available to students with vocational backgrounds (mostly apprenticeship or medium-level vocational school background). Students at this tertiary institution generally do not pay any fees.

At the time of the interviews the institution offered a special bridging course for students lacking in higher education entrance qualifications entitled 'Studienbefähigungslehrgang'. These students came mostly from the dual education system (vocational apprenticeship) or from a three-year VET (vocational education and training) school. The university of applied sciences offered this course free of charge. Its duration was two semesters (one year), and it was offered as extra-occupational. Students who successfully completed the course qualified for study programmes offered at this particular institution.

Another widening access initiative reported at this institution was a course aimed at women who want to return to the labour market. The undergraduate course on product design and technology-related communication was developed in cooperation with the regional public employment service (AMS). Potential female participants were prepared by the public employment service and received information and financial support there. The course was aimed at strengthening female participation in technical study programmes at the institution. Its other aim was to provide mothers who wanted to (re-)enter the labour market with a qualification that would enable them to hold jobs in technological fields. Gender segregation is a strong phenomenon within the Austrian labour market, but also within the education system, where the participation rate of females in technological education programmes is still very low.

Case study 7.5: A Flemish college of higher education

The college was established in 1995 as the result of mergers involving 16 institutions of higher education. It has over 15,000 students and around 2,000 members of staff. Students in traditional universities tend to have higher socioeconomic status than those at colleges of higher education (see **Table 7.2**), and recent migrants are under-represented in higher education. The main difference between higher education colleges and traditional universities is that the former cannot award PhDs but they can offer tuition up to Masters level.

Tuition fees are low and the Flemish government provides a limited number of scholarships and grants to Belgian and foreign students. The scholarships are only granted if students fulfil specific conditions, such as not repeating an academic year and being registered as a regular student. There are also opportunities for students to apply for other scholarships offered by international organisations, such as Erasmus mobility scholarships, Tempus and Erasmus Mundus scholarships.

The college has centres for study advice and student support. The first offers educational guidance and the latter student services such as accommodation, catering, cultural events, sports, medical assistance, transport and guidance for disabled students.

The normal admission requirement to a Bachelor programme is an upper secondary certificate, or an official equivalent, such as another certificate or diploma at a higher level. A relatively high proportion of students come from a vocational upper secondary background in comparison with students in universities. Students can gain entry through accreditation of prior learning and a member of staff offers support to students through the process.

The institution recognises that literacy difficulties can affect students' learning and offers additional support to these students. According to one member of staff interviewed, this is more likely to be a problem for students with a technical upper secondary education. Students are identified through a screening test offered to all new entrants to ensure that there is no discrimination or stigmatisation. The literacy support offered in order to remedy a possible lack of literacy and linguistic skills consists of three steps:

1   an e-learning environment for individual study. This is in fact an e-learning application with different levels (from basic to advanced) to exercise literacy and linguistics in an individual way;

2   literacy workshops. These workshops give students the opportunity to exercise literacy skills (also oral language skills) in a direct way;

3   personal counselling. During office hours some of the students will be able to get feedback on their test results.

The literacy project is funded by the government. The idea of the project is to create a transversal policy on literacy and language that will link all fields of study and will influence the agenda of all policy domains and faculties.

At the time of interviewing, the social work and welfare studies faculty was developing a diversity policy. Its aim was to produce a single policy and it was therefore general in nature and did not name particular underrepresented groups. An interviewee commented:

"One of the basic principles for the plan was: we will not focus on specific target groups. For instance, we will not focus on deaf and hard of hearing students, although they are under-represented in our institution. We could have done so, we could have attracted some interpreters, but this would cost a lot in terms of money and time with no guaranteed success." (Lecturer and member of steering committee)

The policy aimed at developing teaching methods that were inclusive as well as providing information on support facilities available to students. This included software for students with dyslexia, books with different font types for students who are visually handicapped and special support for students such as those with ADHD and ADD.

These institutional case studies reveal important similarities and differences in approaches to widening access to higher education in different parts of Europe. In all countries there has been a considerable expansion of higher education, but students from lower socioeconomic backgrounds tend to be found in newer colleges of higher education and universities of applied sciences rather than in traditional elite institutions. Elite institutions are competing in a global market for the best qualified students and, increasingly, those who are able to pay the highest fees. Institutions also vary with regard to the extent to which they monitor patterns of participation, identify certain groups as being in need of additional support and promote student support services and initiatives. In different types of higher education institutions across Europe it is possible to identify positive action programmes aimed at under-represented groups. However, these cannot possibly redress the economic, social and cultural advantages enjoyed by middle-class students, which enable them to monopolise access to elite higher education institutions across Europe.

Conclusion

It is evident that participation in tertiary education has expanded across Europe, driven in part by social justice concerns, but also by the fear that, unless workers are educated to a much higher level, Europe will be unable to compete with emerging economies in a globalised market. The marketisation of higher education is evident across Europe, with elite universities competing for the most highly qualified students, and often for those who are willing and able to pay increasing student fees. Countries with more liberal economic regimes, such as Estonia and Scotland, are witnessing a marked intensification of institutional hierarchies, with students from lower socioeconomic backgrounds markedly under-represented in the most prestigious institutions.

Social groups have benefited to very different degrees from the rapid expansion of higher education. Women, particularly those from middle-class backgrounds, have clearly been winners, now outnumbering men in many countries. Despite their success in gaining entry to the academy, women continue to be over-represented in arts and humanities and under-represented in maths, science, technology and engineering, the latter group of subjects generally leading to higher paying jobs. Disabled students have also benefited greatly in some countries such as Scotland. However, it is worth pointing out that here, too, there is an intersection with social class, since more than half of disabled higher education students in Scotland have a diagnosis of dyslexia and come from professional and managerial backgrounds. Students with more significant impairments and from poorer backgrounds still find it very difficult to access higher education.

By way of contrast, students from lower socioeconomic backgrounds have benefited to a much lesser extent from the expansion of higher education. They have tended to gain places only when middle-class participation has reached saturation point, and institutions vary greatly as to whether they regard widening access as a central part of their mission. New universities in many countries locate themselves within the widening access market, accepting additional support from government to support non-traditional students and deliberately trying to increase recruitment from this group. By way of contrast, more prestigious universities are less likely to provide open access arrangements and student support services. While data on participation by students from lower socioeconomic backgrounds are available in most countries, monitoring of progress over time varies greatly. For example, Slovenia does not appear to gather data at institutional level on student social background, and does not make any special efforts to increase recruitment of students experiencing economic deprivation. As government funding of higher education reduces in the wake of the global financial crisis, the outlook for newer higher education institutions geared towards widening access appears to be somewhat bleak.

A key question is the extent to which the expansion of higher education has diminished or intensified social inequality. As we noted in Chapter Two, the expansion of higher education has coincided with the growth of social inequality across Europe. Despite the differential labour market benefits garnered by different groups as a result of gaining a higher education qualification, it is still the case that graduates are much more likely to be in employment than non-graduates, for whom labour market opportunities and earnings have declined markedly since the 1970s. As noted by Brown and Lauder (1996) and Brine (2006), within knowledge economies there is a real danger that non-graduates are seen as deficient and therefore deserving of economic marginalisation. This of course ignores the fact that risk and opportunity are not distributed randomly, but are socially structured. As discussed further in the Conclusion, the challenge for the coming decades will be to develop a European economy and lifelong learning system that not only provides opportunities for all those who want to participate in higher education, but also ensures that those with low or no qualifications are not constantly struggling for survival.

Revisiting the question of whether the expansion of higher education has resulted in the reduction of social inequalities, it would appear that some progress has been made in widening the social class base of those with tertiary-level qualifications. For example, drawing on her analysis of Scottish data, Iannelli (2011) points out that since the 1970s people from lower socioeconomic backgrounds increased their rate of participation in higher education but did not increase their share of professional and managerial occupations. This indicates, she suggests, the enduring power of social class structures in Scotland, reflected in selective recruitment practices and the use of social capital to protect advantage. Education, it would appear, may contribute to producing a more equal society, but cannot entirely compensate for the effects of wider social inequality. As noted earlier, there is a clear commitment to the further expansion of participation in higher education at European level. However, in the wake of the ongoing financial crisis across Europe, there is a danger that governments will turn their backs on the widening access agenda, allowing market forces to determine the size of the higher education population and the social profile of those gaining places in the most prestigious institutions.

Acknowledgement

Thanks to Vida A. Mohorčič Špolar, Slovenia, Triin Roosalu, Estonia, Stephanie Rammel, Austria and Lode Vermeersch and Anneloes Vandenbroucke, Flanders, Belgium, who provided the case studies that are included in this chapter.

References

Brine, J. (2006) 'Lifelong learning and the knowledge economy: those that know and those that do not – the discourse of the European Union', *British Educational Research Journal*, vol 32, no 5, pp 649-65.

Brown, P. and Lauder, H. (1996) 'Education, globalization and economic development', *Journal of Education Policy*, vol 11, no 1, pp 1-25.

CEC (Commission of the European Communities) (2000) Lisbon European Council, 23 and 24 March 2000, Presidency Conclusions (available at http://www.europarl.europa.eu/summits/lis1_en.htm#a).

EACEA (Education, Audiovisual and Culture Executive Agency) (2010) *Focus on higher education in Europe 2010: the impact of the Bologna Process*, Brussels: Eurydice.

European Commission (2006) *The history of European cooperation in education and training: Europe in the making – an example*, Luxembourg: Office for Official Publications of the European Communities.

European Communities and HIS, Hochschul-Informations-System GmbH (2009) *The Bologna Process in higher education in Europe: key indicators on the social dimension and mobility*, Luxembourg: Office for Official Publications of the European Communities.

Eurostat (2011) *Trends in European education during the last decade, Statistics in focus 54/2011* (available at http://epp.eurostat.ec.europa.eu/cache/ITY_OFFPUB/KS-SF-11-054/EN/KS-SF-11-054-EN.PDF).

Hills, J., Brewer, M., Jenkins, S., Lister, R., Lupton, R., Machin, S., Mills, C., Modood, T., Rees, T. and Riddell, S. (2010) *An anatomy of economic inequality in the UK*, London: London School of Economics.

Hingel, A. (2001) *Education policies and European governance* (March), Report from Unit A1 (Development of Educational Policies) Director-General for Education and Culture to the Interservice Groups on European Governance, Brussels: European Commission

Hirsch, F. (1976) *The social limits to growth,* Cambridge, MA: Harvard University Press.

Iannelli, C. (2011) 'Educational expansion and social mobility: the Scottish case', *Social Policy and Society,* vol 10, no 2, pp 251-64.

Keeling, R. (2006) 'The Bologna Process and the Lisbon Research Agenda: the European Commission's expanding role in higher education discourse, *European Journal of Education,* vol 41, no 2, pp 203-23.

Lažetić, P. (2010) 'Managing the Bologna Process at the European level: institution and actor dynamics', *European Journal of Education*, vol 45, no 4, pp 549-62.

Leuven/Louvain-la-Neuve Communiqué (2009) *The Bologna Process 2020 – The European Higher Education Area in the new decade, Communiqué of the Conference of European Ministers Responsible for Higher Education*, Leuven and Louvain-la-Neuve, 28-29 April 2009 (available at www.ond.vlaanderen.be/hogeronderwijs/bologna/conference/documents/Leuven_Louvain-la-Neuve_Communiqué_April_2009.pdf).

London Communiqué (2007) *Towards the European Higher Education Area: responding to challenges in a globalised world* (available at http://www.ond.vlaanderen.be/hogeronderwijs/bologna/documents/MDC/London_Communique18May2007.pdf).

Marginson, S. (2008) 'National and global competition in higher education', in B. Lingard and J. Ozga, J. (eds) *The RoutledgeFalmer reader in education policy and politics,* London: Routledge, pp 131-53.

Official Journal of the European Union (2008) *2008 joint progress report of the Council and the Commission on the implementation of the 'Education and Training 2010' programme – 'Delivering lifelong learning for knowledge, creativity and innovation'* (2008/C 86/01) (available at http://eur-lex.europa.eu/JOHtml.do?uri=OJ:C:2008:086:SOM:EN:HTML).

Osborne, M. (2003) 'Increasing or widening participating in higher education? A European overview', *European Journal of Education*, vol 38, no 1, pp 5-24.

Riddell, S. (2012, forthcoming) *Policies and practices in education, training and employment for disabled people in Europe*, Network of Experts in Social Sciences of Education and Training, Brussels: European Commission.

Robertson, S. (2009) 'Europe, competitiveness and higher education: an evolving project', in R. Dale and S. Robertson (eds) *Globalisation and Europeanisation in education*, Oxford: Symposium Books, pp 65-83.

Unger, M., Zaussinger, S. and Gottwald, R. (2010) *Studierenden-Sozialerhebung 2009 – die soziale Lage der Studierenden in Österreich (2010), Studie im Auftrag des BMWF*, Vienna.

EIGHT

Conclusion: the role of lifelong learning in reducing social inequality at a time of economic crisis

Sheila Riddell, Centre for Research in Education Inclusion and Diversity, University of Edinburgh

Introduction

The LLL2010 project began in 2005 during a period of social optimism, following the expansion of the EU and a decade of sustained economic growth. Lifelong learning was regarded as having important economic and social benefits in terms of producing a flexible workforce, supporting social mobility and stimulating personal growth and development. The LLL2010 project had a particular focus on exploring the extent to which lifelong learning could contribute to social inclusion, as countries struggled to adjust to the challenges of globalisation, the shifting of economic power to East Asia and, latterly, the threatened collapse of the European Union itself. Building social cohesion was a particular challenge for new member states in Central and Eastern Europe, adapting to the collapse of the old Soviet Union and the demands of the EU to develop new institutions and systems of governance. At the end of the LLL2010 project, the economic and social outlook has changed from one of optimism and growth, to a much more pessimistic prospect of relative and absolute economic decline in many European countries, a faltering currency and the threatened implosion of the state in several countries. Questions therefore arise about the future survival of lifelong learning as a force for building social cohesion, promoting social mobility and contributing to the task of economic rebuilding. In this concluding chapter we consider some of the overarching themes and questions to emerge from the preceding chapters. It should be noted that writing a conclusion to a book of this type at the present point in time (December 2011) is extremely challenging because of huge levels of uncertainty in relation to the global economy, the eurozone and, consequently, the social welfare systems of European countries, including their systems of lifelong learning.

Bounded agency and the motivation of adult learners in different European countries

To begin on a note of optimism, it is evident that adult learners at all levels have considerable enthusiasm to engage in learning for a variety of reasons connected with securing their financial future, but also to feel rooted within their local community and wider society. The survey of adult motivation described in Chapter Four demonstrated that intrinsic motivation was important in all countries and to learners at all levels, suggesting that economic instrumentalism is very far from the sole, or even the main, driver of the decision to participate in adult education. The love of learning, the desire for personal growth and the urge to exert some control over future life events clearly play a major role in individual decision making. Our research suggested that in all countries and across all groups individuals tend to be motivated by an interconnected mix of intrinsic and extrinsic factors. It was evident that people's initial decision to enrol in a course might be driven by extrinsic factors such as the need to obtain further qualifications to secure a promotion or as a result of active labour market policies, which increasingly require participation in education or training as a condition of benefits receipt. However, the act of engaging in learning of whatever type generally stirs a desire for further learning experiences. For groups such as newly arrived immigrants the provision of lifelong learning opportunities may be particularly important because of the need to gain qualifications for particular jobs, but also to establish connections within the new society. These findings point to the inadequacy of human capital theories in explaining the motivation of adult learners, since such theories place undue emphasis on rational economic planning, which offers at best only a partial explanation of motivation.

The survey of adult learners' motivations was informed by the notion of bounded agency developed by Rubenson and Desjardins (2009), which emphasises the importance of individual psychological motivation, but also recognises that decisions on participation are always socially contextualised rather than taking place in a social vacuum. Within particular countries and regions, the nature of the national and local welfare state, the lifelong learning regime and the architecture of educational institutions, including the curriculum and qualifications framework, are critical determinants of which groups of people participate in adult education. Boeren et al (see Chapter Four) found that the flexible systems of lifelong learning that have developed in Anglo-Celtic countries promoted higher levels of participation and satisfaction amongst learners from diverse social backgrounds. By way of contrast, the more rigid systems found in continental European countries and the countries of Central and Eastern Europe led to lower participation rates and reduced learner satisfaction. Learners in Central and Eastern European were generally much less satisfied with their learning environment, reflecting the lack of focus on teaching methods appropriate to the education of adults in these countries. Furthermore, in Central and Eastern Europe, extrinsic factors related to the labour market and job scarcity appear to be of great importance in influencing participation. Economic insecurity is clearly a major motivator in these countries, but may explain, at least to some extent, the lower levels of satisfaction with educational experiences that were reported. Overall, the survey findings indicate that if politicians and policy makers see lifelong learning simply as a tool of economic growth, they are likely to reduce rather than enhance adults' commitment to education and self-development. This may be a very important message for politicians and policy makers, who, in the context of rising levels of unemployment, are likely to prioritise even further vocational education and training at the expense of other types of learning that have less immediate and obvious economic benefits.

Access to formal education in the workplace

Given the glaring inequality in educational outcomes produced by the initial education system, workplace learning, the subject of Chapter Six, has been identified by governments as an important means of helping those who were deprived of earlier opportunities to gain qualifications. In addition, supporting workers to retrain and upskill while in employment is seen as essential in terms of allowing companies and countries to retain their competitive edge. Overall, workplace learning opportunities are unevenly distributed across Europe, with new member states in Central and Eastern Europe having lower levels of provision than richer countries in the North and West. However, far from targeting those with the lowest level of initial qualifications, workplace learning is dominated by highly skilled workers who are often employed in professional and managerial occupations. It is evident that the bulk of training provided in the workforce is of an informal variety and is geared towards helping the company perform better, rather than helping individuals realise their own learning objectives, which are linked to their wider life goals. Courses studied, which are classified as formal education, may be highly work-relevant and useful to the person's present employment, but may also be portable, enhancing an individual's career prospects. Because employers may be sceptical of the value of qualifications that are not immediately relevant to the business, or may fear losing good employees to competitor firms, they may be very reluctant to provide support in terms of help with fees or opportunities to study in company time. However, these fears may be counter-productive since individuals who elect to take additional courses while in employment are likely to be highly motivated and willing to contribute in terms of both time and money.

Despite workers' willingness to participate in workplace learning, they often encounter discouraging attitudes in the workplace, where managers may be fearful of losing their workers to rival employers and are therefore reluctant to channel profits into workforce development. As discussed by Hefler and Markowitsch in Chapter Six, there is a strong relationship between the training cultures within firms and their willingness to support participation in formal adult education. Unsurprisingly, firms with reactive training cultures are likely to take little interest in, or actively discourage, participation in formal adult education, while those with expansive training culture are likely to provide systematic or individualised support. About a quarter of SMEs that featured in our case studies had weak training cultures, but nonetheless offered reasonably generous levels of support to employees who were, of their own volition, undertaking courses leading to formal qualifications. This suggests that self-motivated study may be a very important driver of workplace learning and that its significance may have been severely underestimated. In relation to workplace learning, organisations have been encouraged by local and national government to think about their companies' training needs rather than their employees' educational interests. However, the implicit or explicit under-playing of individual workers' interests and learning ambitions in workplace learning policy is likely to be counter-productive, since effective engagement in learning requires strong intrinsic motivation, not merely compliance with business priorities. Clearly, workplace learning can be an important route to social mobility, but the present climate of economic uncertainty across Europe is unlikely to lead firms to increase their investment in this area, particularly for low-skilled workers who are in greatest need of workplace development.

The expansion of higher education and the growth of social inequality

One of the paradoxes of the massification of higher education across most of Europe over the past two decades is that it has coincided with, and contributed to, the growth of economic inequality. Until the early 1990s higher education across much of Europe was the preserve of an elite group of mainly young people drawn predominantly from the middle classes. As the discourse of the knowledge society became increasingly dominant across Europe, higher education assumed centre stage, since it was seen as the means of preparing a workforce able to work in knowledge-intensive industries. In addition, widening access to higher education was identified as an important means of facilitating social mobility and inclusion. As demonstrated in Chapter Seven, these objectives have been only partially achieved. Clearly, participation in higher education has increased dramatically in most member states. However, some new member states in Central and Eastern Europe have bucked this trend, educating a smaller proportion of the population to higher degree level than was the case under the Soviet regime. In most (but not all) countries, women have been the principal beneficiaries of the expansion. The economic need for a more highly qualified workforce has, therefore, been at least partially met.

With regard to the objective of attracting a more socially diverse group of students to study to degree level, the verdict is much more mixed. Higher education expansion has mainly benefited those from middle-class backgrounds, where participation is virtually at saturation point. Those from less socially advantaged backgrounds have also benefited from the expansion but to a lesser extent, and are more likely to study in newer institutions that prioritise widening access. Elite institutions, whose graduates dominate the old professions such as medicine and law, continue to attract disproportionate numbers of students from socially advantaged backgrounds. While all higher education graduates have better chances of being employed than non-graduates and have higher earnings, the graduate premium varies greatly with regard to the institution and subject studied. A significant minority of graduates are employed in non-graduate occupations, especially in countries such as Ireland where the supply of graduates from an expanded higher education sector has outstripped labour market demand, particularly following the recession.

The case studies presented in Chapter Seven suggest that widening access policies have been introduced with different degrees of enthusiasm and success in a range of countries and types of institution. For example, **Case study 7.1** illustrates the efforts of an elite Scottish institution to recruit a more diverse student body, backed by support from the Scottish Government and Funding Council. Activities include outreach work in schools in deprived neighbourhoods, summer schools, learning support and financial assistance. Participation rates are monitored both within the university and at national level in relation to social class, disability, gender, race and age. Benchmarks are set and a publicly available annual report comments on progress over time and presents a future action plan. However, despite these efforts, the student profile has changed very little and middle-class students, drawn disproportionately from the independent school sector, continue to claim the lion's share of places. In contrast, the Slovenian government has no monitoring systems in place to analyse the social characteristics of the student population and no special measures or initiatives are targeted at under-represented groups (see **Case study 7.2**).

Overall, although higher education clearly has the potential to promote social mobility and equality, far more determined efforts would be needed to realise this goal. There is some evidence that the policy tide has turned against the widening access agenda. In Scotland, where the government for more than a decade has encouraged widening access, recent government pronouncements suggest that there will be a new focus on diversity of mission, with some universities emphasising widening access and others focusing on research and fee-paying undergraduate and postgraduate students. There is also a trend towards privatisation of higher education across Europe. The decision of the UK government to triple university fees from 2012 onwards for English-domiciled students signals the view that higher education should be seen primarily as a benefit to the individual rather than to society. Privatisation of higher education is also progressing in Estonia, where the majority of new universities are in the private rather than public sector. While the state continues to pay the fees of some students in public institutions, it is also possible to attend as a private fee-paying student. The trend towards privatisation suggests that increasingly higher education places are likely to be awarded on the basis of ability to pay rather than ability to study.

An ambitious aim of the EU's 2020 education and training strategy was to remove the link between students' family background and their educational outcomes. This would imply that in higher education, for example, the composition of the student population in all institutions would reflect the social profile of the wider population, and that similar proportions of students from more and less advantaged areas would obtain degree level qualifications. At a time when education is being seen increasingly as a positional good (Marginson, 2009), with increasing competition from middle-class groups to secure and retain their social advantage, this may be an impossible goal to achieve.

Barriers to inclusion and exclusion in lifelong learning across Europe

The importance of the social, economic and cultural context within which lifelong learning takes place is underlined by the analysis of Adult Education Survey data in Chapter Five. There is much evidence to support the notion that, across Europe, lifelong learning is currently operating in a way which cements, rather than undermines, established inequalities. Those with low initial qualifications, particularly early school leavers, who generally come from socially disadvantaged backgrounds, are much less likely to participate than their more socially advantaged and well-educated peers. In many countries, the problems of exclusion from lifelong learning are particularly acute for low skilled men, reflecting the socially demoralising effects of the collapse of manufacturing industries which provided employment and a sense of identity for this group. Even in countries like Austria and Belgium (Flanders), where manufacturing still makes up a significant part of the economy, the focus has been on the creation of more highly skilled jobs to produce higher-value added products. The problem of escalating levels of economic and educational inequality, evident across Europe since the 1980s, is likely to intensify over coming years (OECD, 2008; Förster, 2011).

While recognising the general pattern of exclusion of low-skilled workers from lifelong learning, there are also significant cross-European differences in the nature and intensity of sociodemographic barriers. New member states in Central and Eastern Europe are currently much less successful than old member states in the North and West in hooking socially disadvantaged people into lifelong learning and employment. Disavowing their socialist past, these countries have adopted particularly brutal versions of capitalism with regressive fiscal regimes and limited social welfare, with a strong emphasis on competitive individualism and little focus on promoting social cohesion. With the exception of Slovenia, they have also been much less successful in securing the equal participation of women in workplace learning and in the economic sphere more widely. By way of contrast, Scandinavian countries such as Norway and Sweden have been much more successful in removing barriers to participation for women and for people from lower socioeconomic backgrounds. Walby (2009) comments on the 'public gender regime' that has been created in the Scandinavian countries, encouraging gender equality across the public sphere. In addition to promoting equal participation in lifelong learning, important measures have included the provision of state-supported childcare, the criminalisation of violence against women and the provision of quotas for women in parliament. Green and Janmaat (2011) point to the importance of securing equal levels of female participation in the public sphere, since women have become strong supporters and defenders of social democracy. The 'presence democracy' (Walby, 2009) fostered in Scandinavian countries has resulted in stronger gender and social class solidarity that is reflected in patterns of participation in lifelong learning as in other social spheres.

Knowledge-extensive policies and the elusive goal of equality of outcome

As noted in earlier chapters, systems of education and lifelong learning have the potential to either widen or reduce existing patterns of social inequality. At the time of writing, the expansion of educational opportunities over the past two decades appears to have cemented rather than eroded social divisions. This is illustrated by **Figure 8.1**, which demonstrates a strong association between level of education and risk of poverty. A persistent concern raised in this book is that, rather than acting as a mitigator of poverty, education and lifelong learning actually drive the social reproduction of inequality because of their unequal distribution across the population. In knowledge economies, individuals with higher levels of education generally have professional jobs that provide much greater levels of financial security and social respect than experienced by those with low levels of education. Those enjoying social advantage, particularly in countries like the UK, may increasingly resemble a separate caste, educating their children in private fee-paying schools to secure their future educational advantage, making social mobility for others much harder to achieve.

The policies of the EU and member states have over recent years emphasised the potential of lifelong learning to make an equal contribution to the goals of economic growth and social inclusion. During their 2000 Spring Summit in Lisbon, European leaders agreed on a common growth strategy that would build on knowledge as a key asset in global competition, 'making the EU the most dynamic and competitive knowledge-based economy in the world, capable of sustainable economic growth with more and better jobs and greater social cohesion' (www.europarl.europa.eu/summits/lis1_en.htm). The new Europe 2020 education and training strategy, adopted in the spring of 2010, essentially continues along the same lines, with the goal of delivering 'smart, sustainable and inclusive growth' (http://eur-lex.europa.eu/LexUriServ/LexUriServ.do?uri=OJ:C:2011:070:0001:0003:EN:PDF). Boldly, the EU asserts that it wishes to sever the association between an individual's social origin and their educational outcomes. However, the evidence to date suggests that the knowledge society tends to sustain, rather than weaken, inequality. This raises the question of whether inequality will inevitably increase to the point of social fracture, or whether this trend can be reversed.

Figure 8.1: Risk of poverty by education level in different European countries

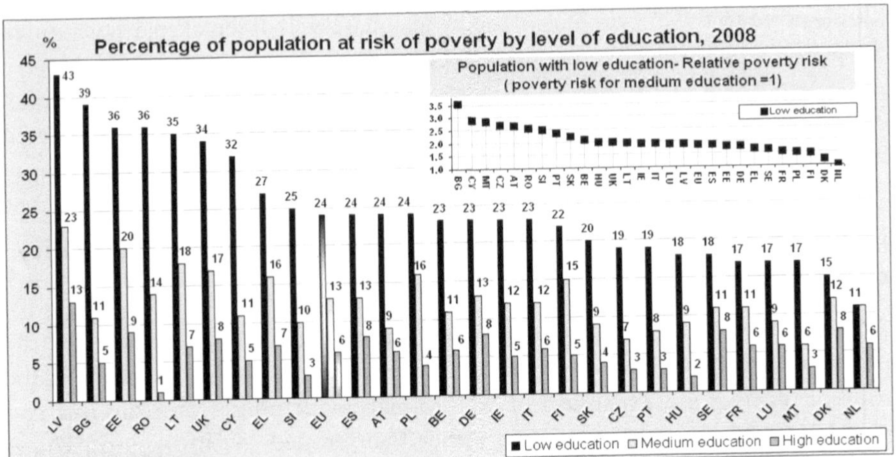

Key: LV = Latvia, BG = Bulgaria, EE = Estonia, RO = Romania, LT = Lithuania, UK = United Kingdom, CY = Cyprus, EL = Greece, SI = Slovenia, EU = EU-27, ES = Spain, AT = Austria, PL = Poland, BE = Belgium, DE = Germany, IE = Ireland, IT = Italy, FI = Finland, SK = Slovakia, CZ = Czech Republic, PT = Portugal, HU = Hungary, SE = Sweden, FR = France, LU = Luxembourg, MT = Malta, DK = Denmark, NL = Netherlands

Source: Nicaise (2010)

As argued by Brakman (2006) and Nicaise (2010), the dominant distribution pattern within the knowledge economy has been one of skill-biased technological growth, with technological innovations boosting the demand for better-skilled jobs, while low-skilled jobs are displaced and either disappear or sink lower on the status and pay ladder (see Chapter Two). As noted earlier, the OECD reports an overall picture of growing income inequality in the EU (OECD, 2008; Förster, 2011), a trend that began in the 1980s. The inequality in *individual labour incomes* has in fact risen significantly more than the inequality in *total household incomes*, partly as a result of widening wage gaps and partly as a result of an increase in atypical employment, especially among the low-skilled (part-time work, temporary work, and so on). This suggests that labour markets in the EU have indeed undergone a radical shift towards more *knowledge-intensive* services (Gottschalk and Smeeding, 1997; Gregory and Russo, 2005). The recent prospective analysis of labour market trends, carried out by Cedefop (2008), shows that this trend is likely to continue in the next 20 years, resulting in further imbalances at the expense of low-skilled workers. In other words, the knowledge-based society has until now widened inequality.

This does not imply that the knowledge society is per se harmful for social cohesion and social inclusion. It simply necessitates an appropriate policy mix, with a better balance between *knowledge-intensive* policies, which concentrate education and training on an already privileged group, and *knowledge-extensive* policies, which attempt to spread education and training more widely among the whole population. Policies that extend knowledge focus on its dissemination and distribution among the population. They concentrate on investments in education and training, particularly among adults at the bottom of the education ladder. The wide dissemination of knowledge through education and training is equally favourable for economic growth, but not at the expense of greater inequality, because knowledge-extensive policies operate at the supply side of the labour market. Education and training transform unskilled into skilled labour, reducing the labour supply at the bottom of the ladder, while increasing the supply in higher-skilled segments. In this way, the supply of labour is better able to track the trends in demand, and consequently the employment rate and pay levels of vulnerable groups can be maintained at decent levels, reducing the risk of poverty. Of course, there also needs to be a political will to ensure that the living standards of those with lower levels of education are maintained. This might involve encouraging and extending trade union membership and ensuring that trade unions are fully involved in a range of activities as important social partners. This means that education and training must be seen as a cornerstone of social policy in the knowledge-based society. Social inclusion will fail or succeed, depending on the commitment of the EU and its member states to invest in the human and social capital of all citizens. The Council conclusions of 11 May 2010 on the social dimension of education and training are a significant signal in this direction (Council of the European Union, 2010), but are not necessarily reflected in the actions of national governments, which have moved to the right in the wake of the economic crisis.

The economic crisis and the future of social Europe

What, then, are the chances of achieving the knowledge-extensive policies described above? As noted by Holford and Mohorčič Špolar (see Chapter Three), commentators such as Dale (2009) have characterised the EU as primarily an imperialist force driving forward the agenda of neoliberal globalisation. At the same time, EU policy documents have argued the case for combining equity and efficiency, with the Scandinavian social market economies, rather than the Anglo-Celtic neoliberal economies, providing a template for the new European socioeconomic model. There is a particular recognition that public education and lifelong learning systems may be used to promote social mobility and act as a brake on extreme forms of free market capitalism. As argued by Lawn (2006) and Giddens (2006), it is possible to identify a European space in which social justice policies can be developed. However, much of the more optimistic commentary on the prospect of an emergent social Europe was written prior to the ongoing economic crisis. Over the past decade there has been a general shift to the right in the political complexion of governments across Europe. While it is clear that the neoliberal agenda of free trade, free movement of labour and deregulation has not succeeded in producing lasting economic growth, there appears to be little appetite across Europe at the time of writing for redistributive policies and stronger state intervention to boost economic growth. The continued dominance of neoliberalism is particularly evident in the failure to regulate the financial services industry, which, particularly in the UK and Ireland, contributed to the collapse of the economy and to the growth in inequality (Förster, 2011; Stewart, 2011). Anti-capitalist protest movements are growing across Europe, promoting the view that globalisation has been far from benign or neutral in its consequences. However, there is as yet no clearly articulated political response to the crisis, as European governments swither between attempting to stimulate the economy through public investment while cutting public sector jobs, thus creating great insecurity and stifling demand. Keynes' view that at times of economic crisis governments should concentrate on creating jobs rather than cutting public spending is given short shrift. Holford and Mohorčič Špolar remain optimistic that the ideals of social Europe will survive, and that these will continue to influence the development of lifelong learning, but the evidence on the ground is not encouraging.

In conclusion

Throughout this book we have pointed to the inherent paradoxes within Europe's knowledge society. To date, education and lifelong learning within the knowledge society have tended to reinforce existing patterns of inequality by concentrating knowledge and skills among those who are already socially advantaged. However, as argued above, the knowledge society has the potential to spread skills more widely across populations, contributing to greater social and economic equality. Stiglitz (2002) expressed the belief that globalisation, of which the knowledge society is a key element, has the potential to be a force for good, enriching 'everyone in the world, including the poor' (Stiglitz, 2002, p ix). The problem, he suggested, is not with globalisation per se, but with how it is managed. As we have demonstrated, even though lifelong learning is regarded primarily within European policy as a means of developing human capital, there is also a strong counter theme urging the use of lifelong learning to promote greater social equality and cohesion. While most European governments have responded to the economic crisis by radically reducing public expenditure, including investment in education and training, the response has not been uniform. It is interesting that the countries that have survived the economic crisis relatively unscathed are those in the Scandinavian group, where levels of educational and economic inequality are less marked. Ozga and Lingard (2007) question the assumption that globalisation in education, as a product of neoliberal politics and economics, has an inevitable homogenising influence. This conceals, they suggest, 'the extent to which local, vernacular globalisation is called forth and energised in response to homogenising tendencies and trends' (Ozga and Lingard, 2007, p 79). As Europe emerges from the economic crisis, we must hope that, far from vanishing, the social dimension of lifelong learning will be strengthened, democratising access to knowledge and skills and producing more equal, rather than less equal, societies.

References

Brakman, S. (2006) *Nations and firms in the global economy: an introduction to international economics and business*, Cambridge: Cambridge University Press.

Cedefop (2008), *Future skill needs in Europe. Medium-term forecast synthesis report*, Luxembourg: Office for Official Publications of the European Communities.

Council of the European Union (2010) *Council conclusions of 11 May 2010 on the social dimension of education and training, Official Journal of the European Union*, 26 May 2010.

Dale, R (2009) 'Introduction', in R. Dale and S. Robertson (eds) *Globalisation and Europeanisation in education*, Didcot, Oxfordshire: Symposium Book, pp 7-19.

Förster, M. (2011) *Divided we stand*, Paris: OECD.

Giddens, A. (2006) 'A social model for Europe?', in A. Giddens, P. Diamond and R. Liddle (eds) *Global Europe, social Europe,* Cambridge: Polity Press, pp 14-36.

Gottschalk, P. and T.M. Smeeding (1997) 'Cross national comparisons of earnings and income inequality', *Journal of Economic Literature*, vol 35, no 2, pp 633-87.

Green, A. and Janmaat, J.G. (2011) *Regimes of social cohesion: societies and the crisis of globalization*, Basingstoke: Palgrave Macmillan.

Gregory, M. and Russo, G. (2005) 'The employment impact of differences in demand and production structures', in I. Marx and W. Salverda (eds) *Low-wage employment in Europe: perspectives for improvement*, Leuven: Acco, pp 21-31

Lawn, M. (2006) 'Soft governance and the learning spaces of Europe', *Comparative European Politics,* vol 4, pp 272-88.

Marginson, S. (2008) 'National and global competition in higher education', in B. Lingard and J. Ozga, J. (eds) *The RoutledgeFalmer reader in education policy and politics*, London: Routledge, pp 131-53.

Nicaise, I (2010) 'A smart social inclusion policy for the EU: the role of education and training', Paper presented at the Belgian Presidency Conference on Education and Social Inclusion, Ghent, 28–29 September 2010.

OECD (2008) *Growing unequal? Income distribution and poverty in OECD countries*, Paris: OECD.

Ozga, J. and Lingard, B. (2007) 'Globalisation, education policy and politics', in B. Lingard and J. Ozga (eds) *The RoutledgeFalmer reader in education policy and politics*, London: RoutledgeFalmer, pp 65-82.

Rubenson, K, and Desjardins, R. (2009) 'The impact of welfare state regimes on barriers to participation in adult education', *Adult Education Quarterly*, vol 59, no 3, pp 187-207.

Stewart, M.B. (2011) 'The changing picture of earnings inequality in Britain and the role of regional and sectoral differences', *National Institute Economic Review*, vol 18, no 1, pp 20-32.

Stiglitz, J. (2002) *Globalization and its discontents*, Norton: New York.

Walby, S (2009) *Globalization and inequalities: complexity and contested modernities*, London: Sage.

Technical annex to Chapter Four

Survey methodology

In order to obtain a diverse range of adult learners in our sample, and to guarantee a sufficient number of adult learners at the lowest course levels, each national sample was stratified by ISCED level of the current course, with four subsets of respondents:

- ISCED 1+2 – primary and lower secondary/basic level   250
- ISCED 3 – upper secondary level   250
- ISCED 4 – post secondary (non tertiary) level   250
- ISCED 5 – tertiary level   250.

Although this sample is not representative of the entire population of adult learners in the formal education system, it allows us to analyse similarities and differences by educational level of the current course. Especially in the Eastern European countries, it was difficult to find 250 respondents at ISCED 1 and 2 levels as the educational provision for early school leavers who want to complete secondary school usually start at ISCED 3 level. Moreover, the aim was to include low-qualified adults in the ISCED 1 and 2 courses, but particularly in Flanders, and also partly in the UK, more highly educated adults were also found on lower level courses. In Flanders, this is because of high enrolments of learners with an ISCED 5 background on arts programmes that span ISCED levels 1 to 4. The database was weighted to take the original sampling structure of 4×250 into account. Each country in the analysis counts 250 adult learners at ISCED 1-2 courses, 250 at ISCED 3 courses, 250 at ISCED 4 courses and 250 at ISCED 5 courses.

In order to exclude students from initial tertiary education, adult learners were not defined on the basis of age, but rather narrowly as people who have left full-time formal initial education – e.g. to enter the labour market – and who, at some point, decide to participate in formal education again. The time span between leaving full-time formal education and re-entering must be at least two years. Respondents thus had to be adult *returners*.

The definition of adult education used in this chapter is based on the final report of the task force on the Adult Education Survey (Eurostat, 2007):

> Formal education is education provided in the system of schools, colleges, universities and other formal education institutions that normally constitutes a continuous 'ladder' of full-time education for children and young people, generally beginning at age of five to seven and continuing up to 20 or 25 years old. In some countries, the upper parts of this 'ladder' are organised programmes of joint

part-time employment and part-time participation in the regular school and university system. Formal learning is intentional from the learner's point of view. It leads to certification which leads to the next educational level.

Because of the different needs and abilities of the adult learners, a mixed survey method was used. Although each national team was allowed to choose a survey methodology adapted to their possibilities and budget, recommendations were made by ISCED level of the current course:

- ISCED 1+2: face-to-face interviews;
- ISCED 3+4: written questionnaire with the help of an interviewer (in group);
- ISCED 5: written questionnaire, administered groupwise, or by post or online (via e-mail, not through web survey).

The questionnaire for the learners consisted of four main parts:

A: **Educational background**, which included questions about date and reasons for leaving full-time initial education, highest educational level achieved, discipline of highest educational level, interrupted studies at a higher level, and attitudes towards learning;

B: **Participation in formal adult education**, which included questions about enrolment in other formal courses, discipline of current study, start and end date, reasons for starting the programme, and whether they had been encouraged or assisted when making the decision to start the course programme;

   B1: Characteristics of the institution attended, which included questions about entry requirements, exemptions, preparatory programmes, time spent studying use, teaching modes, and organisation of the programme;

   B2: Costs of the entire course, which included questions about the person who pays the enrolment fee, the fee, extra costs, grants, whether paid leave was available, and services provided by the institution;

   B3: Learning process during the entire course, which included questions: about the classroom environment, support provided to students, barriers to learning, and satisfaction with the learning experience;

C: **Personal details**, which included questions about sociodemographic characteristics such as gender, age, nationality, country of birth, first language, educational level and nationality of parents, marital status and household composition;

D: **Day-to-day activities of the learner**, which included questions about main activity (in work, retired, student, etc), occupational status, type of contract, sector of employment, date of entering the labour market, general time use, participation in social and cultural activities, and monthly income.

Questions were based as much as possible on existing scales and questionnaires. One important source for constructing the students' questionnaire was the Eurostat Adult Education Survey codebook (Eurostat, 2007). Questions measuring the attitudes of the adult learners were based upon the Adult Attitudes towards Continuing Education Scale of Blunt and Yang (1995). Within their scale, three dimensions of attitude were found: enjoyment of learning, importance of adult education and intrinsic value. Each dimension consists of three items, nine in total. Reasons for participation and the relevance of the course were measured by means of the Education Participation Scale developed by Boshier (1977, 1991). This scale was used by Garst and Ried (1999), who used factor analyses and identified six dimensions of relevance: competency-related curiosity, interpersonal relations, community service, escape from routine, professional advancement and compliance with external influence. The scale measuring the experiences of the learning process was based on the Adult Classroom Environment Scale of Darkenwald and Valentine (1986). Previous research revealed seven dimensions of these learning process characteristics (O'Fathaigh, 1997): affiliation, teacher support, task orientation, personal goal attainment, organisation and clarity, student influence, and involvement.

The multiple regression analysis that was used to identify the main determinants of satisfaction (see **Figure 4.11** as well as **Table A.1** later in this annex) started with a regression analysis that included only personal characteristics in the first step. This resulted in determination coefficients as small as 0.02–0.04 (2-4%, depending on the country cluster). This meant that personal background variables (that is, age, sex, educational attainment and occupational status) contribute only marginally to the explanation of differences in satisfaction between individual participants. The second step examined the inclusion of the 'barriers' hindering participation as independent variables, but this increased the explanatory power of the model only marginally (by 4-6%). In step 3, addition of the classroom environment variable produced a different result as it demonstrated that around 28-33% of the variance could be explained by this variable. This indicates that differences in the classroom environment explain differences in satisfaction to a large extent. Finally, in step 4, it appeared that organisational aspects of the course and the institution (such as admission requirements, teaching methods and modular systems), add another 0-6% of the variance. Organisational aspects may be important as such, but contribute little to the understanding of the variation in satisfaction among adult learners.

Data reduction

In the questionnaire, we used Likert item scales to measure motivation and the perception of the classroom environment. All these items ranged from 1 (totally disagree) to 5 (totally agree). In the final analyses, we reduced these items into a number of key dimensions by means of principal component analysis. The decision on how many dimensions to use was based on the following criteria:

an eigenvalue higher than 1, a component load higher than 0.25 (mostly indeed above 0.40), explanation of at least 10% of the variance by every single component and obvious interpretation (coherent concept) of each component (Mortelmans and Dehertogh, 2008). Furthermore, Cronbach's Alphas were calculated to check for internal consistency.

The scale measuring motivation was reduced into two components: intrinsic and extrinsic motivations. Both dimensions had a Cronbach's Alpha higher than 0.700, so these were reliable components. A Kaiser–Meyer–Olkin measure of sampling adequacy of 0.843 and a Bartlett's test of sphericity with a significance of $p<0.001$ confirmed that the data were suitable for principal component analysis.

Factor loadings for extrinsic versus intrinsic motivation

	C1	C2
to learn more on a subject that interests me	0.527	-
to earn more	-	0.529
because my employer required me to enrol in the programme	-	0.685
to participate in group activities	0.612	-
to contribute more to my community	0.691	-
to gain awareness of myself and others	0.755	-
to get a break from the routine of home and work	0.468	-
to do my job better	-	0.423
because someone advised me to do it	-	0.527
to start up my own business	-	0.465
because I was bored	-	0.270
because I was obliged to do it (for example to claim benefits, to avoid redundancy)	-	0.695
to get a job	-	0.561
to learn knowledge/skills useful in my daily life	0.597	-
to contribute more as a citizen	0.694	-
to meet new people	0.686	-
to be less likely to lose my current job	-	0.688
to obtain certificate	-	0.368

Cronbach's Alpha=(T) 0.816 & (C1) 0.801 & (C2) 0.739; Kaiser–Meyer–Olkin=0.843; Bartlett's $p<0.001$

The scale measuring the classroom environment was reduced into one component. This dimension had a Cronbach's Alpha score of 0.828, which means that the component is reliable. The Kaiser–Meyer–Olkin measure of sampling adequacy (0.912) and the highly significant Bartlett's test of sphericity ($p<0.001$) confirmed that the data were suitable for principal component analysis.

Factor loadings for classroom environment

The study programme provides opportunities for making new friends	0.462
Students often ask the teacher questions	0.601
The teacher makes every effort to help students succeed	0.726
Students can select assignments that are of personal interest to them	0.412
Activities not related to the study programme are kept to a minimum	0.248
Most students in the study programme achieve their personal learning goals	0.620
The teacher respects students as individuals	0.740
Getting work done is very important in the study programme	0.638
The study programme is well organised	0.706
The teacher insists that you do things his or her way	-
Students feel free to question study programme requirements	0.435
The study programme has a clear sense of direction	0.667
Most students enjoy the study programme	0.719
The students in the study programme enjoy working together	0.681
Participants in the training discuss real-life examples based on their personal experiences	0.547

Cronbach Alpha=0.828; Kaiser–Meyer–Olkin=0.912; Bartlett's $p<0.001$

Regression analyses

We conducted multiple linear regression analyses in order to analyse the relation between learner satisfaction and four sets of independent variables (the personal characteristics of the learner, barriers hindering participation, perception of the classroom environment, the characteristics of the course and the institution). **Figure 4.11** shows the increase of the variance (Adjusted R-square – this shows how much of the variation in satisfaction was explained by each set of variables). We conducted separate analyses by cluster. **Table A.1** contains the standardised beta coefficients (including the level of significance) of each variable in the complete model, for each of the three clusters. As indicated by **Figure 4.11**, the perceived 'classroom environment' index was strongly related to the participants' level of satisfaction. This mechanism was found in all European regions in our dataset, as well as in all separate countries.

Table A.1: Micro and meso level variables influencing learner satisfaction: detailed results of the regression analysis summarised in Figure 4.11

FINAL MODEL	Standardised Beta coefficients		
	AT and BE	UK and IE	CEE
STEP 1 Individual background characteristics			
Female (reference)			
Male	0-.013	0.012	0.022
Age group -25 (reference)			
Age group 25-40	0.055*	.050*	0.032
Age group 40+	0.095***	0.076***	0.079***
Highest educational level – low (reference)			
Highest educational level – medium	-0.019	-0.065**	-0.035
Highest educational level – high	-0.100***	-0.112***	-0.036
Employed (reference)			
Unemployed	0.010	0.012	-0.030
Inactive	0.002	-0.013	-0.026
Level of the current course – ISCED 1–2 (reference)			
Level of the current course – ISCED 3	-0.038	0.014	0.002
Level of the current course – ISCED 4	-0.020	0.042	0.000
Level of the current course – ISCED 5–6	0.034	0.026	-0.049
STEP 2 Barriers/problems hindering participation			
Transportation problems	0.002	0.034	-0.009
Troubles arranging for childcare	0.011	-0.001	-0.010
Financial problems	-0.012	-0.026	-0.020
Studies scheduled at an inconvenient moment	-0.140***	-0.026	-0.063***
Too little time for studying	-0.021	-0.029	-0.035
Lack of preparation for the study programme	-0.017	-0.080***	-0.071***
Difficulties competing with younger students	-0.015	-0.066	-0.046*
Family problems	-0.056**	0.005	-0.051**
STEP 3 Perception of classroom environment (factor score)	0.561***	0.612***	0.566***
STEP 4 Characteristics of the institutions and courses			
APEL (Accreditation Prior Experiential Learning)	0.014	0.018	-0.034
APL (Accreditation Prior Learning)	0.024	-0.015	-0.002
Entrance/admission test and/or interview	0.060***	-0.042*	0.012
Module based courses	-.047**	-	-0.003
Duration of the course	0.002	-	-0.028
Classes more than 3 times a week	0.013	0.070***	0.003

Classes during daytime	-0.030	-0.026	0.028
Classes during weekends	-0.014	0.041*	0.052**
Classes during evenings	0.026	-0.040	0.036
Whole class teaching	0.008	0.065***	0.067**
Individual teaching	-0.017	-0.029	0.047*
Distance teaching	0.074***	0.006	0.033
Working in groups	0.036*	0.000	-0.013
Financial support	-	0.026	0.015
Paid for the course him-/herself	-	0.012	0.022
Adjusted R-Square	0.427	0.421	0.397
F(df)	33.947 (32)***	35.652 (32)***	24.603 (34)***

Effect significance: ***p<0.01; **0.01 ≤p<0.05; *0.05≤p<0.10

Key: AT=Austria, BE=Belgium (Flanders), CEE=Central and Eastern European countries. IE= Ireland, UK=United Kingdom (England and Scotland)

Note: Categories in italics refer to the reference group within each category (i.e. gender, age, educational attainment, activity status and ISCED level of the current course).

References

Blunt, A. and Yang, B. (1995) *An examination of the validity of the Education Participation Scale (EPS) and the Adult Attitudes Towards Continuing Education Scale (AACES)*, Proceedings of the Adult Education Research Conference (AERC), University of Alberta.

Boshier, R. (1977) 'Motivational orientations re-visited: life-space reasons for participation and the education participations scale', *Adult Education,* vol 27, pp 89-115.

Boshier, R. (1991) 'Psychometric properties of the alternative form of the education participation scale', *Adult Education Quarterly,* vol 41, pp 150-69.

Darkenwald, G.G., and Valentine, T. (1986) 'Measuring the social environment of adult education classrooms', Paper presented at the Adult Education Research Conference, Syracuse, NY.

Eurostat (2007) *Task force report on Adult Education Survey*, Luxembourg: Eurostat.

Garst, W.C. and Ried, D. (1999) 'Motivational orientations: evaluation of the Education Participation Scale in a nontraditional Doctor of Pharmacy program', *American Journal of Pharmaceutical Education,* vol 63, pp 300-04.

Mortelmans, D. and Dehertogh, B. (2008) *Factoranalyse*, Leuven/Voorburg: Acco.

O'Fathaigh, M. (1997) 'Irish adult learners' perceptions of classroom environment: some empirical findings', *International Journal of University Adult Education*, vol 36, pp 9-22.

Roosmaa, E.-L., Boeren, E., Nicaise, I. and Saar, E. (2011) *Adult learners in formal adult education: experiences and perceptions. Subproject 3 comparative report*, Leuven: HIVA/Tallinn: Tallinn University.

Glossary of terms and abbreviations

Adult education survey (AES)	The adult education survey is a household survey which collects data on participation in lifelong learning in European and associated countries. The first, a pilot survey, was carried out between 2005 to 2008 and included 29 countries.
Adult education survey participating countries	**Austria**, **Bulgaria**, **Belgium**, Cyprus, **Czech Republic**, Germany, **Estonia**, Spain, Finland, France, Greece, Croatia, **Hungary**, Italy, **Lithuania**, Latvia, the Netherlands, **Norway**, Poland, Portugal, Sweden, **Slovenia**, Slovakia, **the UK**. A further five participated but have not been identified on the Eurostat website. The countries shown in bold are those that were part of the LLL2010 consortium.
Compulsory education	Refers to the period of time that children are legally required to attend school. The starting age of compulsory education varies between countries, it is normally between the age five to seven. The leaving age also varies but is normally around the age of 16.
Continuing education and training	Continuing education and training for adults is defined as all kinds of general and job-related education and training that is organised, financed or sponsored by authorities, provided by employers or self-financed (OECD glossary).

Country abbreviations	AT	Austria
	BE	Belgium
	BG	Bulgaria
	CZ	Czech Republic
	CY	Cyprus
	DK	Denmark
	DE	Germany
	EE	Estonia
	EL	Greece
	ES	Spain
	FI	Finland
	FR	France
	HR	Croatia
	HU	Hungary
	IT	Italy
	IE	Ireland
	LT	Lithuania
	LU	Luxembourg
	LV	Latvia
	MT	Malta
	NL	Netherlands
	PL	Poland
	PT	Portugal
	RO	Romania
	SI	Slovenia
	SK	Slovakia
	SE	Sweden
	UK	United Kingdom
	NO	Norway
	RU	Russia
Early school leavers	The percentage of the population aged 18-24 with at most lower secondary education and not in further education or training. It refers to persons aged 18 to 24 in the following two conditions: the highest level of education or training attained is ISCED 0, 1, 2 or 3c short and respondents declared not having received any education or training in the four weeks preceding the survey. (Labour Force Survey, Eurostat).	
Economic activity	The number of people who are in employment or unemployed expressed as a percentage of the relevant population (Annual Scottish Labour Force Survey 2004/05).	
Economic inactivity rate	The number of economically inactive people expressed as a percentage of the relevant population (Annual Scottish Labour Force Survey 2004/05).	
Economically inactive persons	Economically inactive people are those not in employment and do not satisfy the criteria to be classed as 'unemployed'. For example, students not working or seeking work and those in retirement are classed as economically inactive. (Annual Scottish Labour Force Survey 2004/05).	

Educational attainment level	Educational attainment level is expressed by the highest completed level of education, defined according to the International Standard Classification of Education (ISCED) (OECD glossary).
Employment protection legislation (EPL)	Employment protection legislation refers to the extent to which there exists legal protection for employees in relation to their employment; for example in relation to being made redundant or sacked.
Employment rate	The Employment rate is calculated by dividing the total number of persons aged between 15 and 64 by the total population of the same age group. (Eurostat Yearbook 2006–07)
European Credit Transfer System (ECTS)	This system expresses learning outcomes in terms of credits achieved and aims to enhance transferability of learning between different contexts and across national boundaries with the European Union.
European Qualification Framework (EQF)	This is a framework currently being developed which will allow national frameworks of accredited learning to link to an overarching European framework to allow for easy transfer of qualifications between countries.
Formal education and training	Formal education and training corresponds to education and training in the regular system of schools, universities and colleges (Eurostat Yearbook 2006–07).
Gross Domestic Product (GDP)	GDP is a measure for the economic activity. It is defined as the value of all goods and services produced less the value of any goods or services used in their creation (Eurostat).
Informal learning	Informal learning can be either intentional (e.g. participation in short lectures or reading books or journals) or unintentional (occurring by chance or as a by-product of everyday activities) (OECD glossary). The lack of clarity in this term has led to Eurostat leaving it out of its statistics as from year 2004.
Internal labour market	In this type of labour market the links between the initial education system and the labour market are weaker than in an occupational labour market. The initial education system is general and academic and does not develop all the technical and job related skills required by an individual.

ISCED levels	International Standard Classification of Education. The ISCED was adopted by Unesco in 1976 and it groups educational programmes according to their content into 7 levels, numbered 0 to 6: ISCED 0: pre-primary education ISCED 1: primary education ISCED 2: lower secondary education ISCED 3: lower-upper secondary education ISCED 4: post-secondary non-tertiary education ISCED 5: tertiary education (first stage, not leading directly to an advanced research qualification) ISCED 6: tertiary education (second stage, leading to an advanced research qualification) (Eurostat).
Job-related continuing education and training	Job-related continuing education and training refers to all organised, systematic education and training activities in which people take part in order to obtain knowledge and/or learn new skills for a current or a future job, to increase earnings, to improve job and/or career opportunities in a current or another field and generally to improve their opportunities for advancement and promotion (OECD glossary).
Labour force	The total labour force consists of all people employed and unemployed but not those economically inactive.
Labour Force participation rate	This refers to the percentage of the population in the same age group who are either in employment or unemployed. It is defined according to ILO guidelines (OECD glossary)
Labour Force Survey	This is a quarterly household survey gathering labour market statistics. From time to time it includes ad hoc modules on specific themes. Data on lifelong learning was gathered in an ad hoc module in 2003. The adult education survey will take over as the main survey for statistics on lifelong learning participation.
Lifelong Learning Indicator	The Lifelong learning indicator is calculated from the responses of persons aged 25 to 64 who participated in the Labour Force Survey and indicated that they received education or training in the four weeks preceding the survey. These responses are compared to those in the same age group in the survey who did not receive education or training. Self learning activities are no longer included in this indicator (European Union Labour Force Survey, EU LFS).
Non-formal education and training	This includes all types of taught learning activities which are not part of a formal education programme (Eurostat yearbook 2006-07).

Occupational labour market (OLM)	This type of labour market is characterised by a close link between the initial education system and the requirements of skills in the labour market. In countries with an OLM employees develop technical and job relevant skills in their initial education.
Post-compulsory education	This refers to any learning that an individual engages in after having reached compulsory education leaving age (see above). This could include upper secondary education as well learning in university or college.
Unemployment	The ILO definition of unemployment covers people who are: not in employment, want a job, have actively sought work in the previous 4 weeks and are available to start work within the next fortnight, or out of work and have accepted a job which they are waiting to start in the next fortnight (Annual Scottish Labour Force Survey 2004/05).
Unemployment rate	The unemployment rate is based on the number of unemployed persons (according to Labour Force Survey definition of unemployment) as a percentage of the overall labour force. (Eurostat Yearbook 2006-07)
Vocational programmes	Vocational education prepares participants for direct entry, without further training, into specific occupations. Successful completion of such programmes leads to a labour-market relevant vocational qualification. Some indicators divide vocational programmes into school-based programmes and combined school- and work-based programmes on the basis of the amount of training that is provided in school as opposed to training in the workplace (OECD glossary).

Index

Note: The following abbreviations have been used – *f* = figure; *n* = note; *t* = table. Individual European country entries are highlighted in bold.

A

access *see* widening access
'active citizenship' 12
activity-oriented learners 67
Adult Classroom Environment Scale 76
adult education 7, 11, 13, 18, 23, 31
Adult Education Survey (EuroStat) 6, 10, 11, 13, 23, 35, 67, 70, 88–9, 105, 106
adult educators 82
Adult Learning: it is never too late to learn (Commission of the European Communities) 49
age
  higher education 133*f*, 134*f*, 136, 137*f*, 138*f*, 139*f*
  participation and 93, 94, 95*t*, 96*t*
Aiginger, K. 24, 25
Anglo-Celtic liberal market regimes 18, 22, 25, 33, 34, 35, 36*n*, 152, 159
  higher education 130
  key characteristics 28*t*, 29*t*
  learner satisfaction 79, 80*f*
apprenticeships 26, 120
ARCS model of motivation 66, 67, 77
Austria 2, 8, 10, 14
  barriers to participation 94, 95*t* 96*t*, 97*f*, 98*t*
  case study 113–14
  formal adult education 69, 70, 75, 103, 105, 107*f*, 119, 120
  higher education 130, 131*t*, 132, 133*f*, 134*f*, 135*t*, 136*f*, 137*f*, 138*f*, 139*f*, 140*f*
  risk of poverty by education level 158*f*
  socioeconomic factors 20*f*, 21*f*, 28*t*, 29*t*, 30, 31, 34, 36
  tertiary-level education 126*t*
  universities 144–5

B

Bauman, Z. 20
Beck, U. 4
Becker, G. St. 107
Belgium 8, 10, 30, 31, 36, 69, 75, 80, 127*t*

barriers to participation 94, 95*t*, 96*t*, 97*f*, 98*t*
formal adult education 105, 106, 107*f*
higher education 130, 131*t*, 132, 133*f*, 134*f*, 135*t*, 136*f*, 137*f*, 138*f*, 139*f*, 140*f*, 145–6
risk of poverty by education level 158*f*
socioeconomic factors 20*f*, 21*f*, 22, 28*t*, 29*t*
benchmarks 9, 47, 56, 128, 155
  Europe 2020 55, 56
  Lisbon Strategy 48, 49, 50, 53, 54
Benn, Tony 55
Bologna Declaration/Process (1998) 14, 42, 74, 128, 129
Bologna Process in Higher Education (European Communities/Hochschul-Informations-System (HIS)) 130, 136, 143
Boshier, R. 40, 67
bounded agency model 4, 12, 23, 64, 65*f*, 88, 100, 152–3
Bourdieu, J.-P. 88
Brakman, S. 158
Brine, J. 148
British Left 55
Brown, P. 20, 148
Bulgaria 69, 75
  barriers to participation 94, 95*t*, 96*t*, 97*f*, 98*t*
  formal adult education 105, 106, 107*f*, 119
  higher education 131*t*, 134*f*, 135*t*, 136*f*, 138*f*, 139*f*, 140*f*
  risk of poverty by education level 158*f*
  socioeconomic factors 19, 20*f*, 21*f*, 28*t*, 29*t*, 30, 32, 34, 36

C

capitalism 17–18, 23, 44, 55
career patterns 120–1
carers: children 93, 94, 95*t*, 96*t*
Castells, M. 2
catching-up model 25–6, 36
CEC *see* Commission of the European Communities
Cedefop 158

Central and Eastern Europe 1, 2, 11, 18, 64,
151, 152
  barriers to participation 94, 95*t*
  formal adult education 70, 75, 79, 80*f*, 81
  higher education 130, 137*f*
  socioeconomic factors 26, 27, 28*t*, 29*t*, 31,
  32, 33, 34, 35, 36
  workplace learning 153
citizenship 41
classroom environments 75–6, 77*f*, 81, 82
Coleman, J.S. 72
Commission of the European Communities
  (CEC) 5, 9–11, 40–1, 42, 43, 46, 47, 49,
  52–5
'common interest approach' 48
Communication from the Commission
  to the Council and the European
  Parliament (2006) 5
comprehensive school systems 27, 28*t*, 30,
  32, 99
Conclusions 'on the social dimension of
  education and training' (Council of the
  European Union) 50–1, 56
'conservative-corporatist' welfare state 24
Continental coordinated market economy
  model 25, 28*t*, 29*t*, 33, 35–6, 79, 80*f*, 99
continuing professional education 120
Continuous Vocational Education and
  Training Survey (CVTS) 105, 106
cooperation 44, 51, 56
copper production enterprises: United
  Kingdom 112
Council of the European Union 41, 47,
  48–9, 50–1, 53, 54, 56
course organisation: formal education 73,
  74*f*
Cousins, M. 34
Croatia
  barriers to participation 94, 95*t*, 96*t*, 97*f*,
  98*t*
  formal adult education 69, 75, 80, 105,
  106, 107*f*
Cross, K.P. 87
cross-generational social mobility 14
Cyprus
  barriers to participation 94, 95*t*, 96*t*, 97*f*,
  98*t*
  formal adult education 105, 107*f*
  risk of poverty by education level 158*f*
Czech Republic 69, 73
  barriers to participation 94, 95*t*, 96*t*, 97*f*,
  98*t*
  formal adult education 107*f*
  higher education 131*t*, 132, 133*f*, 134*f*,
  135*t*, 136*f*, 138*f*, 139*f*, 140*f*
  risk of poverty by education level 158*f*

socioeconomic factors 20*f*, 21*f*, 28*t*, 29*t*, 30

D

Dale, R. 42, 43, 44, 55, 56, 159
Darkenwald, G.G. 76
Dehmel, A. 57
demographic barriers to participation 93,
  94, 95*t*, 96*t*, 97*f*, 98*t*
Denmark 158*f*
Desjardins, R. 12, 64, 65*f*, 87, 88, 99, 152
Desmedt, E. 64
Directorate-General for Education and
  Culture (DG-EAC) 46, 48, 49–50, 57*n*
disability 6, 14, 131*t*, 142, 144, 146, 147
Disabled Students Allowance (DSA) (UK)
  142
distance learning 31

E

EACEA *see* Education, Audiovisual and
  Culture Executive Agency
early school leavers 100
Eastern Europe *see* Central and Eastern
  Europe
economic crisis 1, 3, 5, 11, 17, 19, 35, 52, 54,
  129, 159–60
economic efficiency 6, 8, 10, 33, 35
economic growth 7, 12, 152, 157, 160
economic 'pecking order' 7
education 3, 4, 5, 10
  European liberal tradition 6–7
  expenditure 30
Education, Audiovisual and Culture
  Executive Agency (EACEA) 129, 131*t*
Education, Directorate-General for 46
Education Participation Scale 67, 68*t*
educational attainment 70, 71*f*, 139*f*
*Efficiency and Equity in European Education
  and Training Systems* (Commission of the
  European Communities) 49
employment rates 1, 30, 138, 139*f*, 140*f*, 141,
  155
'Erasmus' 45, 49, 128, 145
Esping-Andersen, G. 24, 64
Estonia 70
  formal adult education 69, 75, 80, 105,
  106, 107*f*, 119
  higher education 127, 130, 131*t*, 132, 133*f*,
  134*f*, 135*t*, 136*f*, 137*f*, 143–4
  labour market advantage 138*f*, 139*f*, 140*f*
  participation 95*t*, 96*t*, 97*f*, 98*t*
  risk of poverty by education level 158*f*
  socioeconomic factors 19, 20*f*, 21*f*, 28*t*,
  29*t*, 30, 31, 32, 34
ethnicity 6, 9

EU Sixth Framework Project 'Towards a Lifelong Learning Society in Europe: The Contribution of the Education System' (LLL2010) 1, 9–11, 69*f*, 70*f*, 151
EU-25 30, 105, 136
EU-27 133*f*, 134*f*, 135*t*, 137*f*, 139*f*, 140*f*, 158*f*
EU-LFS *see* European Union Labour Force Survey
EU-SILC *see* European Union Statistics on Income and Living Conditions
Eurobarometer 88
Europe 2020: A strategy for smart, sustainable and inclusive growth (Commission of the European Communities) 2, 5, 52–5, 56, 156, 157
'Europe of Knowledge' 128
European Commission *see* Commission of the European Communities (CEC)
European Higher Education Area 42
European Qualifications Framework 129–30
European semester 57–8*n*
European Union (EU) 1–2, 4, 5, 12, 17, 20*f*, 21*f*, 57*n*, 73, 130
  economic and social aims 40–1
  formal adult education 69, 75, 80, 107*f*
  general objectives for learning 40, 46, 48–9, 53–4, 125
  higher education policies 128–30, 136, 143
  historic role of education/lifelong learning 44–51
  member states 43–4
  policy processes and spaces 41–2
European Union Labour Force Survey (EU-LFS) 10, 22*f*, 23, 90, 105, 130
European Union Statistics on Income and Living Conditions (EU-SILC) 130
European Year of Lifelong Learning (1996) 46
'Europeanisation' 40, 42, 43, 50, 56
Eurostat 6, 10, 11, 13, 23, 27, 35, 67, 88–9
  higher education 130, 133*f*, 134*f*, 136*f*, 137*f*, 138*f*, 139*f*
  socioeconomic factors 20*f*, 21*f*
Eurostudent III 130, 137*f*
Eurydice 27
expansive training cultures 115*t*, 116–17, 118*t*
expectancy value theory 66
extrinsic motivation 67, 68*t*, 69*f*, 70*f*, 80–1, 152

F

family-orientated welfare regime 99

Faure Report 40, 63
Field, J. 39
Finland
  barriers to participation 94, 95*t*, 96*t*
  formal adult education 69, 75, 80, 92*f*, 105, 106, 107*f*
  risk of poverty by education level 158*f*
firm-specific experience 107
Flanders 10, 30, 31, 36, 69, 75, 80
  higher education 127*t*, 130, 131*t*, 145–6
Focus on higher education in Europe 2010: the impact of the Bologna Process (Education, Audiovisual and Culture Executive Agency) 129
foreign students 49
formal adult education 11, 13, 22*f*, 63–4, 80–3, 103–5, 153
  ARCS model of motivation 66
  bounded agency model 64, 65*f*
  characteristics of institutions/courses 72, 73*f*, 74*f*, 75*f*, 76, 77*f*
  European Union policies 69, 75, 80, 107*f*
  initial education and 89*f*, 90
  learner satisfaction 77, 78*f*, 79, 80*f*
  reasons for participation 67, 68*t*, 69*f*, 70*f*, 71*f*
  research methodology 66–7, 108–9, 163–5, 166*t*, 167*t*, 168*t*, 169*t*
  small to medium-sized enterprises 105–6, 107*f*, 108, 109*t*, 110*t*, 111*t*, 112–14, 115*t*, 116–21
Foucault 40
France
  barriers to participation 94, 95*t*, 96*t*, 97*f*, 98*t*
  risk of poverty by education level 158*f*
free-riding 108
Friedman, M. 2–3

G

gender 6, 14, 93*f*, 94, 95*t*, 96*t*, 133, 154
  higher education 131*t*, 134*f*, 135*t*, 136*f*, 139*f*, 143, 145, 147
general skills 107
Germany 1, 22
  barriers to participation 94, 95*t*, 96*t*, 97*f*, 98*t*
  formal adult education 107*f*
  risk of poverty by education level 158*f*
Giddens, A. 159
Gini coefficient 18, 19*f*
globalisation 2–6, 10, 14, 17, 22, 23, 46, 160
  'Europeanisation' and 40, 42, 43, 50, 56
goal-oriented learners 67
Greece 20
  formal adult education 105, 107*f*

risk of poverty by education level 158*f*
Green, A. 2, 4, 8, 17, 26, 157
Gross, M. 82
Growth, Competitiveness, Employment
    (Commission of the European
    Communities) 43, 46
Guger, A. 24
Gypsy Travellers 9, 132

H

headline targets 53, 54–5
Hefler, G. 109*t*, 110*t*, 111*t*, 114
High Level Group 47–8, 52
higher education 9, 14, 21, 44, 51, 120,
    147–9
  age differences in participation 133*f*, 134*f*,
    136, 137*f*, 138*f*
  data sources 130
  development of European policy 128–30
  European Union policies 128–30, 136,
    143
  expansion across Europe 132, 133*f*, 154–6,
    157
  gender differences in participation 131*t*,
    133, 134*f*, 135*t*, 136*f*, 139*f*, 143, 145, 147
  institutional case studies 141–7
  labour market advantage and 130, 138,
    139*f*, 140*f*, 141
  socioeconomic differences in participation
    135, 136*f*
  socioeconomic status of students 125,
    126*t*, 127*t*, 128
  under-representation in higher education
    129, 130, 131*t*, 132, 135, 143, 147
Hingel, A. 128
Hirsch, F. 126
Hochschul-Informations-System (HIS) 130,
    137*f*
Holford, J. 49
Houle, C. 67
household income inequality 18, 19, 20*f*
human capital 2, 5, 6–8, 12, 31–2, 87, 125,
    152, 160
human resource development (HRD) 103,
    114, 118
Hungary
  barriers to participation 94, 95*t*, 96*t*, 97*f*,
    98*t*
  formal adult education 105, 106, 107*f*
  higher education 131*t*, 132, 133*f*, 134*f*,
    135*f*, 136*f*, 138*f*, 139*f*, 140*f*
  risk of poverty by education level 158*f*
  socioeconomic factors 20*f*, 21*f*, 28*t*, 29*t*, 30

I

Iannelli, C. 135, 148
identity: individual and group 4
ILO (International Labour Organisation) 22
IMF (International Monetary Fund) 4
immigrants 6, 7, 9, 152
inclusive liberalism 14
income distribution 19
indicators 48–51, 56
inequality 5, 8–9, 10, 12, 14, 41, 148–9, 160
  expansion of higher education 154–6, 157
  factors underpinning the growth in 17,
    21*f*, 22
  growing trend towards 18, 19*f*, 20*f*, 21
  household income 18, 19, 20*f*
  knowledge-extensive policies 157, 158*f*,
    159
  national typologies 26, 35
  reasons for growth in 22–3
informal learning 11
initial education system 89*f*, 90, 92, 93
institutions: case studies 141–7
intergenerational learning 51
Internal Labour Market (ILM) 99, 100
International Adult Education Survey 9
International Adult Literacy Survey (IALS)
    26
International Labour Organisation (ILO) 22
International Monetary Fund (IMF) 4
intrinsic motivation 67, 68*t*, 69*f*, 70*f*, 80–1,
    82*n*, 108, 152, 154
Ireland, Republic of 7–8, 18
  case study 115–16
  higher education 131*t*, 132, 133*f*, 134*f*,
    135*t*, 136*f*, 138*f*, 139*f*, 140*f*
  risk of poverty by educational level 158*f*
  socioeconomic factors 19, 20*f*, 21*f*, 28*t*,
    29*t*, 30, 31
Irish Green Paper on Adult Education
    (1998) 8
ISCED levels 21*f*, 66–7, 68, 69*f*, 72, 73*f*, 74*f*,
    75*f*, 81, 108, 139*f*, 140*f*
  formal adult education 66–7, 68, 69*f*, 72,
    73*f*, 74*f*, 75*f*, 81
Italy
  formal adult education 105, 107*f*
  risk of poverty by education level 158*f*

J

Janmaat, J.G. 8, 17, 157
Jogi, L. 82

K

Keeling, R. 128

Keller, J.M. 66, 67, 77
Key Competences for Lifelong Learning:
European Reference Framework (DG-EAC)
49–50
Keynesianism 3, 5, 160
knowledge economy 2–6, 12, 17, 22, 24, 32,
35, 63, 125, 160
equality of outcome 154, 157, 158*f*, 159
neoliberalism 41, 44, 46, 47, 48
Kok, Wim 47–8, 52

L

labour markets 3, 4, 7, 9, 12, 17, 19, 22, 25
higher education and 130, 138, 139*f*, 140*f*,
141
knowledge-extensive policies 158*f*, 159
participation and 89*f*, 90, 91*f*, 92*f*, 93*f*, 99
languages 40, 47, 50
Latvia
barriers to participation 94, 95*t*, 96*t*, 97*f*,
98*t*
formal adult education 69, 75, 80, 107*f*
liberal market regime 32
risk of poverty by education level 158*f*
Lauder, H. 20, 148
Lawn, M. 41–2, 159
Lažetić, P. 129
learner satisfaction 77, 78*f*, 79, 80*f*
learning difficulties 23
learning society 2, 7, 8, 40, 41, 46, 121
learning-oriented learners 67
Leonardo da Vinci programme 46, 49
Leuven/Louvain-la Neuve Communiqué
(2009) 129
Levitas, R. 8, 20
liberal market regime 26, 30
'liberal' welfare state 24
life-cycle-oriented personnel management
105–6
Lingard, B. 5, 40, 46, 160
Lisbon Strategy (2000) 2, 11, 63, 65
neoliberalism and 41, 42, 43, 44, 46–8, 52,
53, 55
Lithuania
formal adult education 69, 75, 107*f*
higher education 131*t*, 132, 133*f*, 134*f*,
135*t*, 136*f*, 138*f*, 139*f*, 140*f*
participation 95*t*, 96*t*, 97*f*, 98*t*
risk of poverty by education level 158*f*
socioeconomic factors 19, 20*f*, 21*f*, 28*t*,
29*t*, 30, 31, 32, 34
LLL2010 *see* EU Sixth Framework Project
'Towards a Lifelong Learning Society
in Europe: The Contribution of the
Education System'
London Communiqué (2007) 128

low-skilled workers 23
Luxembourg 158*f*

M

Maastricht Treaty 4, 43, 45–6, 47, 128
Malta 158*f*
Marginson, S. 125
Markowitsch, J. 114
Master of Business Administration (MBA)
120
Matthew effect 89, 90, 98
Maurice, M. 99
Mediterranean model 25
Mexico 18
Meyer, W.J. 121
middle-classes 9, 22, 135, 147, 154
motivation factors 13, 23, 64, 66, 68*t*, 69*f*,
70*f*, 80–1, 152–3
Müller, W. 99

N

National Qualification Frameworks 73
National Reform Programmes (NRPs) 54
national typologies 18, 25–6, 27, 28–9*t*,
30–2, 32–5
neighbourhood regeneration strategies 7
neoliberalism 2–6, 8, 10, 14, 32, 36, 39,
55–8, 159
areas of debate 40–4
education/lifelong learning in the EU
44–6
indicators and politics 48–51
lifelong learning in 'Europe 2020' 52–5
Lisbon Strategy 46–8
Netherlands
formal adult education 97*f*, 107*f*
risk of poverty by education level 158*f*
new European socioeconomic model 24,
25, 35, 159
New Zealand 18
Nicaise, I. 158*f*
non-formal training 2, 13, 31, 103, 108, 112,
117, 119, 143
non-participation 87
non-traditional learners 7, 31, 51, 130, 136*f*,
137*f*, 138
Norway 7, 10, 88
barriers to participation 94, 95*t*, 96*t*, 97*f*,
98*t*
case study 112
formal adult education 69, 75, 80, 105,
106, 107*f*, 119
higher education 131*t*, 132, 133*f*, 134*f*,
135*t*, 136*f*, 138*t*, 139*f*, 140*f*

socioeconomic factors 20*f*, 21*f*, 28*t*, 29*t*,
30, 31, 35

O

Occupational Labour Market (OLM) 99,
103
occupational social class 9
OECD *see* Organisation for Economic
Cooperation and Development (OECD)
O'Fathaigh, M. 76
Official Journal of the European Union 135*t*
open access 31, 73
Open Method of Coordination (OMC) 17,
47, 48, 49
Open University (UK) 73
Organisation for Economic Cooperation
and Development (OECD) 18, 20–1, 39,
130, 137*f*, 158
Ozga, J. 160

P

parental level of education 14, 135, 136*f*
part-time study 31, 138
participation 64, 66, 67, 68*t*, 81, 82, 87,
98–100, 154, 155
data sources 88–9
formal adult education in enterprises
105–6, 107*f*, 117
higher education 130, 131*t*, 132, 133, 134*f*,
135*t*, 136*f*, 137*f*, 138*f*
labour market status and 89*f*, 90, 91*f*, 92*f*,
93*f*, 99
overview of barriers to 87–8
socioeconomic differences in 135, 136*f*
socioeconomic obstacles by country 93–4,
95*t*, 96*t*, 97*f*, 98*t*
tertiary level education 132, 133*f*, 134*f*,
135
partnership arrangements 25, 31, 56, 117
personal growth 6, 31, 32, 35, 151, 152
Pickett, K. 5, 17, 19
Poland 43
formal adult education 107*f*
risk of poverty by education level 158*f*
Policy making in the European Union
(Wallace) 41
policy processes 4, 41–2, 128–30
'poor jobs' 20
Portugal
barriers to participation 94, 95*t*, 96*t*, 97*f*,
98*t*
formal adult education 107*f*
risk of poverty by education level 158*f*
poverty: risk of by country 158*f*
Prague Communiqué (2001) 128

presence democracy 157
principle of subsidiarity 45, 47

Q

qualifications 2, 14, 19, 31, 53, 56, 81, 103,
104, 119–120
labour market advantage 138, 139*f*, 140*f*,
141
socioeconomic factors 20, 21*f*, 22*f*, 23
tertiary level 132, 133*f*
widening access and 128, 129–30

R

rational choice theory 108
reactive training cultures 114, 115*t*, 116,
117, 118*t*
redistribution 24, 25, 30, 35, 160
regulation 24, 25, 35
responsibility 24–5
retention policies 104
returners to formal education 9, 10, 14, 18,
92*f*
Rizvi, F. 5, 40, 46
Robertson, S. 5, 42, 43, 44, 48, 56, 129
Romania 32, 158*f*
Romany people 9, 132
Rome, Treaty of (1957) 128
Rose, N. 40
Royce, S. 82
Rubenson, K. 12, 64, 65*f*, 87, 88, 99, 152
rural areas 93, 94, 95*t*, 96*t*
Russian Federation 7, 10, 35, 70
case study 116–17
higher education 131*t*, 136*f*, 140*f*

S

Saar, E. 32
Scandinavia 18, 22, 24, 64, 157, 159, 160
barriers to participation 94, 95*t*, 96*t*, 97*f*,
98*t*
formal adult education 69, 75, 80, 105,
106, 107*f*
risk of poverty by education level 158*f*
social market economy model 25, 28*t*, 29*t*,
32–3, 159
socioeconomic factors 90, 91*f*, 92*f*
school systems 30
Schuetze, H.G. 65, 72
Scotland 141–2, 148, 155
Scott, R.W. 121
Scottish Funding Council 141, 142, 155
Scottish Widening Access Programme
(SWAP) 141
self-employment 90–1

Sennett, R. 3
service sector 22, 134
Shavit, Y. 99
skilled/unskilled labour 22–3
skills assessment 73
Slovakia
  barriers to participation 94, 95*t*, 96*t*, 97*f*,
    98*t*
  formal adult education 69, 75, 80, 107*f*
  risk of poverty by education level 158*f*
Slovenia
  barriers to participation 94, 95*t*, 96*t*, 97*f*,
    98*t*
  chemical production enterprises 113
  formal adult education 69, 75, 80, 92*f*, 105,
    106, 107*f*, 119, 120
  gender 14
  higher education 130, 131*t*, 132, 133*f*,
    134*f*, 135*t*, 136*f*, 137*f*, 147, 155
  labour market advantage 138*f*, 139*f*, 140*f*
  risk of poverty by education level 158*f*
  socioeconomic factors 20*f*, 21*f*, 28*t*, 29*t*,
    30, 32, 33, 34, 36
  universities 142–3
Slowey, M. 72
small to medium-sized enterprises (SMEs)
  9, 10, 13, 36, 103–5, 153–4
  approaches to support for participation in
    formal adult education 109*t*, 110*t*, 111*t*,
    112–14
  case study methodology 108–9
  future outlook 119–21
  interdependence of support patterns for
    formal adult education and training
    cultures 117, 118–19
  statistical accounts of formal adult
    education in enterprises 105–6, 107*f*
  theories of support for formal adult
    education 107–8
  training cultures in enterprises 114, 115*t*,
    116–17
social capital 2, 6–8, 12, 31–2
social class 6, 9, 135, 147
social cohesion 17, 18, 41, 125, 151, 160
human/social capital 5, 7, 8, 11, 12, 14
social control 7, 8, 12
social democratic regime 26
social exclusion 7, 8, 10, 156–7
social inclusion 2, 7, 8–9, 10, 12, 18, 41, 87
  barriers to 156–7, 159
  neoliberalism 54, 55
social integrationist discourse 20
social market regime 26, 99
social mobility 4, 14, 23
social partnership 25
social transfers 4, 18, 20*f*, 25

social welfare regimes 8, 12, 13, 18, 23–6,
  27, 28*t*, 29*t*, 32–4, 88
'social-democratic' welfare state 24
'societal effects' school 119
sociodemographic barriers 93, 94, 95*t*, 96*t*,
  97*f*, 98*t*
socioeconomic context 18, 35–6
  contrasting approaches to lifelong learning
    and social welfare 23–6
  difficulties encountered in developing
    national typologies 34–5
  extended typology of lifelong learning
    and welfare systems 27, 28*t*, 29*t*
  factors in wider context 17, 20*f*, 21*f*, 22,
    28*t*, 29*t*, 30, 31, 34, 36, 136*f*
  reasons for growth in inequality 22–3
  similarities and differences between
    European countries 30–2
  trend towards growing inequality 18, 19*f*,
    20*f*, 21
  typologies of lifelong learning and welfare
    regimes 32–4
Socrates programme 14, 46, 49, 128
SONAR database 127*t*
Soviet-style education 8
space: educational 41–2, 55, 159
Spain
  barriers to participation 94, 95*t*, 96*t*
  formal adult education 107*f*
  risk of poverty by education level 158*f*
Standing Group on Indicators and
  Benchmarks (SGIB) 49
stepwise multiple regression analysis 78–9,
  80*f*
Stiglitz, J. 3, 160
stratified school systems 27, 28*t*, 30, 32, 33
subsidiarity, principle of 45, 47
Sweden 22, 90, 91*f*
  barriers to participation 94, 95*t*, 96*t*, 97*f*,
    98*t*
  formal adult education 69, 75, 80, 105,
    106, 107*f*
  risk of poverty by education level 158*f*

T

Task Force on Human Resources,
  Education, Training and Youth (TFRH)
  57*n*
teacher training 82
*Teaching and learning: towards a learning
  society* (Commission of the European
  Communities) 40–1, 46
tertiary level education 31, 32, 33, 49, 70,
  72, 80, 82, 90, 125
  Austria 126*t*

EU participation targets 132, 133*f*, 134*f*, 135

Flanders 127*t*

labour market 140*f*

socioeconomic factors 136*f*

vocational training 132

'three worlds of welfare capitalism' 24

trade unions 10, 22, 25, 31, 159

training cultures 1, 3, 4, 5, 114, 115*t*, 116–17, 118*t*

Treaty of Maastricht (1992) 4, 43, 45–6, 47, 128

Treaty of Rome (1957) 128

Turkey 18

U

under-representation: higher education 129, 130, 131*t*, 132, 135, 143, 147

UNESCO (United Nations' Educational, Scientific and Cultural Organisation) 39

UNESCO-OECD-Eurostat data collection (UOE) 130, 137*f*

Unger, M. 126*t*

United Kingdom 7, 8, 10, 14

case study 112

formal adult education 69, 75, 80, 103, 105, 106, 107*f*, 120

higher education 128, 130, 131*t*, 132, 133*f*, 134*f*, 135*t*, 136*f*, 137*f*, 138*f*, 139*f*, 140*f*, 141–2, 155

labour market advantage 138*f*, 139*f*, 140*f*

participation 90, 91*f*, 100

risk of poverty by education level 158*f*

socioeconomic factors 18, 19, 20*f*, 21*f*, 28*t*, 29*t*, 30, 31

teacher training 82

United Nations' Educational, Scientific and Cultural Organisation (UNESCO) 39

United States 8, 18, 19, 24

universities 125, 126*t*, 127*t*, 130, 141–7, 148

Ure, O.B. 32

V

Valentine, T. 76

Visigrad countries 32, 34, 35, 36*n*

vocational education and training 4, 45–6, 49, 53, 55, 99, 132

Vroom, V.H. 66

W

Wallace, H. 41

widening access 9, 10, 21, 51, 147–9, 153–6

age differences in higher education participation 136, 137*f*, 138*f*

data sources 130

development of European policy for higher education 128–30

expansion of higher education across Europe 132, 133*f*

gender differences in higher education participation 133, 134*f*, 135*t*

institutional case studies 141–7

labour market advantage and 138, 139*f*, 140*f*, 141

socioeconomic differences in higher education participation 135, 136*f*

under-representation in higher education 129, 130, 131*t*, 132, 143, 147

Wilkinson, R. 5, 17, 19

working class 22

workplace 6, 9, 10, 13, 36, 103–5, 153–4

approaches to support for participation in formal adult education 109*t*, 110*t*, 111*t*, 112–14

case study methodology 108–9

empowerment and 20

future outlook 119–21

interdependence of support patterns for formal adult education and training cultures 117, 118–19

learning 13, 64, 153–4

statistical accounts of formal adult education in enterprises 105–6, 107*f*

theories of support for formal adult education 107–8

training cultures in enterprises 114, 115*t*, 116–17

World Values Survey 26